ABORTION POLITICS
IN THE
UNITED STATES
AND
CANADA

ABORTION POLITICS IN THE UNITED STATES AND CANADA

Studies in Public Opinion

EDITED BY
Ted G. Jelen
and
Marthe A. Chandler

PRAEGER

Westport, Connecticut
London

Library of Congress Cataloging-in-Publication Data

Abortion politics in the United States and Canada : studies in public
   opinion / edited by Ted G. Jelen and Marthe A. Chandler.
      p.   cm.
   Includes bibliographical references and index.
   ISBN 0–275–94561–8 (alk. paper)
      1. Abortion—United States—Public opinion.   2. Abortion—Canada—
   Public opinion.   3. Public opinion—United States.   4. Public
   opinion—Canada.   I. Jelen, Ted G.   II. Chandler, Marthe A.
   HQ767.5.U5A267   1994
   363.4'6'0973—dc20   93–43074

British Library Cataloguing in Publication Data is available.

Copyright © 1994 by Ted G. Jelen and Marthe A. Chandler

Library of Congress Catalog Card Number: 93–43074
ISBN: 0–275–94561–8

First published in 1994

Praeger Publishers, 88 Post Road West, Westport, CT 06881
An imprint of Greenwood Publishing Group, Inc.

Printed in the United States of America

The paper used in this book complies with the
Permanent Paper Standard issued by the National
Information Standards Organization (Z39.48–1984).

10 9 8 7 6 5 4 3 2 1

Contents

ABORTION POLITICS
IN THE
UNITED STATES
AND
CANADA

1 The Body in Late Capitalism: An Introductory Sketch

John H. Simpson

"Council Considers Penalties for Abortion Clinic Violence"
To combat violence outside abortion clinics, a majority of the New York City Council is sponsoring a bill that would stiffen penalties against people who physically harass women and medical staff members as they try to enter the clinics.
—*The New York Times,* April 22, 1993

"This Weekend's March on Washington May Rock Clinton's Delicate Tightrope Act on Gay Issues"
As gay men and lesbians, as many as a million, take over almost every available public accommodation in the capital, President Clinton will be conveniently absent, meeting Democratic legislators in Virginia and giving a speech in Boston. But whether here or there, Mr. Clinton will feel the heat.
—*The Wall Street Journal,* April 23, 1993

"It's Like Being Inside a TV Tube when the Set is Tuned to MTV"
New York—Night Owls can have a hoot time in the old town tomorrow night. The Ritz nightclub is offering to keep them wide-eyed with an 11-hour "omnisensorial sweepout." The futuristic extravaganza . . . will feature three dance floors, 77 musicians, "vibrating platforms," the highest indoor strobe waterfall, a flying human and a variety of other attractions for $15. . . . The idea is to create so much confusion that people won't be able to hear one another, will lose their identity and rely on body language instead, says Mr. Airaldi [the organizer]. "People become more human once they lose their identity. It's a regression in a sense. We call it sensoria."
—*The Wall Street Journal,* April 23, 1993

In recent years a number of issues focused on the control, display, and use of the body have engulfed public arenas. The visibility and salience of the issues and the passionate attitudes and committed actions that they arouse have attracted widespread attention and caused legislative bodies, the courts, and executive officials to respond in various ways. Why have pornography, euthanasia, homosexuality, the content and bounds of heterosexuality, child abuse, so-called family values, and abortion generated so much public controversy, political attention, and judicial deliberation in recent years? This chapter addresses that question.

Two key notions inform the answer to the question. First, the interrelated structural properties of late capitalism are proposed as a source of diffuse moods and orientations underwriting a cultural resource—the "body-sensibility" of late capitalism—that can be used to provoke conflicted public discourse and foment a politics of the body.

The second key notion is that the body-sensibility of late capitalism is a necessary resource but not *both* a necessary and a sufficient resource for generating public discourse and controversy about the body. What is added to the body-sensibility of late capitalism in order to produce "body-controversy" is a set of action possibilities that can be located with reference to what has been called the "patric body" (Simpson, 1993)—a metaphor or image of the nuclear family under modern industrial capitalism. It is the deconstruction of the patric body in the context of late capitalism's body-sensibility, I will argue, that provides the sufficient condition for realizing the politics of the body.

The analytic approach that is proposed in this chapter differs from (but also complements) other approaches that recognize the body and body-oriented issues as major features of the social and political landscape of our time. Some dwell on the historical, philosophical, and social-theoretical sources that inform and provide insight into body concerns in the contemporary situation (for example, Turner, 1984). The analysis in this chapter complements those approaches by sketching the systemic elements or structural features that are, in effect, assumed by historical, philosophical, and social-theoretical approaches to the body question. Others have dealt with the proximal sources and empirical consequences of specific body-controversies such as abortion (for example, Cook, Jelen, and Wilcox, 1992). This chapter complements those approaches by proposing a way of considering the distal or deep-structural aspects of the contemporary situation to which the manifestations of body concerns and body politics can, eventually, be traced. Thus, for example, the United States Supreme Court's decision in the case of *Roe v. Wade*—a decision that made legal abortion in America more accessible—has, clearly, been a major source of controversy in recent years. This chapter is not concerned with the many consequences of *Roe v. Wade* as a social and political resource. It is, rather, focused on the systemic features of late capitalism that congealed in American society and made the *Roe v. Wade* decision a possibility or likelihood within its institutional framework.

A brief sketch of the meaning of the phrase "late capitalism" follows. That sketch is a prelude to the second section of the chapter, where I argue that late capitalism provides a generative context that strongly encourages the thematization of body-oriented issues.

LATE CAPITALISM

The phrase "late capitalism" has both an ironic twist and some useful analytic scope. The phrase was inspired by the widespread political and expressive revolt among youth in Europe and North America during the sixties. From a progressive/Marxist perspective, the problem at the time was to explain why some students and intellectuals but not workers, organized labor, or "downscale" minorities had, apparently, become the "driving force of history." One prominent answer focused on the emergence of the "third technological revolution" in the capitalist system (Mandel, 1975).

According to Mandel (1975), the first technological revolution entailed a move from handcraft production to production by handcrafted machines, a move identified with the classic industrial revolution of the eighteenth century. The second revolution occurred at the end of the nineteenth century. It involved the application of machine-made machines (electric and steam) to the production of industrial goods (steel, oil, etc.) and consumer commodities. The third revolution took place after World War I. It resulted in the automatically controlled production of machine-made raw materials, for example, plastics.

Successive technological transformations subordinated workers to machines and increasingly removed workers from direct control of the production process. Crudely put, the point of critical dependence or vulnerability of capital to labor shifted from the operatives in the factory and on the shop floor to, eventually, the designers, programmers, and operators of the machines that, in turn, make and control the machines that are responsible for production. The revolt of the sixties, then, was in some sense a strike to establish rights in time of war by those who would provide the brainpower that was needed to reproduce the system of late capitalism. The "strikers" were, obviously, not the heirs of the "WORKINGMEN" *(sic)*, that is, the laboring bodies addressed by Marx and Engels in *The Communist Manifesto* of 1848.

The irony of Mandel's "late capitalism" lies in the supposition of capitalism's decline and the apprehension of a victorious socialism, with the disruptive events of 1968 serving as the "leading indicator." Ahead, however—but who could tell in the early seventies—lay an opposite course: the rise of Margaret Thatcher, the regime of Ronald Reagan, and, eventually, the *former* Soviet Union. Still, the British sociologists Scott Lash and John Urry, writing in 1987, would interpret the shift to the right in the 1980s as *The End of Organized Capitalism*. Given the subsequent unification of Germany, the collapse of the Warsaw Pact, and the demise of the Soviet Union, their title could now be glossed as a parody on the end of organized socialism.

Lash and Urry (1987:3–9), however, do provide a useful description of the most recent phase of capitalist development, which they label "disorganized" and which they contrast with the earlier phases of "organized" and "liberal" capitalism. Lash and Urry's phases are roughly coincident with Mandel's revolutions. The terms "organized" and "disorganized" are relative to one another and capture a sense of some of the changes that have taken place in recent years in the political economies of certain advanced Western nations: Britain, France, (West) Germany, Sweden, and the United States. The terms "organized" and "disorganized" are also used to describe differences between those nations regarding the degree of organization and interpenetration of capital, labor, and the state. Thus, for example, the United States relative to other nations has had the most highly organized capital sector, with close ties between banks and industry and with the state, more often than not, serving as an instrument of capital. On the other hand, labor in the United States has historically been less organized than elsewhere.

While Lash and Urry, then, recognize that capitalism is not a uniform entity even in the most advanced Western nations, they also argue that certain general changes can be detected in the systems of capitalism characteristic of those nations. Those changes can be conceptualized as a shift from "organized" to "disorganized" capitalism where disorganization is read as a devolution from one system state to another. "Disorganized," then, does not mean "unorganized" but, rather, indicates movement in a new direction.

Following Kocka (1974), Lash and Urry describe organized / modern capitalism and unorganized / late capitalism in terms of a number of interrelated properties. Those properties provide a general picture of the structural characteristics that constitute fields or limitations and possibilities for the actions of individuals and groups. While they are systemically interrelated, the structural characteristics of modern and late capitalism should not be viewed as indicators of closed determinate systems. They are, rather, contexts or conditions that vary as proximate and distant sources of action depending upon what is being examined.

According to Lash and Urry, then, organized, industrial, or modern capitalism has the following properties:

Capital. Capital is highly centralized, cartels proliferate, and special attention is given to the production of capital or producer's goods.

Ownership and Control. Ownership becomes separated from control, and control is vested in bureaucratically organized managerial hierarchies.

Occupational Change. There is marked growth in the managerial, scientific, and technological occupational sectors.

Organization of Interests. Workers and managers are organized in national unions and associations.

Redistribution of Wealth and Income. Class-specific welfare legislation is developed pursuant to the interests of the state and large monopolies in minimizing social conflict.

The State. Empires are expanded in order to control overseas markets and production. The attainment of national objectives is emphasized, and the state expands by incorporating many social categories and persons into the political process.

Extent of Capitalist Relations. Capitalist relations are concentrated in a few industries and in a small number of significant nation-states.

Dominant Sectors. Large numbers of workers are employed in the dominant industrial sectors of extraction and manufacturing.

Geographic Concentration/Dispersion. There is a high degree of regional industrial concentration. Large industrial cities dominate regions and provide centralized commercial and financial services.

Plant Size. Industrial plants grow in keeping with the logic of economies of scale.

Culture and Ideology. A cultural-ideological configuration embracing rationality, scientism, and nationalism is ascendent. The celebration of technical and scientific progress and national identity become central elements of public culture.

According to Lash and Urry, the current phase of capitalism—that is, disorganized or late capitalism—has the following properties:

Capital. Capital becomes less centralized at the level of the nation-state, cartels decline, and industrial, banking, and commercial enterprises are increasingly oriented to a world market. Consumer goods and services vastly outweigh capital goods as major sources of profits.

Ownership and Control. Ownership spreads to fiduciary institutions, for example, pension funds, where large pools of capital are managed on behalf of third parties who are neither direct owners nor managers.

Occupational Change. The white-collar and service sectors continue to expand. The absolute and relative size of the core manual working class declines.

Organization of Interests. Collective bargaining declines at the national level and increases at company and plant levels.

Redistribution of Wealth. The control of the state over large firms is diminished, and the centralized universalistic welfare state is challenged from the right and the left.

Growth/Change. Industrial capitalism spreads to the Third World, and proletarian jobs are exported from the First World to the Third World. There is a marked decline in class politics and an incorporation into the state of class-based interests.

Extent of Capitalist Relations. There is an expansion of the number of nation-states and the number of sectors within nation-states that are organized on the basis of capitalist relations of production.

Dominant Sectors. The number of workers employed in the manufacturing and extractive sectors declines, with concominant increases in the service sector and growth in the comodification of human relations, dependence on mental skills, and increases in the feminization of labor.

Geographic Concentration/Dispersion. The size of industrial cities diminishes as does their dominance of regional hinterlands. The regional concentration of industries and the shaping of politics and social relations by regional economies diminishes.

Plant Size. Average plant size declines.

Culture and Ideology. Cultural and ideological configurations that challenge science, aesthetic modernism, and nationalism appear and are distributed on a mass basis.

CAPITALISM AND THE BODY

No more than a casual glance at the TV or newspaper these days quickly reveals that the body—in one way or another—is on the public mind and that body-related matters have become a source of contentious and sometimes bizzare behavior. The range of phenomena include controversies about the social rights and organizational roles of gays and lesbians, definitions and revelations of sexual harrassment and sexual abuse, intense and sometimes violent behavior by those who favor or oppose abortion, and debate and action regarding the border separating art and pornography. Daily confessions in the media and the mass distribution of sexually explicit images and narratives of all forms and types define and produce a public presence for what in living memory would have once been viewed as the most intimate and hidden details regarding the body, its processes, uses, and treatment. Writing over twenty years ago, when abortion had newly emerged as an issue on the American public agenda, Nancy Howell noted that the "explanation of why a subject [like abortion] is taboo at one time and au courant soon after is not obvious" (quoted in Lee, 1969:3). The same could be said, today, for sexual harrassment and abuse, public discourse on sexual orientations, and, more generally, the diffuse "eroticization" of the public arena in recent times.

What, then, are the linkages between the structural characteristics of modern and late capitalism and changes that have occurred in the thematization and construction of the body as an object and source of social action and, especially, as a "revealed" or uncovered element in public discourse? Three trends in particular have left their traces on the body: (1) the growth of new forms of work, (2) significant increases in the production of consumer goods and services, (3) an intertwined set of forces deconstructing what has been called the "patric body" (Simpson, 1993).

The growth of new forms of work and the rise of consumerism, I will argue later, have produced a diffuse public sensibility—"an energized field of salience"—that privileges the body as a source and focus of action. That sensibility or field functions as a context, backdrop, or implicit stage where specific body-oriented issues are scripted and played out.

While dependent on the body-sensibility of late capitalism, the body-oriented issues that are, today, so much in the public eye—homosexuality, pornography, abortion, and so forth—find their proximate, immediate stimulus in the decline of the "patric body" or the ebbing of the hegemony of the male-dominated nuclear family. Thus, where the body-sensibility generated by late capitalism is conjoined to the forces operating to deconstruct the hegemony of the patric body, the contemporary politics of the body arises.

Under industrial or modern capitalism, nine of out ten people did manual work, making or moving things, in manufacturing, in farming, in mining, in transportation (Drucker, 1993:40). While the professional and managerial occupational sectors significantly expanded under industrial capitalism, they essentially constituted structures of command and control for skilled and unskilled workers whose hands and bodies performed primary production work. Modern capitalism required disciplined, trained bodies, bodies that moved as machines and often, in effect, became parts of machines. In other words, the modal form of work under modern or industrial capitalism was executed by and depended on controlled bodies.

While late capitalism still needs some controlled bodies to perform work, many manual jobs have been exported to the Third World. That trend plus a growth in jobs that require the invention, acquisition, and application of knowledge have shifted the critical dependence of late capitalism away from controlled bodies to proficient minds. In late capitalism there is less emphasis on making and moving things—particularly capital goods—and more emphasis on creating and applying knowledge in the production and marketing of consumer goods and services. Disciplined bodies are needed less and educated or creative minds more.

The differential needs of industrial and late capitalism for disciplined bodies and educated minds are reflected in the spatial distributions of populations in each case. Under industrial capitalism, populations were concentrated in large urban agglomerations. At the heart of the industrial city stood the factory, assembly line, mill, refinery, and power plant where, on a daily basis, workers, managers, and professionals were aggregated and concentrated. Work for most persons meant being in a given geographically precise spot for a given amount of time on a daily basis. To be "on time" and "on the line" meant that one was "at work." That is still true for many workers, but it holds true less for educated minds than for disciplined bodies.

Under industrial capitalism, manual workers brought their bodies to machines where they did their work. Under late capitalism, knowledge workers connect their minds to storehouses of knowledge—libraries, electronic databases, "hardened" knowledge in the form of machines that create or process facts and information—and then use their minds to reconfigure knowledge and produce new knowledge. From an ecological or spatial point of view, there is no need for the knowledge worker's body to be in any particular place as long as access to knowledge is available. Sometimes the knowledge worker only needs access to her or his brain. In a very diffuse sense, then, late capitalism underwrites a model of work that is increasingly indifferent to the spatial concentration and patterned movement of bodies in dedicated slots of time. In late capitalism, the disciplined body becomes a fixture and symbol of the past, an icon of the age of industrial capitalism, when work, more often than not, constrained the body to appear at appointed times and places in order to perform a repetitive sequence of regimented tasks.

Work in industrial capitalism not only constrained the body, but it was also part of a general system that focused on the production of capital goods and, as Marx (1954) noted, tended to maintain the retail consumption of workers at subsistence levels. Thus, industrial capitalism encouraged the rationalization and discipline of the body as both a dedicated producer and a consumer with limited horizons.

In late capitalism, the emphasis shifts from production to consumption. The hero of late capitalism (from the perspective of its center) is not the diligent worker. The hero of late capitalism is the unsatiated consumer desirous of new things and experiences. In late capitalism, much surplus value is allocated to a fiduciary system of capital formation that operates to smooth consumption over the life course by collectivizing savings in social security and pension funds. The remaining portion of surplus value—that which is not saved—must then be spent on goods and services in order to maintain the system. In late capitalism, fewer domestic units exist at the subsistence level than was the case for long periods of time under industrial capitalism. The relatively high level of economic well-being over all actors—individual and collective—in the system of late capitalism, then, requires the extraeconomic stimulation of demand. Thus, where industrial capitalism fostered the control of desire and the subjection of the body in order to implement the production of capital goods and capital formation based on the limitation of consumption, late capitalism encourages forces that stimulate desire in an economic order requiring a high rate of consumer demand for products and services. From the perspective of the history of human economic endeavor, many of those goods and services can only be labeled "sumptuous," that is, far beyond the requirements of ordinary necessity itself.

One can discern, then, an associative or correlative pattern in late capitalism between, on the one hand, the relaxation of controls over the body in the world of work as indexed by, say, the decreased need to concentrate workers at a particular place for a certain length of time and, on the other hand, the requirement that desire be stimulated in order to encourage the consumption of goods and services. It is perhaps trite to observe that advertising or, more generally, the images produced in the broad field of public relations in late capitalist societies are designed to stimulate desire by invoking sexualities of all kinds. What is, however, not so obvious is that the sexuality of contemporary public imagery goes hand-in-hand with the loosening of time/space constraints on the body in the world of work. Thus, mutually reinforcing moods and images arise in the realms of work and in public arenas as constructed in the media and its extensions. Those moods and images form an intertwined system of feedback, amplification, and gain that tends to measurably heighten a widespread sense of the body as an expressive primordial unit or a fundamental unit of action. Thus, it might be argued that the body in late capitalism has taken over, or, perhaps, added to the action, possibilities that were once attributed to the self under modern or industrial capitalism (Mead, 1934). In either case body and self are to be viewed as metaphors of action at the individual level.

Late capitalism, then, underwrites and engenders a diffuse sensibility that privileges the body as a source and focus of action. That sensibility originates in the orientations and moods derived from central tendencies in the organization of work and consumption characteristic of late capitalism, and it functions as a context, backdrop, or implicit stage where specific body-focused issues are scripted and played out in the contemporary situation. The "body-sensibility" of late capitalism is a cultural resource that can be used to frame issues in the public arena, issues that define and provoke the conflicts surrounding such matters as homosexuality, pornography, abortion, and, more generally, so-called family values. The specificity and definition of those issues is, however, not a singular consequence of late capitalism's body-sensibility. Rather, the politics of the body in late capitalism is a joint consequence of late capitalism's body-sensibility and the simultaneous deconstruction of what I have elsewhere called the "patric body" (Simpson, 1993)—a metaphor for the modal nuclear family characteristic of industrial capitalism.

The patric body exists where the family is a specialized unit of consumption and socialization (but not production), and public and private arenas are constructed as separate domains of masculine and feminine action, all subject to dominant masculine influence and control. The patric body is, metaphorically, a "distinctively gendered heterosexual body—male or female—producing and reproducing instrumental male dominance and expressive female submission" (Simpson, 1993:157).

The patric body is now under siege for three reasons: (1) Medical science has provided women with safe and effective means (including abortion) for controlling reproduction. Women can now be self-willed instruments of choice rather than unwilled objects victimized by the desire of the other. (2) The expansion of the service, information/knowledge production, and light industrial sectors and the "degendering" of traditional male jobs in late capitalism have widened the scope and enhanced the demand for female labor force participation. Thus, the nature and organization of work in late capitalism undoes the sense of necessity associated with the sharply gendered, heterosexually oriented division of labor characteristic of industrial capitalism. Where brainpower counts, it makes little difference what the gender or sexual orientation of the brain is. (3) The global institutionalization of human rights supports the allocation of social rights to previously "unrighted" bodies—women in general and gays and lesbians in particular (Simpson, 1992a:25). Where, under the hegemony of male heterosexuality, gender and sexual orientation were once excluded as bases for claims to resources, they can now at the limit be invoked (usually informally) as reasons for the differential allocation of resources or "discrimination" favoring woman, gays, and lesbians. More often, formal administrative and legal claims are expressed in terms of nondiscrimination in the distribution of resources. In either case, claims are, in the final analysis, founded on the global institutionalization of human rights as a set of evaluative standards for judging the actions of nation-states and the institutions and collectivities within their bounds.

Laid against the background of late capitalism's body-sensibility, the deconstruction of the patric body, then, generates a field of combat thematizing a host of issues that, essentially, focus on the body as a primary unit of social action. Who has the right to control the reproductive process? What kinds of work can be done by what kinds of gendered and sexually oriented bodies? How are resources, in general, to be distributed to differentially gendered and sexually oriented bodies? When and how does the body become gendered and sexually oriented and who has the right to define and control that construction? How extensive are the social, economic, and political rights of differentially gendered and sexually oriented bodies? What are the legitimate pleasures and pursuits of differentially gendered and sexually oriented bodies? Are the interests of differentially gendered and sexually oriented bodies ultimately reconcilable or not? Are differential gender and sexual orientations the fundamental conditions of otherness that constitute the human condition? All of those issues and questions assume that the body is a fundamental unit of social action and all arise from the deconstruction of the patric body in the context of the body-sensibility of late capitalism.

It is, then, from the perspective of the body as a constructed social unit and contested site of action in late capitalism that, say, the issue of abortion can be approached and understood. But abortion, it should be clear, does not stand alone. The forces that encourage bitter conflicts between supporters and opponents of free access to abortion clinics in America also underwrote the convergence of one million gays, lesbians, bisexuals, and transgendered persons on Washington, D.C., in April 1993 in support of equal rights. The specific manifest focus of action in each case is quite different. The underlying latent cause is the same: action possibilities, orientations, purposes, and resources that can be traced to the deconstruction of the patric body against the background of the body-sensibility generated by late capitalism. The contemporary politics of the body arises in that context.

CONCLUSION

Late capitalism, I have argued, thematizes the body as a fundamental unit of social action and thereby makes a politics of the body possible. By underwriting the intensification of body-sensibility in the context of the deconstruction of the patric body, late capitalism creates a systemic capacity for the politics of the body. Typifying and analyzing late capitalism, as has been done here, provides an answer to the question regarding *why* a politics of the body exists in the contemporary situation. *How* the politics of the body are shaped and contested in concrete action—a topic that is beyond the scope of this chapter—depends largely on the structure of the public and political arenas where such politics is a possibility. Insight into how the structure of public arenas constrain and mold the politics of the body would be gained by comparing societies that are similar in their exposure to the forces of late capitalism but different in terms of the structure of their public arenas and the social characteristics, attitudes, and beliefs of the individual and collective actors in those arenas. (At the individual level of analysis the minimal list of properties would include age, education, sex, religious tradition, religiosity, and location in the economic system.) On the other hand, where public arenas are similar (that is, are held constant) but the structure of capitalism varies (modern, late, contemporary Asian, etc.), the likelihood of an intense politics of the body should covary with the structure of capitalism.

While this chapter provides a conceptual guide for empirical work, as suggested in the previous paragraph, it also raises questions regarding the development of interpretive perspectives that enable us to grasp the complexities of the contemporary situation and render them sensible in terms of an adequate theoretical discourse. In that regard I have argued here that there is a broad correspondence between the structural characteristics of late capitalism and the thematization of the body as a unit of social action.

That type of argument has a clear line of descent from the perspectives found in the sociological classics and, in particular, in Marx (1990) and Durkheim (1964), who, in various ways, posited a correspondence between ideologies or cultural categories and the structural characteristics of human systems of action. Some, today, would cast aside that notion, claiming that it is inadequate.

In his monumental work *Communities of Discourse*, Robert Wuthnow (1989) argues forcefully and at length against the classic sociological notion of correspondence between ideology, culture, and social structure on the grounds that the posited relationship is seldom, if ever, accounted for in a satisfactory way. Furthermore, where an empirical association is found between ideology or culture and social structure, it is usually interpreted or justified in terms of being simply an instance of the posited association, which, of course, is no justification at all since the consequent is assumed by such an argument.

Wuthnow's argument is cogent and attractive (Simpson, 1992). Why, then, would one want to pursue the type of analysis presented herein? A clue may be found by considering Wuthnow's notion of culture and my fleeting observation (made earlier in this chapter) that "the body in late capitalism has taken over, or, perhaps, added to the action, possibilities that were once attributed to the self under modern or industrial capitalism."

According to Wuthnow, culture is a visible empirical "product." Culture is texts, or, more generally, public observable symbols. In Wuthnow's view culture is not internalized beliefs, values, and attitudes. In the classic sociological tradition, the self is conceived as a set of internalized beliefs, values, and attitudes (Mead, 1934). However, that notion—that is, the notion of the self as a set of internalized beliefs, values, and attitudes or a representation of the social structures and processes in which the organism is embedded—has, in effect, been questioned and attacked in contemporary postmodern analysis, where the "death of the social" and the substitution of a "hyperreal" world of imagery for a "real" world of social interaction are proclaimed (Baudrillard, 1983; Kroker and Cook, 1986). Whatever they may be, selves in postmodern thought are not representations or internalizations of social structures and social processes. Thus, in a very broad sense Wuthnow's view of what culture is—visible artifacts, not internalized beliefs, and so forth—resonates with postmodern suspicions about the "classical" self, suspicions that are consonant with rejections of correspondence theories of social structure and the self.

If there is little basis for the "classical" self in the situation of postmodern late capitalism, there clearly is no room for a correspondence theory of the self and social structure, since there is no self to correspond with anything. But now, if you will, consider the body in late capitalism. The body in late capitalism, it would seem, is a visible artifact, a text, or publicly observable symbol. In other words, the body in late capitalism is an element of culture in Wuthnow's sense of that term. Of course, one might still be uneasy and reticent about pursuing a correspondence theory of culture and social structure with special attention to the body even if one grants that the body is a cultural element, perhaps the fundamental cultural element in late capitalism and the only adequate metaphor for individual action in the contemporary situation. I hope the substance of this chapter mitigates any uneasiness and reticence that might constrain the development of perspectives that would provide us with a deeper understanding of the correspondence between the body as a cultural element and the political economies in which the body is embedded in the twilight of the twentieth century.

2 Seeking a Sociologically Correct Name for Abortion Opponents

James R. Kelly

There is little doubt that the movement that arose in the mid-1960s to defeat efforts to make abortion legal was and is a social movement. All serious students of the abortion controversy agree that the label "social movement" fits (Leahy, 1975; Kelly, 1981; Luker, 1984; Francome, 1984; Spitzer, 1987; Cuneo, 1989). But what kind of social movement is it, how should we describe it, and—for this is also relevant to naming it—what are we to think of it? "Naming," "describing," "explaining," and "judging" are distinct but interrelated acts wherein what we think about a movement decisively affects our scholarly descriptions. In not always apparent ways, the undertow of moral judgment deeply affects our descriptions of all social phenomena but especially of social movements. For as McAdam and his colleagues (1988:727) astutely note, most sociologists are interested in social movements because they are interested in their outcomes as "an important force for social change." Probably all judgments about the appropriate name of a social movement involve some anticipation of final outcomes. By "final outcome" I mean the scholar's guess as to whether future generations will think of the movement as representing human progress, human loss, or some complex combination of both.

It is also worth noting that when labels are contested, the winning label can tell us something about the interests of society's most dominant sectors and groups. Although the general public remains ambivalent,[1] the media labeling of the movements promoting and opposing legal abortion, and the evaluation of each, has just about been decided. Promoters of legal abortion have won and abortion opponents have lost.

In a November–December 1989 memo sent out electronically to its news service subscribers, *The New York Times* informed inquiring editors that the *Times*'s policy is to describe opposition to abortion not as prolife but as antiabortion. Regional and local practice have come to imitate the elite media's acceptance of the term "prochoice" and its rejection of "prolife" or "right-to-life" (see Sipe, 1989). In his three-part series on abortion reportage, *Los Angeles Times* Pulitzer award winner David Shaw (1990b) concluded that major print and television media almost always report about abortion in terms favoring those who defend it. Ethan Bronner of the *Boston Globe* told Shaw that "opposing abortion, in the eyes of most journalists, is not a legitimate civilized position in our society."

It's likely that editors think of their use of these terms as value-neutral. Gans (1979:191–92) astutely observes that the majority of elite journalists consider themselves nonideological. Even more astutely, he adds, "At the same time, the journalists' definition of ideology is self-serving, if not intentionally so, for it blinds them to the fact that they also have ideologies, even if they are largely unconscious." For example, the following appears in the *New York Times* (1989) memo sent around the country about the use of fair terms in abortion reporting, "WE DO USE: women, not mother, in reference to a pregnant woman. Everyone agrees she's a woman; some say she isn't a mother until she gives birth. WE DO USE: fetus, not baby, in reference to the embryo *[sic]* she carries. There's agreement that it's a fetus, no agreement that it's a baby." Needless to say, these choices are not morally innocent. Critics could point out that they prejudge the entire moral debate in subtle ways and, in effect, settle it.

Indeed, legal abortion activists knew from the start how important it was to avoid or to neutralize any reference to the object of abortion. Faux (1988:236) reports that the coordinator of *amici curiae* pro-*Roe* briefs promoted the term "prochoice" in the briefs and "cautioned brief writers never to use the word 'baby' [or] the strident, hackle-raising expression 'abortion on demand.'"

More than most social movements, the ones that emerged around abortion have dealt with conflicts about "correct naming." What do we call the object of abortion? Abortion opponents speak of unborn babies, while proponents prefer "fetal tissue" or "the products of conception." Science has not helped, for those with acknowledged scientific credentials can be produced by protagonists to describe the object of abortion as "human life" or as merely "potential human life." See, for example, the extensive testimony given on April 23, April 24, and May 20, 1981, during the Hearings before the Subcommittee on the Judiciary of the United States Senate on S. 158, called "The Human Life Bill," whose section 1 declared: "The Congress finds that present day scientific evidence indicates a significant likelihood that actual human life exists from conception."[2]

Gans (1979:184) makes the interesting observation that "although journalists may not be aware of it, they are perhaps the strongest remaining bastion of logical positivism in America." In reporting on the controversy about abortion, media elites have adopted language that suppresses the very moral conflict that abortion opponents claim has prompted their activism. What about sociologists? Do social scientists show more reflexivity than elite journalists?[3] The few sociological studies of the abortion controversy with comprehensive aims already show clear tendencies, like the national media, to confidently reject the movement name chosen by abortion opponents themselves. Petchesky (1990:chap. 7), Staggenborg (1991:188), and Davis (1985:237) describe the movement opposing legal abortion not only as "anti"-abortion but also as "anti"-feminist. Davis (1985:15, 12) adds, "She could not ethically" study the movement "that calls itself 'right-to-life' " and acknowledges that she writes from "the point of view of abortion partisans." In their authoritative chapter "Social Movements" for Neil Smelzer's *Handbook of Sociology* (McAdam, McCarthy, and Zald, 1988:711) McAdam and colleagues characterize the opposition against legal abortion as a "reactionary movement" that "emerged in opposition to the feminist movement." Their momentarily authoritative academic appraisal probably reflects the sentiments of large numbers of sociological professionals. Even the more sensitive scholars show strong tendencies to judge abortion opponents as perhaps sincere but morally limited by their "traditional ethic" regarding abortion (Luker, 1984:207).

WHAT DO WE MEAN BY "SOCIAL MOVEMENT"?

Among the defining characteristics of social science are the search for phenomenological accuracy and objective analysis, elusive goals that are severely tested in the continuing conflicts raised by abortion. Here especially studies conducted over time by women and men of different cognitive and moral orientations will be necessary for the complex understandings sought by scholarship. As a start, it makes some sense to begin with the terms and approaches in the social movement literature that seem more unproblematically to fit what is empirically known so far about abortion activists. Then we can move to issues of naming, which, as I have already mentioned, involve questions of evaluation and even anticipations about the future. My argument will be that it still is not clear what label appropriately fits abortion opponents and that any worthy resolution of the labeling issue hinges on whether most remain an antiabortion countermovement or continue to evolve more fully into a prolife social movement. This evolution, in turn, greatly hinges on the movement's continuing capacity to enter new coalitions, including some that are prochoice but not proabortion.

Some Social Movement Perspectives

Technical definitions aside, for scholars and others the main point of using the term "social movement" is to quickly communicate something of the flavor of many thousands of people who feel strongly and certainly about something in a situation where "politics as usual" fails them and who, despite many differences and obstacles, form an evolving collective consciousness prompting them to create new organizations. The social identity of a movement links together the individual motivations of each activist, creating bonds among them far deeper than the transient alliances among political actors. For this very reason, the internal politics and the shifting trajectories of movement strategies are even less predictable than conventional politics. The very term "movement" suggests the fluidity that defeats, or at least thwarts, the intellectual mastery scholars seek. While the category of an "authorized" biography makes sense, an "authorized study of a social movement" is a nonsense term precisely because a social movement (as long as it remains one) has no single authorized voice.[4] Which of the competing, indeed warring, social movement organizations would accept as authoritative any analysis other than their own current version? Indeed, an authoritative account would signify that the movement had ended, either by a final defeat or by assimilation into a contemporary stage of "politics as usual." Till their demise as victors or forgotten losers, social movements remain mostly messy and unpredictable, especially since they seek innovative approaches to counter the failure (for them at least) of politics as usual.

Even after their emergent stages, "social movements" have no central address, no one official spokesperson, no single zone of activity that the investigator can approach for a definitive account of exactly what is happening and why. A social movement will appear unitary and coordinated only to its ideological opponents. It is no surprise that in the conclusion (1988:728–29) of their overview for the *Handbook of Sociology,* McAdam, McCarthy, and Zald note that while there are many studies of the emergence of social movements, "we know comparatively little about the dynamics of collective action over time." Social movements are too messy, too much in flux, and they take too long. Social movements with any vitality follow centrifugal forces of moral and strategic analyses and outlive the intellectual career of any scholar or even generation of scholars, if the reason for the movement touches deeply some central dimension of the meaning of community and the worth of the mostly ordinary people who live within it.

Defining a Social Movement

In their overview of social movements for the *Handbook of Sociology,* McAdam and his colleagues never actually define a social movement.

While not explicitly apologetic, they do note the difficulties of even de-scribing "the range of phenomena lumped together under the heading of social movements" (1988:695). Still, definitions of social movements abound. In fact, two of the three authors of the *Handbook* sans definition overview have elsewhere (Zald and McCarthy, 1987:20) defined social movements as "a set of opinions and beliefs in a population representing preferences for changing some elements of the social structure or reward distribution, or both, of a society. A counter movement is a set of opinions and beliefs in a population opposed to a social movement. As is clear, we view social movements as nothing more than preference structures directed toward social change, very similar to what political sociologists would term *issue cleavage*."

Especially since it embraces the notion of "counter movement," this contemporary definition of social movements can serve as our starting point. As McAdam and his colleagues (1988:722) note, a necessary task hardly begun by students is "to map the chesslike interaction that charac-terizes movement-countermovement relations." It might even be the case that the terms "movement" and "countermovement" cannot be univo-cally, much less permanently, applied to social movement protagonists. Unsurprisingly, McAdam and his colleagues acknowledge there is no the-ory of "movement development," "no real theory of the effect of move-ment participation on the individual," (1988:729) and little knowledge of what happens "in between" the emergence of a social movement and its social outcomes. This caution is especially worth remembering when we discuss both abortion opponents and supporters, and I will return to it in my conclusion.

But most nonspecialists, such as myself, turn to the social movement literature more pragmatically, as a source of terms, perspectives, and in-sights formed by the many scholars who have studied the many different kinds of people who shared a catalytic experience when elites dismissed their moral claims and in response formed the fledgling organizations and searched for the arguments to change what they had come to see as an intolerable state of affairs. For the study of the controversy over abortion it makes sense to conjoin the more contemporary emphasis on "resource mobilization" with the older scholarly tradition—characterized as the "hearts and minds" approach—that gave more explicit emphasis to the moral grievances experienced by activists. Besides, the controversy over abortion is likely to outlive the momentary emphases of contemporary fashions in social movement analyses.

Some Applicable Social Movement Terms

Gamson (quoted in Zald and McCarthy, 1987:6) has warned that in "resource mobilization" perspectives "the meanings that participants give to their involvement in collective action are made to seem largely irrelevant." In explaining the origins of social movements, resource mobilization perspectives stress the role of structural factors (such as the availability of time, money, expertise, organizations, government support) rather than, as in past studies, the grievances held by a segment of the population. Zald and McCarthy (1987:337–38) respond that while it makes sense to note that in a culture stressing equality and rights there will always be large pockets of "grievances" waiting for mobilization (and so speak of moral entrepreneurs and the bureaucratization of social discontent), they wish to correct, not replace, the earlier emphasis on the consciousness of social movement activists. The study of the abortion controversy especially shows the need to link "resource mobilization" perspectives with the earlier focus on motivations. Studying the movements originating in the dispute about legal abortion solely in terms of "structural resources" would be analogous to the critic analyzing interpretations of *Hamlet* solely in terms of the differences in Elizabethan and Broadway production costs. Above all, collectively shared moral sentiments are precisely what "moves" social movements, which is precisely why they cannot easily be assimilated into politics as usual. Indeed, politics as usual typically reproduces social order by masking moral disputes with the neutralizing language of efficiency and management. The inattention of contemporary "resource mobilization" perspectives to the motivations and arguments of movement activists, and thus to their moral claims, means that it can only partially serve in an analysis of the abortion controversy. But we can begin with it, for both protaganists.

ALL RESOURCES ARE NOT EQUAL

Both the term "grass roots" and the term "social movement" apply far more to abortion opponents than to proponents. Staggenborg (1991) has shown, both before and after *Roe*, the difficult and often failed attempts of the full-time staff of national abortion rights groups to maintain a grassroots presence and the local activities characteristic of authentic social movements. McCarthy (1987:33) describes the prochoice movement in terms neatly fitting the core premises of the "resource mobilization" perspective. Groups supporting legal abortion are characterized by paid functionaries, formal bureaucracies, and philanthropic funding. "Its relative lack of usable social infrastructures compared with the pro-life movement leads it to depend far more heavily upon modern mobilization technologies in order to aggregate people and resources." McCarthy (1987:33) concludes that it "can be safely said that pro-life is more dense in numbers, more grass-roots in nature, more variegated in organizational form" than prochoice organizations. McCarthy found (1987:59) that the membership of a main abortion rights social movement organization, the National

Abortion Rights Action League (NARAL, originally the National Association for the Repeal of Abortion Laws), were highly educated (55 percent with some graduate training), rarely active in local chapters (only 13 percent, and 60 percent explicitly said they would not join), and most (77 percent) did not know if any of their friends were members. Indeed, McCarthy describes the membership of each of the major groups associated with the protection of legal abortion—the American Civil Liberties Union, the National Organization for Women (NOW), Planned Parenthood, and Population Control groups—as comprised of large numbers of isolated members whose involvement is limited to paying dues and receiving newsletters. Their isolated members can only be mobilized for "one shot emergency appeals which can be elegantly coordinated with legislative and movement struggle" (1987:60). Prochoice attempts to create stable grassroots groups have been generally unsuccessful. Both pre- and post-*Roe,* legal abortion groups had and have, in McCarthy's phrase, "thin infrastructures." A cofounder of the National Association for the Repeal of Abortion Laws (Lader, 1973:vii) recalled that until the late 1960s their movement was a "lonely" one consisting of "only a few clusters in a few states." Staggenborg (1991:57) writes that it was *Roe* itself that "created legitimacy for the movement." Rubin (1987:1) characterizes the legal abortion movement not as a "grass roots" campaign but as a "litigation campaign," where pressure group activity was "tailored to fit the format of a lawsuit but specifically designed to produce broad social change rather than to vindicate the private rights of the parties." Litigation campaigns originate not with grass-roots groups but with elites who control significant economic and social resources. Rubin points out (1987:3) that litigation campaigns are extremely costly: "To control, organize, and manage a carefully selected sequence of cases, it is also necessary to have sizable resources in money, legal talent, and experience. Funding is especially important, for litigation is expensive." In litigation campaigns, the characteristic resource is not grass-roots volunteers but routine access to elite networks. Ordinary people start social movements; elites start litigation campaigns.

Litigation campaigns are relatively new. Faux (1988:233–36) describes what she calls, for that time, the novel strategy of the "Association for the Study of Abortion" which, with an active membership of only 20 (Staggenborg, 1991:15), solicited and orchestrated "amici curiae briefs" from medical, professional, academic, religious, and women's groups. The only failure was the attempt to organize briefs from black women and from prominent American women who had had abortions. Faux (1988:234) recalls that the coordinator "felt the idea died mostly because abortion was still enough of a taboo in the United States to dissuade women from taking so personally revealing a stand." (It was not until eighteen years after *Roe* that a book—Angela Bonavoglia's *The Choices We Made* [Random

House, 1991]—was published in which public personalities discussed their own abortions.) Faux does not offer any explanation why the brief by black women failed, though elsewhere Fried (1990:Introduction) suggests that the mainstream prochoice movement—especially NARAL and NOW—failed to "mobilize women of color" on the grass-roots level because it narrowly serves the interests of white middle class women.

Abortion Opponents Had Mostly People, Abortion Reformers Had Mostly Connections

The Association for the Study of Abortion obtained forty-two briefs, a record at the time, showing that abortion movement activists, in Staggenborg's phrase (1991:13, 17), were "in no way 'outsiders' " to national and local centers of power. Their abortion opponents lacked this movement centralization and commanded no similar elite support. The Supreme Court received only four prolife briefs: Americans United for Life, National Right to Life, LIFE (the league for infants, fetuses, and the elderly), and "certain physicians of the American College of Obstetricians and Gynecologists." While very few Americans would recognize the three groups signing prolife briefs, signers of pro-*Roe* briefs included well-known and prestigious professional groups, such as the American Medical Association, the American Psychiatric Association, the American Women's Association, NOW, the National Board of YWCAs, as well as many prominent women. Staggenborg (1991:37) describes as especially important resources for legal abortion proponents the American Civil Liberties Union and the Law Center for Constitutional Rights. She acknowledges that legal abortion lacked widespread grass-roots support: "It was important that the victory was achieved by movement participation in an arena in which the countermovement was comparatively weak." Lader, a cofounder of NARAL, recalled that the elective abortion found constitutional in *Roe* "came like a thunderbolt. . . . It was even more conclusive than any of us had dared to hope." In short, the evidence strongly supports Rubin's description of legal abortion activists as conducting a "litigation campaign" (1987:1) rather than starting a "social movement." Staggenborg (1991:33) reports that when the "National Association for the Repeal of Abortion Laws" began in 1969 they had no more than five hundred individual contributors and only eighteen "organizational members," who planned strategy and tactics without consulting even their small membership. A member of the first abortion activist group, the "California Society for Humane Abortion" (1961), told Staggenborg (1991:47), "Really, our major accomplishment was in talking about abortion, saying the word outloud rather than using euphemisms." At that time abortion lacked the moral legitimacy necessary to generate a vital grass-roots movement. Staggenborg's (1991:29) informants recalled that "the word 'abortion' could barely be mentioned in public when the movement began."

But while abortion was still considered disreputable (Davis, 1985:xiii), and thus outside conventional politics, legal abortion activists had routine access to powerful political support. The immediate bridge was the growing government interest in population control and the putative threat to American national security posed by a growing Third World population (Donaldson, 1990:25, 27). Donaldson (1990:32) recalls that in the early 1960s "worries about the Soviet Union and the possibility of Communist-inspired revolutions in the Third World were widespread in government and foreign-policy circles." Funding for population control in the Agency for International Development began with a modest $2.1 million dollars in 1965 and quickly reached $185 million by 1980 (also Back, 1989:107). The founders of the National Association for the Repeal of Abortion Law (Staggenborg, 1991:25) were mostly "single-issue activists with backgrounds in the family planning and population movements" who later added a women's rights framework to their campaign. These single-issue activists had ready access to wealthy donors and (Staggenborg, 1991:33) they "routinely received large donations." Back (1989:108) reports that by 1969 global population had become such a salient issue that "even the question of domestic overpopulation started to arouse concern, prompting Congress to establish a Commission on Population Growth and the American Future which included among its recommendations legal abortion and its public funding for poor women."

NARAL Successfully Woos NOW

The abortion activists' ties (Staggenborg, 1991:3) to the population movement were especially important for fund-raising. Staggenborg (1991:19) found a large overlap in the memberships of NARAL and Zero Population Growth (ZPG), noting that "the movement for legal abortion was very small during this period and so needed ZPG's help." Lader, a cofounder of NARAL, was a ZPG board member and author of (1971) *Breeding Ourselves to Death*. Lader also persuaded Betty Friedan that the newly formed National Organization for Women should endorse legal abortion, which NOW did in 1967. Tribe (1990:44) observes that while legal abortion now "virtually defines the women's movement," in her 1963 classic work *The Feminine Mystique* Friedan does not even mention abortion. Staggenborg (1991:20) reports that Friedan's decision committing NOW to abortion advocacy provoked considerable conflict within NOW and did not necessarily represent a majority position. Clarke Phelan, coordinator of NOW's task force on abortion, recalled, "There was no networking [about the decision]. There were phone calls for those that could afford them, but no regular communication" (Staggenborg,

1991:20). When NOW endorsed legal abortion, many delegates resigned (Tribe, 1990:45). Even later, some chapters tried to remove abortion from NOW's "Bill of Rights for Women" because it made their work on other issues in their own communities more difficult. In fact, in 1972 two former members of NOW, one expelled because she objected to including legal abortion in NOW's bill of rights, founded *Feminists for Life of America* (FFL). The inside cover of the FFL quarterly *Sisterlife* explains that "FFL continues the work of over a century of pro-life feminism, working for a society in which women are enabled to make life-affirming choices for themselves and their children. Feminists for Life of America is a member of the Seamless Garment Network, and supports the Network's mission of opposing the violence of war, abortion, poverty, euthanasia, and the death penalty."

Abortion Brakes the Feminist Agenda

Because the prochoice movement remained highly dependent on the population control organizations, grass-roots feminist groups were not able to successfully contest its increasingly single-issue focus (Back, 1989:154ff); Davis, 1985:121, 2; Staggenborg, 1991:110). Staggenborg (1991:44) reports that while "some of my informants confessed a bit of embarrassment in looking back at their own rhetoric, at the time they thought of themselves as part of a larger movement that was challenging basic social, economic, and political institutions. Legal abortion was simply a part of the larger revolution they thought was near. Their goal was to create participatory democratic institutions that would serve human needs rather than corporate interest." More specifically, they wanted to create a nonprofit, high-quality health care delivery system.

But those interested primarily in a single-issue population control approach rejected any feminist linkage of legal abortion with political and economic reforms. Before *Roe,* differences between single-issue abortion movement groups and feminist groups were often intense. After *Roe,* feminist groups had trouble sustaining any linkage between legal abortion and a more comprehensive approach that ensured that women with problem pregnancies and in difficult circumstances had more choices than abortion. No longer were there prominent prochoice groups expressing concerns about the misuse of abortion as a way of controlling the welfare costs of minority and poor populations. For example, after *Roe* The Committee for Abortion Rights and Against Sterilization Abuse and the Reproductive Rights National Network had difficulty attracting either funds or members, and both became defunct. Feminists seeking to promote legal abortion within a "multiissue approach," especially for "women of color," were told that a comprehensive approach was a luxury and were accused of having a "holier than thou attitude" (Staggenborg, 1991:120). Davis

(1985:19–20) more pointedly contrasts feminist approaches to abortion with the "anti-poverty ideology that pervades" the "population control enterprise." Within the "population control enterprise," Davis includes demographers, epidemiologists, public health bureaucrats, drug companies, family planning counselors, and abortion clinics as well as explicit population control groups. These groups, she claims (1985:19–20), share a dominant metaphor of "control by technology" and "a narrow belief in the salvation of rationality, of limiting births as a necessary and sufficient tool of progress." Back (1989:154) warns, "If the principles of family planning and population control are carried to their ultimate logical conclusion, then they will inevitably conflict with many of the principles of other movements who generally support family planning aims." He cautions that population control elites do not openly oppose social welfare policies that encourage childbirth among the poor (such as welfare, maternal benefits, free education) only because at present "this would be tactically unwise" (1989:154). Since supporting legal abortion is not synonymous with supporting "prochoice," perhaps sometime soon someone will write "Seeking a Sociologically Correct Name for Abortion Proponents."

Are the Adjectives "Progressive" and "Retrogressive" Forever Fixed?

Francome (1984:210) has observed a worldwide pattern where economic elites quickly come to support abortion as a way of controlling births among the "unproductive" classes. In the United States the great disparity in elite status between pro- and antiabortion groups can be quickly shown by a breakdown of the *amici curiae* briefs filed in the July 3, 1989, Supreme Court decision *Webster v. Missouri Reproductive Services* which, because it partially returned abortion legislation to the state legislative level, represented a new stage in the controversy. There was massive professional activity against *Webster,* from organizations that include the American Medical Association, the American Psychological Association, the American Academy of Child and Adolescent Psychiatry, the American Academy of Pediatricians, the Population Council, Planned Parenthood Federation of America, the Sierra Club, and many more (see Kelly, 1990:692–93). In contrast, pro-*Webster* briefs came from few professional groups (and only from those formed specifically to dissent from parent organizations, such as the American Association of Pro-Life Pediatricians.)

Although there is presently a pronounced tendency within the social movement literature to describe the movement opposing abortion as a "countermovement" driven by "antifeminist" sentiments (Staggenborg, 1991:188), this judgment stems more from presuppositions than from actual historical or social survey evidence (Cook, Jelen, and Wilcox, 1992:76ff., "Abortion and Gender Role Attitudes"). Besides, an early theoretical closure prevents scholars and others from noting the increasingly complex coalitions sought by some in the movement. It will be some time before the final outcome of the abortion controversy will safely allow commentators to decide which aspects of the social movement organizations it gave rise to warrant the adjective "counter" and "antifeminist" and which warrant different descriptions entirely. To begin, we must first briefly review the history of the movement and its shifting emphases over time.

ORIGINS, EMPHASES, AND DEVELOPMENTS OF ORGANIZATIONS OPPOSING ABORTION

True enough, the first grass-roots opponents of abortion were almost entirely reactive and limited to efforts to maintain the existing abortion laws. While the first public opponents to legal abortion were lawyers and doctors, the grass-roots organizations that began around 1966 attracted more ordinary people. More than half were women, almost always mothers with small children at home (Kelly, 1981:655; Leahy, 1975:51; Luker, 1984:138; Spitzer, 1987:58, 84). While many were active in local voluntary organizations (especially church-related) ones, few had any political experience. Spitzer (1987:58) describes the founders of the Right-to-Life Party (now mostly New York–based) as previously "apolitical." Edward Golden, the first president of the primary social movement organization that opposed abortion, The National Right to Life Committee (NRLC), had to take a course in public speaking. Undoubtedly a majority of the first activists were Roman Catholic, and from the start prochoice leaders exploited this fact. One of NARAL's first projects was "to train local activists and to expose the Catholic Church's backing of the anti-abortion movement" (Staggenborg, 1991:48). "Naral was constantly urging the formation of Catholics for Abortion Repeal" and adopted a policy of support for Catholic legislators favoring repeal" (Staggenborg, 1981:39). Nathanson (1983:173ff.), cofounder of NARAL, reports that the description of opposition to abortion as financed by the American bishops was a conscious distortion by NARAL. It is likely that histories of abortion law changes in particular states will replicate Morrison's (1982:iv) finding in Washington State that legal abortion advocates consciously masked the widespread opposition to abortion by "focusing on Catholics as the source of all opposition."

Yet even the first activists included many Protestants and some Jews (Kelly, 1981:655; Luker, 1984:196; Cuneo, 1989:6). A major reason why Protestant presence in the movement was so delayed was the mistaken Protestant leadership belief that abortion reform would comprise only the so-called hard cases of incest, rape, and severe threats to health and that it would specify that procedures be performed early in pregnancy.[5] Only after *Roe* were arguments publicly advanced defending elective abortion throughout pregnancy.

The accounts given by the first activists themselves differ greatly from those promoted by NARAL and other legal abortion activists. The activists were self-financed and often complained that they received little help from their local clergy. They argued against abortion in purely secular terms, claiming that it offended the foundational principle of the social order, the right to life, and, by eroding the respect for vulnerable life, in time would lead to further erosions, such as infanticide and euthanasia.

Studies of the first grass-roots opponents of abortion describe them as spontaneously experiencing a quick and powerful sense of moral repulsion to legalized abortion (Kelly, 1981:659; Leahy, 1975:45ff.; Luker, 1984:146ff.). They claimed that biology (giving clear evidence that abortion stopped a developing human life) and not theology or sectarian teaching was their determinative frame of reference. The movement's main recruitment tactic was not church teachings but pictures of fetal development and of aborted fetuses, especially from late-term abortions. Dr. Jack Wilke, president of the NRLC during the 1980s, credits the massive distribution of these graphic photos for the defeats of the 1972 Michigan and South Dakota referenda on legal abortion. Activists found it significant that supporters of legal abortion agreed to debate them publicly only after they promised not to exhibit the pictures that they called "proof" but their opponents called "emotional."

The Early Role of American Roman Catholicism

Studies of these activists uniformly find high levels of commitment, time (Luker, 1984:218; Leahy, 1982:68), and self-financing (Luker, 1984:223; Burtchaell, 1982:124–26). But the Roman Catholic Church played an important role in stabilizing antiabortion sentiment. Since 1966 the American Catholic Church monitored the efforts to make abortions legal (first through the Family Life Bureau of the United States Catholic Conference and after *Roe* with an explicit Secretariat for Pro-Life Activities). These offices functioned as a center of information about national trends and arguments, and it was only after the 1973 *Roe* decision that an autonomous and clearly secular national social movement organization called the National Right to Life Committee was formed. Catholicism's contribution to the movement opposing abortion was simultaneously crucial and limiting. Crucial because from the mid-1960s to the mid-1970s no other widely recognized institutional presence lent its direct support to abortion opponents. Limiting because Roman Catholicism's teachings that all directly intended abortions were immoral and that "artificial" forms of contraception violated its moral teaching created tensions with many Protestant opponents of abortion. In 1974, a separate national organization,

American Citizens Concerned for Life (ACCL), formed to take a more flexible approach to legal abortion, accepting restrictive rather than prohibitive laws and, unlike the single-issue National Right to Life Committee, supporting social policies that might lessen the social and economic pressures on women and families who otherwise might think of abortion as the sole way of dealing with unwanted pregnancies (Kelly, 1988:708–11). While the National Right to Life Committee took no position on contraception, ACCL explicitly supported family planning funding and sex education as well as increased welfare benefits and employment training programs. But by 1987, ACCL had found little national attention or interest in its comprehensive approach to abortion, and ceased its activities.

Liberal Protestants opposed to permissive abortion laws found early antiabortion strategies too absolutist, too narrow, too innocent of social realities. It was not easy to place the liberal Protestant conscience within the movement where the Catholic presence was so pervasive. But liberal Protestants opposed to permissive abortion laws could not easily form their own organizations, for by the end of the 1960s the major mainstream Protestant leadership had identified their churches with what they mistakenly took to be the modest reformist goals of those seeking to change the laws. Especially important was the sensitivity of these Protestant leaders to feminists who argued that a ban on all non-life-threatening abortions—the position of Catholic leaders—seemed to regard a woman's future as morally less significant than fetal life (Kelly, 1989b).

The Influence of the Reagan Embrace

The Reagan administration's support politically strengthened the movement opposing legal abortion but obscured its internal divisions, in particular, the existence of the movement's prolife or consistent ethic approaches. Still, the prolife response to legal abortion was present from the start, and after the 1992 defeat of President George Bush, the Republican heir of the Reagan antiabortion legacy, it is becoming increasingly pervasive. There are powerful populist and egalitarian sentiments that animate the movement, sentiments that have always characterized its rhetoric, if not its politics. In the September 1974 edition, the *National Right to Life News* editor, Janet Grant, characterized legal abortion activists as mostly wealthy, upper-class elites whose notion of equality, she observed, stopped at equal access to abortion: "The rich want to 'share' abortion with the poor. But 'sharing' stops when it comes to wealth, clubs and neighborhoods."

The 1989 *Webster* decision has increasingly made evident the long-standing cleavages in the movement that I describe as antiabortion, right-to-life, and prolife (or consistent ethic) wings. Or, to put the argument in more general social movement terms, after the sudden (albeit contested) legitimation given to abortion by the Supreme Court in its 1973 *Roe v. Wade* decision, the countermovement opposing legal abortion slowly but perceptibly moved toward becoming a more proactive social movement (Kelly, 1991:159–61). There have been (with much overlap) several stages in the movement, and more stages undoubtedly will follow (Kelly, 1993b). In the beginning, the movement was primarily reactive, but a proactive social support wing quickly followed. It is of some significance that the first national prolife groups to form were in the service wing. These groups immediately realized the inadequacy of simply opposing legal abortion without trying to help women who were pregnant and did not want to be. In 1970 Louise Somerhill founded Birthright to provide counseling, financial assistance, medical help, and even private "birthright" homes for women whose futures were threatened by an unwanted pregnancy. In 1971 Lori Maier founded Alternatives to Abortion International, which provides similar services. Since then, other groups, such as the Christian Action Council, have started similar services. There are now more than three thousand such centers in the United States.

The term "prolife"—preferred by most abortion opponents—itself suggests the move from reaction to proactive approaches. Quite soon important parts of the movement explicitly moved from a volunteer-based social welfare response to an explicit structural approach based not on "charity" but on "justice." By 1971 the phrase "consistent ethic" referred to efforts to deal with the causes of abortion rather than merely providing a social work type of outreach to women with problem pregnancies (Kelly, 1991:154). But with the Reagan-Bush 1980–1992 embrace, the mistaken belief that political power could effectively halt abortions resuscitated the pre-1973 antiabortion reactive aspects and obscured the internal growth of the movement's explicit "prolife" elements. So too did the rather late entrance of fundamentalist Protestantism into abortion politics in the mid-1970s (Kelly, 1991:158). Since the late 1970s, important parts of the movement saw less reason to break with the earlier National Right to Life Committee position that a single-issue focus on abortion (and euthanasia) was essential to movement unity and to political success. But with *Webster*, the fragile ties between the movement and the fiscal conservatives of the Republican party began their public unraveling, and the earlier development toward a prolife or consistent ethic approach to abortion is now receiving renewed attention.

Fiscal Conservatives Slowly Abandon the Movement

Because the dominant women's rights organizations define elective abortion as an essential requirement for equality, the strong egalitarian sentiment characteristic of abortion opponents is overlooked. But it is pervasive and central to the vitality of the movement. The central philosophical argument of the movement is strikingly simple and central to core Western moral categories: each human life is singularly important and cannot be morally subordinated to the self-interests of those who are more powerful. Arguments based on equality have never been appealing to economic conservatives, and it has become increasingly obvious that policies favoring childbirth and disfavoring abortion, especially among the troubled poor, are economically costly. For example, at the end of 1989 New York State health officials predicted that the cost of the medical intensive care alone, not including long-term welfare costs, for New York State babies born to crack-addicted mothers (which comprised 10 percent of all nonwhite births in 1987) would exceed $1 billion by 1995. A later study (*New York Times*, 1991:B-4) estimated the additional costs of hospital care for babies born to cocaine-addicted mothers as $5.04 million per year. While about 14 percent of American women fall below the poverty line, about one-third of women obtaining abortions do (Henshaw and Silverman, 1988:158–60), and among all women the second most common reason women give for aborting was that "she couldn't afford the child" (Torres and Forrest, 1988:169). In other words, among other results, *Webster* began to show that fiscal conservatives and moral traditionalists opposing abortion do not share compatible positions. Opposing abortion will certainly increase welfare costs and require governmental support, positions rejected by fiscal conservatives. The antiabortion position adopted in the late 1970s by Republican party strategists seeking to expand the party's electoral base visibly weakened. Soon after the 1989 elections, the chairman of the National Republican Committee announced that the "Republican umbrella" included those who explicitly rejected the Republican party platform's endorsement of a Human Life Amendment. Six months after *Webster*, three distinct Republican political action committees were formed specifically to raise funds for Republicans who supported federal funding for abortions.[6] Post-*Webster* Republican strategists openly questioned whether the party could afford to maintain what Phillips (1991:221) described as "their highly effective alliance of economic and religious conservatives." Within days of President George Bush's November 3, 1992, loss to Bill Clinton, leading Republicans launched the Republican Majority Coalition, which they announced would be "inclusive" on social issues. R. W. Apple (1992) of *The New York Times* observed that no abortion opponents were among its founders. There's a logic to the exclusion, for the tactical political coalition partners had different primary worries. While prolife moral conservatives held the rather costly proposition that all human lives, even those just beginning, were intrinsically important and had claims on community resources, fiscal conservatives worried more about the growth of a nonproductive underclass.

The right-to-life component of the movement, best represented by the National Right to Life Committee, has made tactical alliances with the

Republican party since the Reagan administration. But NRLC has supported all opponents of abortion from both parties and has remained constant in its single-issue approach to the "life" issues of abortion, infanticide, and euthanasia. In this respect, NRLC has attempted to separate what it calls the "foundational" principle of the right of life from all conceptions of the "quality of life." NRLC has practiced a "principled pragmatism" supporting laws that restrict abortion but do not prohibit all abortions, hoping to keep open the possibility of gaining in the future greater legal protection for the unborn. This gradualist approach involves support for parental notification laws, the prohibition of abortions performed for reasons of gender, and informed consent statutes. Polls show strong public support for restrictions such as these, but not for laws making most abortions illegal. Laws highlighting the seriousness of abortion and its distinction from other surgeries would begin to make American law more similar to the abortion laws of other Western nations, which typically describe fetal life as human, encourage childbirth, and severely restrict late-term abortions (Glendon, 1987).

With the rapidly eroding political support of fiscal conservatives, the long-range vitality of the movement opposing abortion is likely to come from its publicly ignored component, the prolife, or consistent ethic, wing. This sector has always been present in the movement, but obscured by the alliances between the single-issue social movement organizations and the Republican party. The media has ignored it. Four years before Joseph Cardinal Bernardin's 1983 Fordham address, "A Consistent Ethic of Life: An American-Catholic Dialogue" (Bernardin, 1988:1–11), Judy Loesch formed Prolifers for Survival, whose members argued that their opposition to military spending, capital punishment, and abortion all stemmed from the same root value, respect for human life. The Seamless Garment Network formed at the last convention (March 1987) of Prolifers for Survival. The network's June 1990 publication, *Consistent Ethic Resources* (San Francisco: Harmony), lists fifty-five member organizations, eleven pages of available speakers, and the titles of five consistent ethic journals and newsletters (*Sisterlife, Harmony, Justlife, Sojourners,* and *Salt*). It is significant that the consistent ethic wing of the movement opposing abortion has roots almost entirely within some respected groups on the religious left— such as Pax Christi, Sojourners, and Evangelicals for Social Action. The linkages among opposition to legal abortion, support for government assistance to women and children, support for antipoverty programs, and opposition to the arms race and capital punishment is the official position of the National Conference of Catholic Bishops (1975).

Some Anticipations

I have argued that the eroding tactical political alliances between presently dominant social movement organizations opposing legal abortion and fiscal conservatives dominant in the Republican party makes likely only those abortion restrictions congruent with the actual ruling of *Roe* (protection after viability) and congruent with what appears to be stable public sentiment (regulations ensuring informed consent, parental notification, prohibition of abortion based on gender, restrictions on late-term abortions) and raises to larger moral and cultural significance the prolife sector of the movement and its development of the consistent ethic. The prolife / consistent ethic component defines itself as publicly guarding the foundational principle of all authentic humanisms, namely that each human life, with no regard to its real or potential achievements, has an intrinsic worth and thus has moral claims on the community. This moral insight, dramatically and energetically present throughout the movement, resists all conceptions of a social order based on either meritocracy or efficiency, and thus can be appropriately described as "radical."

While the attempt to frame abortion in a consistent ethic framework has thus far evoked little sympathy from the far more diffuse American Left or from mainstream liberalism, the long-term post-*Webster* unlinking of moral and fiscal conservatives can slowly alter this inattention, at least to some degree. One can find signs, if not clear trends. There is increasing recognition among influential feminist authors that the promotion of abortion rights abstracted from critiques of poverty makes abortion less a "choice" and more a desperate necessity (Davis, 1985:121; Fox-Genovese, 1991:81–84). The career penalization of women who desire to begin families is well known, and coercive pressures to abort exerted by management have already been documented (Martin, 1989).

Some even question whether the term "prochoice" fits all sectors of the legal abortion movement. Hartman (1987:120) notes the class bias among population control groups and their willingness to use coercive incentives and even force to limit births among populations they fear will destabilize existing wealth and power distributions. Hodgson (1991) has documented the powerful influence of eugenics, social Darwinism, and Malthusian notions of poverty on the first generations of population experts in the United States. Hodgson notes that the theme for the 1933 dinner meeting of the Population Association of America was, "Who shall inherit America?" Topics discussed included "Is the quality of our population on the downgrade?" and "Which racial types will predominate in the future?" (Hodgson, 1991:27). It should not be presumed that some kind of progressive enlightenment has forever removed such racist and class biases from American culture or its economic elites. Almost immediately after the announcement of the availability of a contraceptive in which the small tubes implanted in a woman's skin release a pregnancy-preventing hormone over a five-year period, an editorial (December 12, 1990) in the *Philadelphia Inquirer* appeared with the caption, "Poverty and Norplant—Can Contraception Reduce the Underclass?" Indeed, Back (1989:127) in his history of the population planning movement chronicles its contemporary status as part of the political and cultural "establishment" and notes the "transformation of the movement beyond its original goals of removing social barriers to contraception and providing freedom of choice to seeking enforceable norms of birth control." Tribe (1990:238) acknowledges that "it is an uncomfortable truth that the pro-choice movement draws its support disproportionately from various privileged elites, the 'upper echelons' of American society."

The direction anticipated here is that the long-term effect of the *Webster* decision will include the disengagement of the movement opposing abortion from alliances with fiscal conservatives. The prolife components of the movement, gradually winning greater allegiance from right-to-life groups increasingly politically stranded, will assume more prominence as the moral density of opposition to abortion in American culture increases. Following the consistent ethic of life approach, they will slowly create cautious but tactical links with those on the Left, especially the feminist Left (as described by Fox-Genovese 1991, especially 81ff.), increasingly alert to the economically driven pressures to make abortion the preferred solution to pregnancies among the very poor.[7] It will become apparent not only that the equality sought by women does not end with equal access to abortion but that access to legal abortion is slowly becoming the preferred way of dealing with the vast social challenges created by pregnancies among the poor, minorities, and the young. Toubia (1991:7) bluntly observes that "those who control economic resources at both the national and international levels are more interested in investing in family planning programs than in other health or development needs. We will not be able to change their motives to some abstract egalitarianism in which they never believed."

These anticipations of new post-*Webster* coalitions should not be viewed a priori as naive, although the media framing of abortion politics must make them seem so. Shared concerns have already prompted some unexpected coalitions among abortion foes. In New Jersey the National Organization of Women and the American Civil Liberties Union joined with New Jersey Right to Life, Citizens Concerned for Life, and the New Jersey State Conference of Catholic Bishops (and others) to unsuccessfully protest the "additional child provision" of New Jersey's 1992 Family Development Act, which dramatically altered the state's welfare program. The additional child provision stipulated that henceforth any child born to a parent on welfare will bring no additional AFDC funds to the family, thus forcing poor pregnant women to choose between abortion or deeper family poverty. Since other states are actively considering a New Jersey–type approach to welfare costs, other prochoice-prolife coalitions are likely. (For other examples, cf. Kelly, 1993b, "Two Landmark Dates in Abortion Politics," *Commonweal*.)

CONCLUSION

In short, the opposition to abortion will neither succeed nor fail. It will not entirely disappear, after the fashion of the prohibition movement, because most Americans continue to regard abortion as fundamentally different from contraception and do not wish to see elective abortion viewed merely as an indifferent matter of choice. Besides, the continued development of fetology roots the moral disapproval of abortion not merely in religious sentiment but increasingly in direct observation. Readers of the mass media can now learn that (*Newsweek*, 1991) "by the start of the last trimester the brain's neural circuits are as advanced as newborns, capable of paying attention and discriminating new from old." Photos by Lennart Nilson show four-month old fetuses frowning, turning·their heads, squinting, and moving when touched. Some researchers have demonstrated that during the last trimester fetuses "heard and learned something about the acoustic structure of American English" (*New York Times* 1990, "Recognition of Language May Begin in the Womb").

The opposition to abortion that began in the mid-1960s as a reaction to efforts to make some abortions legal will be slowly transformed from a countermovement to a social movement, seeking to lower abortion rates less through legal changes and more by altering the social conditions— such as poverty and employment practices—that in effect favor abortion over childbirth.[8] Coalitions between principled prolife and prochoice activists are no longer unthinkable. This evolution will ensure a continued vital presence in American culture, especially through the religious Left, but will achieve only limited success with regard to the legal and political status of abortion. In all likelihood, the legal restrictions on abortion will simply make American law more congruent with Western abortion law more generally, prohibiting (except to save the mother's life) late-term abortions and ensuring (through waiting period and consent legislation) that abortion is freely chosen and with information about social and medical services for the poor.

Back has suggested (1988:3) the term "permanent nascence" to characterize the possibility of a social movement that cannot be described as either successful or unsuccessful. His oxymoronic neologism appropriately describes the opposition to abortion, which began as a countermovement seeking legal success and slowly and incompletely developed into a social movement with increasing numbers of activists gradually realizing the full implications of their own preferred description as "prolife." The movement will remain on the margins of American power, but this is true of all truly populist movements premised on substantive notions of equality rather than on an equal opportunity animated by meritocratic sentiments, which still characterizes dominant feminism. The continued acknowledgment that abortion stops a developing human life, the concern that the increasing legitimacy given to assisted suicide and euthanasia pose dangers for the incurably sick and the elderly, and the failures of legal abortion alone to appreciably aid the cause of women's equality, along with other factors, will ensure a persisting importance for the prolife movement. In time, the still latent progressive egalitarianism that pervades the movement should be increasingly recognized. While the movement's more explicit linkage between the rights of the unborn and women's rights will not stop the majority of abortions, it will make more luminous its moral center.

A major cultural task is to keep vital for future generations the core principle that the good society protects all humans, not because they meet changing criteria of merit or worth, but simply because they, like us, are human beings. Any other basis for equality is dangerously fragile and sure to break under the weight of the demands for even more privilege by the already privileged.

It will be some time before the movement opposing abortion can be unambiguously labeled and evaluated. This observer anticipates that the future social movement literature will describe it as a single-issue countermovement that evolved into a permanently nascent multi-issue prolife movement. Single-issue social movement organizations survive only as long as there are clear indications that they can slowly win the allegiances of political elites. With the loss of Republican patronage, this possibility has permanently retreated. But the energy of any persistent social movement rests on a charismatic core of beliefs, principles, and visions that by definition must be comprehensive and thus involve multi-issues, for they anticipate changes in society that acknowledge and promote more human dignity and greater equality. As the movement itself more clearly understands that it is prolife rather than antiabortion, its latent egalitarian principles will become increasingly manifest as fiscal conservatives irrevocably withdraw from even tactical alliances with the movement's moral traditionalists.

At the very least, this author doubts that the next generation's version of the *Handbook of Sociology* will describe the movement opposing abortion simply as a "reactionary movement" that emerged "in opposition to the feminist movement" (McAdam, McCarthy, and Zald, 1988:711).

NOTES

1. The battle of labels hasn't yet been settled among the public. The survey commissioned by Americans United for Life found that most Americans identify strongly with neither a "prolife" nor a "prochoice" label. Overall, 42 percent of the Gallup poll described themselves as prolife (but only 26 percent "strongly"), while 33 percent said they were prochoice (and only 17 percent said "strongly.") The Wirthlin poll commissioned by the National Conference of Catholic Bishops found that roughly the same percentage—40 percent—were willing to describe

themselves as prolife as prochoice. But it is significant that Wirthlin found that 68 percent agreed that "the central issue in the abortion debate is who decides—the woman or the government." Wirthlin remarks, "If the battle is framed in terms of 'who decides' and not by what is right or wrong, the abortionists win" (in Kelly, 1991b: 311).

2. The revised bill introduced by Senator Helms on January 19, 1981, on the Senate floor and referred to the Committee on the Judiciary read (*Hearings on the Human Life Bill* [Washington, D.C.: U.S. Government Printing Office, 1982], 117–18; 1117–19):

Be it enacted by the Senate and House of Representatives of the United States of America in Congress assembled, that title 42 of the United States Code shall be amended at the end thereof by adding the following new chapter: Chapter 101.

SECTION 1. The Congress finds that present day scientific evidence indicates a significant likelihood that actual human life exists from conception. The Congress further finds that the fourteenth amendment to the Constitution of the United States was intended to protect all human beings. Upon the basis of these findings, and in the exercise of the powers of the Congress, including its power under section 5 of the fourteenth amendment to the Constitution of the United States, the Congress hereby declares that for the purpose of enforcing the obligation of the States under the fourteenth amendment not to deprive persons of life without due process of law, human life shall be deemed to exist from conception, without regard to race, sex, age, health, defect, or condition of dependency; and for this purpose "person" shall include all human life as defined herein.

SECTION 2. Notwithstanding any other provision of law, no inferior Federal court ordained and established by Congress under article 111 of the Constitution of the United States shall have jurisdiction to issue any restraining order, temporary or permanent injunction, or declaratory judgment in any case involving or arising from any State law or municipal ordinance that (1) protects the rights of human persons between conception and birth, or (2) prohibits, limits, or regulates (a) the performance of abortions or (b) the provision at public expense of funds, facilities, personnel, or other assistance for the performance of abortions.

The Human Life Bill (HLB) was criticized not only in terms of the arguments about the humanity of the result of conception but because, in Senator Daniel Patrick Moynihan's words (p. 159), "This legislation would tell the Court what is a person, and would commence for the first time in our history a serious invasion by the legislative branch of the judicial branch." Among other reasons, the HLB was defeated because it was seen as endangering constitutional processes by prohibiting the Supreme Court from interpreting the application of the Fourteenth Amendment. But the substantive core of the bill did not refer to the "personhood" of the fetus but simply said it was a form of human life. Opponents of the substance of the bill adopted a social constructionist perspective, arguing that since "humanity" is not a scientific term, it must necessarily be a subjective term without scientific validation. At a minimum, it is clear that abortion opponents take no refuge in any irrational flight from biological evidence but argue that the most contemporary data of biology reveal the cogency of opposing legal abortion because it stops a human life. On the very first morning of the hearings, April 23, 1981, scientific testimony supporting the HLB was given by Dr. Jerome Lejeune, professor of fundamental genetics at the Medical College of Paris, Professor Hymie Gordon, Chairman, Department of Medical Genetics, Mayo Clinic, Rochester, Minnesota, and Dr. Micheline M. Matthews-Roth, Principal Research Associate, Harvard University Medical School. Lejeune testified that (pp. 8–10):

as soon as the 23 paternally derived chromosomes are united through fertilization to the 23 maternally derived chromosomes, the full genetic information necessary and sufficient to express the inborn qualities of the new individual is gathered. . . . [E]ach conceptus receives an entirely original combination which has never occurred before and will never again. Each conceptus is unique and thus irreplaceable. . . . To the best of our actual knowledge, the prerequisite for individuation—that is, a stage containing three fundamental cells—is the next step following conception, minutes after it. . . . To accept the fact that after fertilization has taken place a new human has come into being is no longer a matter of taste or of opinion. The human nature of the human being from conception to old age is not a metaphysical contention, it is plain experimental evidence.

Professor Hymie Gordon testified (p. 13) that the zygote meets all criteria for living human matter:

Thus, from the very moment of conception, the organism contains many complex molecules; it synthesizes new, intricate structures from simple raw materials; it replicates itself. By all the criteria of modern molecular biology, life is present from the moment of conception. . . . [W]e can say, unequivocally, that the question of when life begins—is no longer a question for theological or philosophical dispute. It is an established scientific fact. Theologians and philosophers may go on to debate the meaning of life or the purpose of life, but it is an established fact that all life, including human life, begins at the moment of conception.

Dr. Matthews-Roth testified (pp. 13–17) that:

organisms reproducing by sexual reproduction always arise from a single cell and that they are always of the same biological species as their parents—this fact—that a life begins at fertilization—is universally accepted and taught at all levels of biological education. . . . No study or experiment has ever refuted these scientific facts, and no competent scientist denies them. Thus, one is being scientifically accurate if one says that an individual human life begins at fertilization or conception.

Under friendly questioning from the chairman of the subcommittee on separation of powers, Senator John P. East, Dr. Lejeune noted that "When people say that this [the scientific fact that human life begins at conception] has metaphysical connotations, they are perfectly correct, if they wish; but the scientific fact that it is a human being cannot be disputed." Later, Lejeune observed, "We are sure its own life has begun when it has been conceived. There is no scientific escape to that. The only escape could be a theological one." Dr. Matthews-Roth added, "It is a scientific fact, and we have to live with it. . . . I think a function of law is to help preserve the lives of our people, and I think you want to base the laws on scientific fact." Gordon observed, "I have never encountered in my reading of the scientific literature—long before I became concerned with abortion, euthansia, and so on—anyone who has argued that life did not begin at the moment of conception or that it was not a human conception if it resulted from the fertilization of a human egg by a human sperm. As far as I know, there has been no argument about these matters." All three (p. 23) answered affirmatively when Senator East asked, "Are the three of you saying that to pick a point other than the point of conception is arbitrary?"

The afternoon testimony—all substantially agreeing with the scientific testimony given that morning—was given by Dr. Watson Bowes (Division of Perinatal Medicine, University of Colorado) and Dr. McCarthy DeMere (a surgeon and a law professor at Memphis State University). But Bowes observed that while conception marks the clear beginning of human life (p. 25), "the definition of 'the word *person* in biological terms' . . . is, on the other hand, a far more difficult and imprecise task." He added, (p. 26) "If we are to use the philosophical definition which is, 'a self-conscious or rational being,' then a human being, biologically speaking, may not become a person for months, perhaps even years, after birth."

On April 24, 1981, the committee heard from two physicians, Dr. Alfred M. Bongiovanni, University of Pennsylvania Medical School, and Dr. Jasper Williams, Williams Clinic, Chicago, as well as Dr. Leon Rosenberg, Professor and Chairman, Department of Human Genetics, Yale University Medical School, who alone testified against the bill. Rosenberg informed the committee that "a great majority of the American clinicians and scientists in this country would support my side of this argument despite my distinct minority before you in the past two days" (p. 60). Rosenberg (pp. 49–51) did not dispute the scientific points made by the first five witnesses: "There is no reason to debate or to doubt the scientific evidence indicating that conception is a critical event in human reproduction. When the egg is fertilized by the sperm, a new cell is formed that contains all of the genetic information needed to develop ultimately into a human being." But Rosenberg called this not "human life" but "potential for human life" because "I know of no scientific evidence which bears on the question of when actual human life exists . . . the notion embodied in the phrase 'actual human life' is not a scientific one, but rather a philosophic and religious one." Rosenberg added that he could not scientifically answer the question of when he might assert that human as opposed to potential human life begins:

As a scientist I must answer I do not know. Moreover, I have not been able to find a single piece of scientific evidence which helps me with that question. . . . I have no quarrel with anyone's ideas on this matter so long as it is clearly understood that they are personal beliefs based on personal judgments and not scientific truths. . . . [S]cience, per se, doesn't deal with the complex quality called humanness any more than it does with such equally complex concepts as love, faith, or truth. . . . I maintain that concepts such as humanness are beyond the purview of science because no idea about them can be tested experimentally. (p. 50)

And later he asserted (p. 56): "There is no question in my mind that the fertilized ovum is a living cell, but the concept of human life is not a scientific one." For good measure, (p. 51) Rosenberg added that "I believe that those who have preceded me have failed to distinguish between their moral or religious positions and their professional scientific judgments." In short, Rosenberg conceded that a fertilized ovum is a living cell of human origins with a human future but that science allows him to call it only "potentially human" because the term human involves a "moral" or "religious" judgment. He might have, but didn't, add that *not* to call this living cell human life must also involve a moral or religious judgment. He did, however, give reasons for refusing to use the term "human life," referring to "adverse clinical implications." More plainly, he feared that the bill would require the prohibition of birth control pills and intrauterine devices, which prevent implantation. Perhaps even a ban on the aborting of defective fetuses: "Moreover, this bill will protect the conceptus that has no possibility of realizing its human potential" (p. 51). To Senator East's question (p. 58) of when law might consider "potential" human life to be "actual," Rosenberg said he "would protect at the point of viability. I would protect at the point that the human being can exist on its own outside of the uterus." When East responded, "Viability is elusive, isn't it?", Rosenberg agreed: "I am sure there would not be consensus as to the precise point at which viability lies, but I think there is some greater consensus about what we mean by the word 'viability'. . . . However, I cannot help you, Senator East, with the clarity. You are asking me for something that I do not have."

East pressed further:

I am a little troubled about viability being the criterion by which you determine the right to life. Actually, once born, there is not viability if by viability one means the capacity to exist independently. Viability, for example, does not exist then [at birth]. The child is totally dependent upon mother and parents and family. Why, indeed, if we want to expand into a philosphical understanding, no man or woman stands alone. No one is viable in the ultimate moral and ethical sense that we live freely and totally autonomously. Then I think ultimately at the other end of the continuum of the old, the senile, the aged, the infirm, the disabled, the afflicted. If I let loose the concept into the world that viability is the ultimate criterion by which you determine the right to life, I am profoundly troubled with that as a matter of moral and ethical implication, and as a policy position I would have to disassociate myself from it. It would produce all kinds of perverse results, wouldn't it?

But Dr. Rosenberg had nothing more to say: "Senator East, I do not think I have anything more that I can say on the matter" (p. 59).

3. In 1981 Sociologists for Women in Society (then numbered at 1,500) submitted a statement supporting *Roe v. Wade* to the Committee on the Judiciary considering the Human Life Bill from April 23 to June 18, 1981 (ibid., appendix, 231). Their statement claimed "the science of sociology" had shown the necessity of abortion for women's full participation in modern society. The statement also enlisted social science in support of the position denying that fetuses were "humans" possessing rights:

Sociological research has shown that the extent of a woman's involvement in economic and political life outside the home is directly linked to her ability to control her fertility. Drastic limitations on the right to choose when and if to bear a child would severely diminish our members'—and every woman's—potential for professional and political participation. Another major premise of sociology which S. 158 affects is the definition of personhood. A person is not defined by biological viability but by social relationships with people. S. 158 would protect fetuses with coercive social relationships, sacrificing the rights to privacy . . . in the interests, not of bits of living tissue, but of a state-imposed morality.

4. Zald and McCarthy (1987:31) describe the total array of social movement organizations as comprising a "social movement industry." These various social movement groups are "normally differentiated by conceptions of the extremity of solutions required, strategies of goal accomplishment." In Chapter 7, "Social Movement Industries: Competition and Conflict among Social Movement Organizations," they note that mergers among social movement organizations are rare and that social movements and countermovements are characterized by high degrees of internecine conflict (1987:176): "Organizations may wish death on one another; they may want to absorb the other, take over its domain, squash the competition. As we have noted, the greater the commitment to a zealot's view of the proper state of the world, the more one can expect illegitimate, violent, and deadly interorganizational relations."

5. Confusion about the range of abortions made legal by *Roe* continues decades

later. Gallup (see Kelly, 1991b:311) found that only about 10 percent realized that, since health can be interpreted as including psychological and economic factors, *Roe* permitted elective abortion. More than 80 percent acknowledged that they were "not familiar" with *Roe*. Only 24 percent of those who believed they were "very familiar" with *Roe* were able to accurately state its outcome.

6. The chairwomen of the National Republican Coalition for Choice and Republicans for Choice, Ann Stone and Mary Dent, respectively, told reporters (Gwen Ifill, "2 Republican Factions on Abortion Gird for Battle on Party's '92 Platform," *The New York Times*, Sept. 30, 1991, A15) that while they did not expect Bush to reverse Reagan's successful identification with abortion opponents, they did expect that he would "become less publicly identified with it."

7. For those who affirm a "consistent ethic of life," there will be a tendency to focus attention elsewhere than on changes in the law. Antonia Malone, a member of Pax Christi, a Catholic pacifist group officially opposed to legal abortion, makes these points ("Dialogue on Abortion, Continued," *Pax Christi USA* [Spring, 1990]: 28–29): The Second Vatican Council affirmed "the primacy of conscience" and taught "that even when the conscience errs from ignorance it must be respected." She questioned whether legislation would solve the problem of abortion. She noted that in their 1983 pastoral letter entitled *The Challenge of Peace*, the bishops appealed "to men and women in military service" to examine their choices, to consider the alternatives, to ask how their experience affects society, while promising to support them in facing the challenges. And then, she wondered, "Why not a similar approach for abortion?" Finally, she observed that "the Catholic church, while affirming that human life is a continuum from conception to death, has never taken an official stand on when individual personhood begins. That is because there are some things we don't know."

8. The passage of laws protecting the unborn and prohibiting abortions would not signify the complete success of the prolife movement. It cannot not succeed unless it also persuades women not to have abortions. The movement has long recognized this, but probably has not developed truly convincing answers to questions about illegal abortions and their safety. In other words, the movement must be actively concerned with the question of "civic virtue" in ways that those who seek only to regulate sexuality do not. If law prohibited all nontherapeutic abortions there would certainly reemerge many nonlegal groups performing abortions. Jane, also known as The Women's Liberation Abortion Counseling Service, formed in 1968. In Jane women learned how to perform abortions by assisting at abortions (see Staggenborg, 1991:49). Davis (1985:179) reports that during a four-year period, Jane volunteers performed over 11,000 abortions, many performed by self-taught abortionists. Davis describes the abortion methods as easy and safe but notes that for security reasons, no records were kept. RU–486 will certainly have an impact on the ease of obtaining illegal abortions. Besides, there are now nonsurgical alternatives to hysterectomy called "endometrial ablation," which, by destroying the lining of the uterus, acts as a form of birth control by making the womb inhospitable to newly fertilized eggs. Still, the long-term safety of RU–486 and of endometrial ablation are not known (Sandra Blakeslee, "Nonsurgical Means Used as Alternatives to Hysterectomies," *The New York Times*, July 31, 1991, C10).

3 The Abortion Controversy: Conflicting Beliefs and Values in American Society and within Religious Subgroups

Joseph B. Tamney, Stephen D. Johnson, and Ronald Burton

In this chapter we discuss building a model of the reasons people do or do not support legalized abortion. In doing so, we pay particular attention to the cultural or ideological bases of abortion attitudes that were found to be important in a previous study (Tamney, Johnson, and Burton, 1992). Besides exploring why Americans are committed to conflicting positions regarding the abortion question, we also examined how people in various religious groups differed regarding the meaning of legalized abortion.

IDEOLOGY AND LEGALIZED ABORTION

Western culture is rooted, at least partially, in individualism: the belief in the worth of a person as such. This core idea has been elaborated in various ways, including an examination of the value given to political liberties and to self-actualization (Tamney, 1992:21). Some people understand the issue of whether or not abortion should be legal in terms of the secular framework based on individualism. Thus they justify allowing abortions by reference to the individual's right of choice or to the need to protect a person's privacy. The standing opinion of the Supreme Court, as of 1993, is based on the conviction "that the Constitution embodies a promise that a certain private sphere of individual liberty will be kept largely beyond the reach of government" (*USA Today,* 1986). Individualism has also taken on a gender-based meaning relevant to the abortion issue. Feminists argue that a necessary condition for women to be free is to have control of their bodies. Legalizing abortion is part of the struggle to deny that "anatomy is destiny" (Harrison, 1983; Willis, 1985).

Although the tradition of individualism was born in part in the religious ideas exemplified by the Hebrew prophets and the teaching of Jesus, significant opposition to the implications of individualism has come from Christian churches. Christians have tried to brake individualism by emphasizing either the sinful nature of persons or the need for humans to accept a humble role in the scheme of things. In the latter case Christians are not at ease with the modern idea of humanity as designing their destiny, preferring to stress the need for people to accept a God-given order, which includes so-called natural laws. From this naturalist tradition has emerged the idea of the sacredness of human life, and this belief has affected people's attitudes toward the abortion issue. Some Catholic leaders, most notably Cardinal Bernardin, have placed the protest against abortion within the larger ideological framework of the need to preserve all human life (Cleghorn, 1986). From this perspective the rejection of abortion should accompany the condemnation of nuclear warfare as well as capital punishment, and support for programs to eliminate such deadly problems as poverty and malnutrition. All such issues supposedly form a "seamless garment," the purpose of which is the preservation of human life.

Christian opposition to legalized abortion also stems from emphasizing the sinfulness of human nature. In the puritanical perspective, human desires, uncontrolled by right reason or grace, will result in sinful behavior; such desires have no end but physical pleasure or personal comfort. Given the inherent weakness of people, the traditional moral code must be enforced, even legally, for people's own good. As the head of the Pro-Life Action Committee said, "There's more to life than the visceral twitch, and I think using sex purely for pleasure is sort of animalistic" (quoted in Ridgeway, 1985:29). Thus a consistent research finding is that some opponents of legalized abortion hold traditional ideological views about gender and family such as beliefs that woman's place is in the home (Cable, 1984; Luker, 1984:160), that sex education in the public schools is wrong (Schwartz, 1985), and that divorce and pornography must be curtailed if not outlawed (Neitz, 1981:270; Barnartt and Harris, 1982; Johnson and Tamney, 1988). Such attitudes are collectively identified as social traditionalism (Himmelstein, 1983). Thus a further ideological basis for opposition to legalized abortion is a commitment to social traditionalism.

Political conservatism is a secular variant of the puritanical outlook. Conservatives do accept aspects of the libertarian tradition, especially the criticism of state involvement in the economy. At the same time, political conservatives tend to distrust human nature, and for some of them this attitude means accepting that the state should regulate personal behavior (Lenski, 1971; Kirkpatrick, 1982; Tamney, 1992). Not surprisingly, there is a positive relationship between political conservatism and social traditionalism (Tamney and Johnson, 1988), and an antiabortion stand has generally been associated with politically conservative people and groups (Wilcox, 1989).

In sum, acceptance of legalized abortion among Americans is a consequence of individualism, which finds expression in the defense of privacy and feminist ideologies. Opposition to legalized abortion finds ideological justification both in religious tradition, specifically in natural law and puritanical beliefs, and in some politically conservative beliefs. Opponents to legalized abortion, motivated by conservative religious or political ideologies, accept that human life begins at conception, despite the absence of any scientific consensus on this matter (*New York Times,* 1989e), and conclude that abortion is murder, by far the most frequently given reason for rejecting legalized abortion (Jacqueline Scott, 1989).

THE THEORETICAL MODEL

Figure 3.1 depicts the model we tested for explaining abortion attitudes. Such attitudes are understood to be a consequence of believing in the six perspectives just discussed: the right to privacy, feminism, the natural sacredness of human life, a belief in the preservation of all life, sexual traditionalism, and political conservatism. In addition, we believe that conservative religious people are more likely to accept that human life begins at conception and for that reason alone to oppose legalized abortion. The model also suggests that Catholics and conservative Protestants have different motives for opposing legalized abortion. The Catholic church has had an impact on developing antiabortion attitudes through its theology that all life should be preserved and that a human life begins at conception. Conservative Protestants are antiabortion because they are social traditionalists, which relates directly to an antiabortion attitude in our model and indirectly to this attitude via the belief that life begins at conception.

Since valuing control over one's life is an important component of feminism, we predicted that feminism would be related to a privacy orientation. We also argue that the emphasis on individuals submitting to normative control among political conservatives and moral traditionalists would lead both groups to reject arguments based on the importance of privacy because such arguments imply valuing individual autonomy (Tamney, Johnson, and Burton, 1992). Likewise, people who believe that a sacred life begins at conception will find it difficult to define abortion as a private matter (Tamney, Johnson, and Burton, 1992). Other aspects of the model seem straightforward: people who want to preserve all life as well as traditionalists will tend to believe in the existence of sacred life beginning at conception, and political conservatives and social traditionalists will tend not to be feminists.

Three structural variables were added to the model as exogenous vari-

Figure 3.1
Partial Theoretical Model

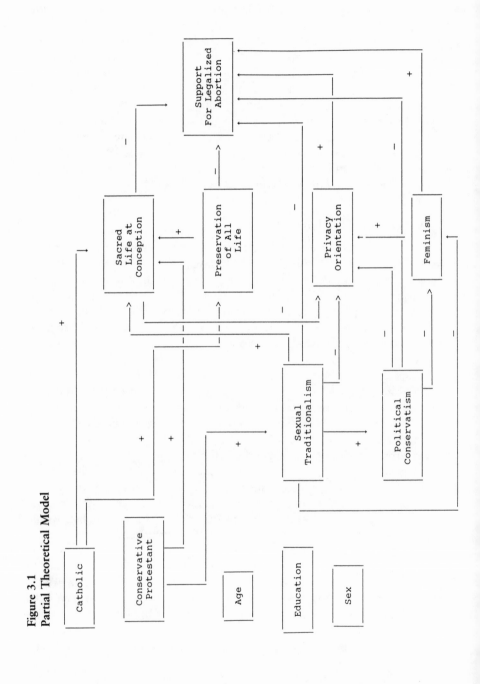

ables: age, education, and sex. These three variables were chosen since they were found to have some role in understanding abortion attitudes in our previous study (Tamney, Johnson, and Burton, 1992). Paths between these three exogenous variables and other variables have not been indicated in Figure 3.1 in order to reduce the "clutter" in the model and thus to make it more understandable to the reader. However, the relationship between each of these three variables with the other variables in the model were assessed in the analysis that was run to test the model. In addition, the Catholicism and conservative Protestant indices were considered exogenous variables in our analysis, that is, the possible causes of these variables is not a concern of our model.

After a test of the model in Figure 3.1, we examined what affected abortion attitude among four religious collectivities: conservative Protestants, Catholics, mainline Protestants, and people with no religious preference.

Methods

The sample consisted of 418 residents of the Lynds' (1929) "Middletown" (Muncie, Indiana) studied in the fall of 1990. Three hundred and fifty of the respondents were randomly selected from the total SMSA (Standard Metropolitan Statistical Area) of Muncie using a random-digit-dialing technique. This sample was selected in such a way that the proportion of people with certain telephone exchanges in this sample was the same as in the total SMSA population. To compensate for a general underrepresentation of people in low-income areas in past Middletown studies, fifty additional people were randomly selected by a staged-sampling technique from the poorest areas of the Muncie SMSA. To increase the percentage of Catholics in the sample and make it more comparable to the nationwide percentage of Catholics, eighteen additional Catholics were selected by randomly selecting telephone numbers throughout the whole Muncie SMSA and then asking the potential respondent if he or she was Catholic; if so, the person was included, and if not, the interviewer went on to another random telephone number.

The interview schedule contained a series of questions measuring basic demographic characteristics such as the respondent's sex, age, race, total income, and education.

The impact of religion on abortion attitude was assessed by creating special indices of conservative Protestantism and Catholicism. For the conservative Protestant measure, a respondent got a score of 4 if he or she belonged to a conservative Protestant church[1] and both believed that every word of the Bible is true[2] and attended church frequently, a score of 3 if he or she was a conservative Protestant and either believed every word of the Bible is true or attended church frequently, a score of 2 if he or she was a conservative Protestant and neither believed every word of the Bible is true nor was a frequent church attender, and a score of 1 if the person was not a conservative Protestant. For the Catholic index, a respondent got a score of 3 if the person was a Catholic and a frequent church attender, a score of 2 if he or she was a Catholic and not a frequent attender, and a score of 1 if he or she was not a Catholic. These two variables were created since it was proposed that Catholics and fundamentalist Protestants who frequently attend church would be the most opposed to abortion. In our later analysis of religious collectivities, respondents were simply classified as conservative Protestant, Catholic, mainline Protestant (i.e., all Protestants not classified as conservative Protestants), or without religious affiliation on the basis of their religious preference and church affiliation.

In this study an aspect of social traditionalism, called sexual traditionalism, was quantified using four questions. The items asked if the respondent did not believe that birth control information and methods should be made available to teenagers, did not think that there should be a law protecting homosexuals from being dismissed from their jobs as teachers in public schools, did believe that premarital sex was wrong, and thought that not controlling one's sexual desires is a sin that God will eventually punish. Responses to these four questions were added to obtain a scale score (alpha = .64).

Another set of questions concerned life issues. Belief in life at conception was measured by asking the respondents when human life begins, and the listed responses were: the moment a woman becomes pregnant, when a fetus can survive, or not sure. This measure was coded 2 if the respondent said life began at the moment of conception and 1 if he or she gave either of the other two responses. Another question asked the extent of agreement or disagreement with the statement that "from the moment of conception a human life is in the hands of God." These two questions were combined to form a measure of belief that a sacred life begins at conception (alpha = .64). Another question asked the respondents the extent to which they thought that in order to preserve life *both* euthanasia and capital punishment should be eliminated. It was an attempt to determine if respondents believed it was wrong as a general principle for one person to take the life of another.

Two ideological positions that support a prochoice stand are belief in the privacy of the abortion decision and feminism. To measure the privacy belief, respondents were asked the extent to which they agreed or disagreed with this statement: "Decisions about divorce and abortion are private matters, and we should not pass laws that regulate these matters." This question was meant to determine if the respondent believed there is a private part of our lives related to family matters from which in general government should be excluded. A measure of feminism was assessed by adding up three Likert items ("Women need to have a much greater say, than they do today, about if and when they will have children," "Males need to take much more responsibility in raising children than they do today," and "American society should change so that women have just as much power as men in making business and governmental decisions"— alpha = .51).

The respondents' general political ideological position was assessed by asking respondents how they would classify themselves along a five-point scale from very conservative to very liberal. This item has been shown in a number of studies to be related to actual positions on a number of political issues (Flanigan and Zingale, 1987:116).

The abortion attitude itself was measured by the following question:

Which of the following statements best describes your opinion about abortion?

1. Abortion should never be permitted.
2. Abortion should be permitted only if the life and the health of the woman is in danger.
3. Abortion should be permitted if, due to her particular situation, the woman would have difficulty in caring for the child.
4. Abortion should never be forbidden.

Results

The percentages of people who took the four basic positions on the abortion measure were as follows: should never be permitted, 9 percent; permitted only if woman's life is in danger, 49 percent; permitted if woman would have difficulty caring for child, 21 percent; should never be forbidden, 21 percent. Although a greater percentage of people opposed legalized abortion, an average person would have split the abortion attitude scale almost exactly in half (mean = 2.54). The latter fact is true because more than twice as many people opposed legal restrictions of any kind on abortion as those who supported outlawing abortion completely.

The path model in Figure 3.1 was tested using a statistical technique called LISREL. This analysis enables researchers to test the whole model all at once and to add or subtract paths (arrows) between variables if by doing so the resulting model will be more consistent with the data. In this analysis, the exogenous variables were sex, age, education, the Catholic index, and the conservative Protestant index. Exogenous variables are ones that are presumed to be completely explained or caused by variables not included in the model; what causes these variables is not of concern (e.g., what causes a person to have a certain level of education is not considered). The remaining seven variables in the model are called endogenous variables. These variables differ from exogenous variables in that an attempt is made to explain these variables by other variables in the model. The correlation matrix indicating the relationships among all of the variables we employed is in Table 3.1. LISREL uses these relationships to build a model.

In the first LISREL analysis, those paths which were found not to be statistically significant were eliminated and the LISREL analysis was rerun. This process, along with adding new paths if the LISREL analysis called for such, was conducted until a model was obtained that best fit the data (Pedhazur, 1982). The resulting model is in Figures 3.2a and 3.2b. Only paths significant at the .01 level are presented in these figures.[3] The probability that this model best describes our sample of people was .32 (according to the chi-square goodness-of-fit test), that is, there was a 32 percent chance that this model, as opposed to any other model, best describes the relationships among the studied variables for our sample of respondents.

A question that interested us was whether people in different religious groups were similarly motivated when reacting to the abortion issue. The impact on abortion attitude of the endogenous variables in the model presented in Figure 3.2a was examined for each of four religious collectivities: conservative Protestants, Catholics, liberal Protestants, and those with no religious preference (or "nones"). The independent variables in these analyses were feminism, a privacy orientation, a consistent life view, a sacred life perspective, political conservatism, and sexual traditionalism. First, the zero-order correlations between these six variables and abortion attitude for each of the four religious groups were examined. Those variables significant at the .01 level were placed into a multiple regression equation with abortion attitude as the dependent variable for each of the four religious groups. The results of backward stepwise analyses are in Table 3.2. For each of the religious groups, the variables that were found to be independently related to abortion attitude, the proportion of variance explained (r-squareds) in abortion attitude by these variables, and the mean score on the abortion scale for that group are shown.

DISCUSSION AND CONCLUSION

As anticipated, support for legalized abortion was related to cultural variables: feminism, a commitment to privacy, a belief that sacred life begins at conception, holding to the seamless garment argument (preservation of all life), political conservatism, and sexual traditionalism. As for the exogenous variables of age, education, and sex (see Figure 3.2b), age was the only one of these variables directly related to abortion attitude— the younger respondents being more likely to support the legalization of abortion.[4]

Regarding religious identity, we failed to predict that being either a Catholic or a conservative Protestant would be directly related to abortion attitude (see Figure 3.2b). However, these results are not surprising. Both

Table 3.1
Correlations for Model Variables

	Abortion Attitude	Feminism	Privacy Orientation	Life Preservation	Sacred Life	Political Conservatism	Sexual Traditionalism	Conservative Protestant	Catholic	Education	Sex
Feminism	.24										
Privacy Orientation	.34	.25									
Life Preservation	-.21	.05	.03								
Sacred Life	-.55	-.09	-.31	.15							
Political Conservatism	-.26	-.13	-.16	.03	.22						
Sexual Traditionalism	-.49	-.17	-.25	.07	.52	.33					
Conservative Protestant	-.35	-.01	-.13	.06	.36	.15	.47				
Catholic	-.09	-.05	-.12	.07	.15	.02	-.11	-.27			
Education	.14	.07	-.02	-.14	-.07	-.02	-.14	-.15	.08		
Sex	.10	.08	.03	.01	.16	.05	.03	.08	-.02	-.08	
Age	-.14	-.14	.03	.04	.08	.13	.30	.02	-.17	-.18	.14

Figure 3.2a
Paths between the Endogenous Variables

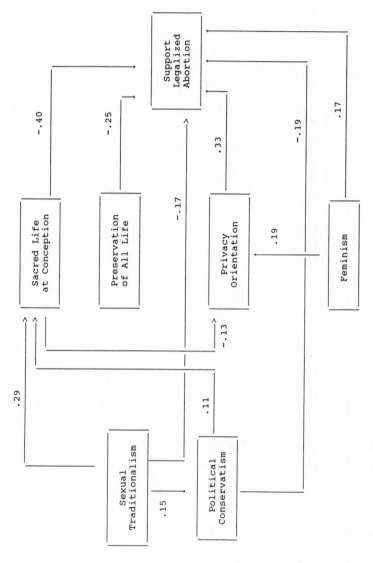

50

Figure 3.2b
Final Model: Paths between the Exogenous and Endogenous Variables

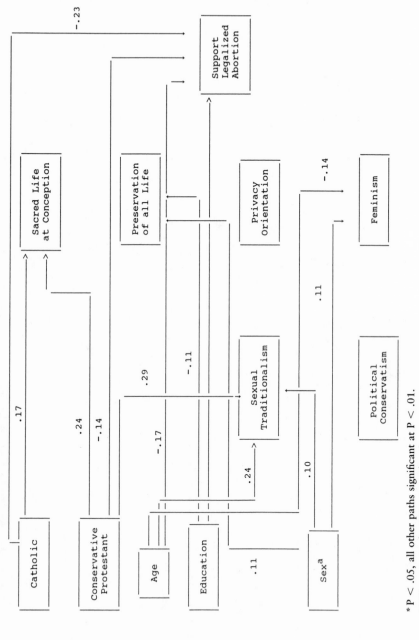

* P < .05, all other paths significant at P < .01.
[a] "1" means male; "2" means female.

51

Table 3.2
Beta Values for Variables Significantly Related to Abortion Attitude by Religious Subgroup

	Conservative Protestants (N=149)	Catholics (N=58)	Mainline Protestants (N=127)	Nones (N=53)
Feminism			.34	
Privacy	.22	.42		
Preserve All Life		-.22*		
Sacred Life At Conception	-.21*	-.33	-.38	-.70
Political Conservatism			-.22	
Sexual Traditionalism	-.25*			
R^2	28 percent	40 percent	39 percent	49 percent
Abortion Means	2.20	2.48	2.70	3.11

*Significant at .05 level; all others significant at .01 level.

conservative Protestants and Catholics say that church leaders have influenced their abortion opinions (Tamney, Johnson, and Burton, 1992). Consistent with this finding, it is the religious conservatives among Protestant ministers who communicate their beliefs about abortion in sermons (Jelen, 1992). Our results suggest that such religious socialization may result in church members having the "right" attitudes even when they do not accept the underlying beliefs for a church's abortion position. Similarly, churches are convincing people that human life begins at conception (see Figure 3.2b), and this belief influences abortion decisions independent of ideological beliefs. In effect, churches are able to establish the "fact" that any abortion is murder.[5]

Examining what related to abortion attitude for the four religious collectivities, notable differences were observed (see Table 3.2). Like the Catholics opposed to legalized abortions, conservative Protestants who were opposed to abortion rejected the privacy doctrine; for both collectivities, so-called private behavior is not a realm of individual choice; rather, the law should be used to ensure that private behavior conforms with religious norms. Among those opposed to legalized abortion, what distinguished the Catholics from the conservative Protestants is that while only the former perceived abortion in the context of defending human life generally, only the conservative Protestants understood abortion within a puritanical or traditionalist framework.

Considering only those who said abortion should *never* be permitted, conservative Protestants were overrepresented. While 19 percent of this group chose the strong stand against legalized abortion, the next highest percentage was 5 percent for Catholics. Conservative Protestants are more likely than others to base moral decisions only on religious norms (Tamney and Johnson, 1985). In addition, people who support social traditionalism tend to be authoritarian, which implies a rigid adherence to rules (Levinson and Huffman, 1955; Johnson, 1986). We suggest that conservative Protestants differ from other groups, in part, because they tend to accept rigidly a smaller universe of values. Thus situations requiring a decision can seem less ambiguous, allowing conservative Protestants to take a strong (extreme) stand on abortion.[6]

Mainline Protestant ministers tend to perceive their ministerial role in a nonauthoritarian manner and the Bible in the light of modern scriptural analysis. Thus in their churches the responsibility of each member to form religious judgments is emphasized (Jelen, 1992). Moreover, clergy usually do not legitimize their libertarian beliefs on religious grounds (Johnson and Tamney, 1988; Tamney, 1992:123). As a result, among mainline Protestants, secular beliefs, specifically feminism and political conservatism, determine abortion attitudes (see Table 3.2).

In light of the Supreme Court's justification for allowing abortion, it is interesting that mainline Protestants who favor legalized abortion do not use the privacy argument. Rather, their attitudes seem to be influenced by feminism and political philosophy. Among mainline Protestants, the stance is that abortion should be legal not because the role of the state must be minimized but because persons need an environment that allows them to be fully human. Both feminism and political liberalism use the language of self-actualization. In this context the right to an abortion is not so much akin to the right to carry arms as to the right to a satisfying job. It is not that the state must leave us alone in our private worlds, but that the state should support individual development.

Neglected in our study is another manifestation of individualism. Some people justify keeping abortion legal for the sake of children. Rather than indirectly condone the existence of children suffering from being unwanted or from being raised by deeply troubled parents, people reluctantly accept that abortion may be justified. Thus the bumper sticker, Pro-Child: Pro-Choice.

For all of the religious groups, the attitude about legalized abortion was related to the belief that a sacred life begins at conception. For people who accept this idea, abortion is both murder and blasphemy. The attitudes of our respondents with no religious affiliation who accepted legalized abortion were influenced only by the belief about the sacredness of life. Among respondents with no religious affiliation, the acceptance of legalized abortion seems to be a result of their rejection of a Judeo-Christian framework for understanding the world. An amazingly high 47 percent of those with no religious affiliation said abortion should *never* be forbidden. The next highest figure, 21 percent, was for mainline Protestants. People who do not identify with the religions in the United States reject the state limiting access to abortion because they understand the development of human life in terms of a process and not a single event. Christians tend to perceive conception as God creating human life. The nones understand conception as a point on a line of development that results in a human being.[7]

The political scientist Ronald Inglehart (1990) has tried to establish the existence of a "culture shift" in Western civilization. Previously Westerners were divided into the Right or the Left on the basis of their attitudes about government control of the economy and the redistribution of income. However, affluence has freed most people from preoccupation with such matters. A new division, which now coexists with the old one, pits Materialists, who support traditional social and religious values, against Postmaterialists, whose primary concern is self-realization. Inglehart elaborated on this new division as follows.

Materialist/Postmaterialist values seem to be part of a broader syndrome of orientations involving motivation to work, political outlook, attitudes toward the environment and nuclear power, the role of religion in people's lives, the likelihood of getting married or having children, an attitude toward the role of women, homosexuality, divorce, abortion, and numerous other topics. (Inglehart, 1990:423)

Based on our study of abortion, we would draw a more complex ideological map. First, there are the fundamentalists. Their primary motivation is religious; although this starting point leads some of them to be politically conservative (see Table 3.1), their main concern is the defense of social traditionalism (New Right). Second, there are committed Catholics whose religion is trying to redefine ideological boundaries, for example, by linking opposition to legalized abortion with the peace movement. Third, there are people whose policy positions are largely the result of accepting secular ideologies such as libertarianism (old Right) or feminism (New Left).

As Jim Kelly has pointed out, the coexistence of distinct religious perspectives on abortion contributes to the privatization of religion (Kelly 1989a:233). As he wrote, the failure to develop an ecumenical framework for the discussion of abortion reinforces "the contemporary tendency to view religion as simply a matter of private interest with little viable or constructive role to play in more public and shared realms of civil life" (p. 227). Starting from different values, religious collectivities develop divergent worldviews within which the issue of legalized abortion is placed. Obviously there is no single Christian position regarding abortion laws. Moreover, within both the Catholic and Protestant traditions there are fundamentalist types whose sole perspective is religious and modern types who struggle to reconcile religious and secular ideologies. Finally, even among Christians who agree on the need to restrict the availability of abortion, there is a lack of agreement about why such restriction is justified. As a result, an American cannot refer to a unitary religious perspective on abortion questions, and as a consequence the capacity of church leaders to influence public policies is weakened.

NOTES

1. Conservative Protestant meant affiliation with the Lutheran Church (Missouri Synod), Baptist churches, the Christian Church (not the Disciples of Christ), the Church of the Nazarene, and other, small nonmainline churches.
2. The item assessing fundamentalism has been shown in a series of previous studies (Johnson, 1986) to have the most reliability and validity of seven items used in these studies to measure religious fundamentalism.
3. In addition, the following relationships were significant at the .05 level: political conservatism—sacred life (beta = .11), preservation of all life—feminism (beta = .10), Catholicism-privacy (−.09), age-conservatism (.10), and preservation of all life—privacy (.09).
4. The expected relationships of the independent variables sexual traditionalism

and political conservatism with feminism were not found. Additional regression analyses indicated that the lack of a relationship between feminism and sexual traditionalism could have been a statistical artifact, since these variables were related significantly when political conservatism was no longer controlled. However, the lack of a relationship between political ideology and feminism was more substantive since conservatism was *not* significantly related to feminism when sexual traditionalism was not controlled. Similarly, in another study no relationship was found between political conservatism and feminism (Tamney et al., 1992). Feminism does not seem to be understandable in terms of the old liberal-conservative continuum (Inglehart, 1990).

5. At least among conservative Protestant ministers, the conviction that human life begins at conception seems to be based on secular rather than religious sources (Jelen, 1992).

6. People opposed to legalized abortion are more likely to use deontological ethics. They base decisions on following set rules. They do not understand ethics as trying to achieve goals (e.g., preserving life) but as compliance with rules (e.g., do not kill). The latter approach is less likely to result in interpreting situations in terms of conflicting frameworks (Lake, 1986). We suggest that conservative Protestants are especially likely to use rule-based ethics.

7. The sacred life measure was based on two questions, one of which referred to human life being in the hands of God. For the subsample of nones we examined the relationship between abortion attitude and the other component of the sacred life measure, which was a question about when human life begins. More than others, nones did not believe that human life begins at conception. For the subsample of nones, the correlations of abortion attitudes with the two-item sacred life measure and the question about when human life begins were almost identical.

4 Abortion and the Popular Press: Mapping Media Discourse from *Roe* to *Webster*

Laura Grindstaff

Scarcely a book or article on abortion begins without emphasizing the polarizing nature of the debate, and this work is no exception. Twenty years ago the *New York Times* heralded the Supreme Court decision in *Roe v. Wade* as "an historic resolution to a fiercely controversial issue" (Weaver, 1973:1). Yet the abortion controversy was far from resolved, and in fact had scarcely begun. Eight years later *Time* magazine called abortion "the most emotional issue of politics and morality that faces the nation today" (1981:20), and eight years after that, when the Supreme Court upheld a restrictive state abortion statute in *Webster v. Missouri Reproductive Services,* a chorus of voices in the popular press echoed the refrain. Studies show that as many as one-quarter of American voters indicate a willingness to vote on abortion alone, and that as a single issue abortion has been more potent than busing, gun control, school prayer, or the Equal Rights Amendment (Conover and Gray, 1983).

Like most feminist scholars, I believe abortion is so intensely divisive because it is deeply enmeshed in much broader beliefs and values about sexuality, reproduction, motherhood, and the family in America. Abortion is one of those issues that highlights the tensions between tradition and change, played out simultaneously on the individual female body and collectively through the social, political, legal, and mass media discourses that constitute it. *Legalized* abortion in particular arouses passionate emotions for both proponents and opponents because it has important symbolic as well as practical consequences. "Legal discourse," writes Condit (1990:97), "carries a kind of direct, performative power open to very few other genres of public address. It marshals the coercive power of the state behind certain vocabularies instead of others." In the case of abortion, it publicly validates and institutionalizes a certain ideology, and corresponding vocabulary, about women's sexuality that is not coterminous with motherhood and procreation.[1] Thus, although the contemporary debate appears on the surface to focus on the relative rights of pregnant women and embryos, it is also a referendum on the meaning of motherhood and a symbolic marker between those who wish to maintain a traditional gendered division of labor and those who wish to challenge it (Luker, 1984). Indeed, without an understanding of the symbolic quality of the issue, the fierceness of the struggle would appear absurd, an observation Gusfield (1963) makes about Prohibition and other "status issues" but which applies equally well to abortion. Abortion is thus a site of conflict between competing ideologies, what Luker (1984) calls "world views," institutionalized over the last two decades as "prochoice" and "prolife."

For feminists who are prochoice, reproductive self-determination—including the option of refusing motherhood by choosing abortion—is an essential condition of women's liberation, since women's reproductive capacity often justifies their oppression. Insofar as feminism challenges traditional patriarchal assumptions about the "nature" of women and the grounds upon which gender relations are enacted, particularly the translation of biological difference into social inequality, one could argue, as many feminist scholars do, that it is feminism—not abortion or the destruction of "life" per se—that is the really disturbing idea to those who oppose abortion (see Cisler, 1970; Willis, 1983, 1990; Faludi, 1989, 1990; Petchesky, 1990; Pollitt, 1990, 1992). As proof they note the increasing incidence of prolife violence, the finding that opposition to abortion correlates positively with support for capital punishment and military spending, and the observation that antiabortion activists seem to care little about pregnant women or their children once they are born.

Antiabortion activists do not necessarily describe their motives in these terms. For them, the fetus is a human being and therefore abortion (whether legal or criminal) is murder. Antiabortion folk share the goal of recriminalizing abortion, however, because they see legalized abortion as symptomatic of other social problems. For example, the women right-to-life activists that Ginsburg (1989) interviewed were concerned that materialism and narcissism (coded by the respondents as male) are replacing older values of nurturance, kin, and community (coded as female). In their view, abortion erodes gender difference critical to biological and social reproduction, and encourages women to become "structurally male" by denying their feminine obligations to reproduction and nurturance (Ginsburg, 1989:216). For many who identify as prolife, feminism does much the same thing, teaching women "a vague but abiding dissatisfaction with their essential physical natures" (Bell, 1987:20; see also Gilder, 1981;

Levin, 1988; Zepezauer, 1988). In this context, the feminist drive for equality is considered perverted because it means women are striving for "sameness"—to be the same as men—thus bringing women down from their pedestal to the level of men (see Sheeran, 1987). Some prolife advocates are themselves feminists who believe that support for abortion rights is actually antifeminist because abortion allows men to escape from responsibility for pregnancy and from committed relationships with women (see the comments of activists interviewed by Paige, 1983, and Luker, 1984) and that abortion is a form of "technological imperialism" designed to better accommodate women to a male-dominated society (Meehan, 1980).

Clearly, abortion represents quite different things to different people. In the words of Lynn Chancer (1990:114): "abortions and fetuses are floating signifiers, an occasion for projecting and displacing a host of cultural contradictions onto a symbolic terrain." This in no way suggests that the consequences of abortion politics are not real or that real women—especially poor women, many of whom are women of color—do not suffer from restrictive laws and policies. It suggests, rather, that a large part of passing laws, formulating policy, and winning public approval for movement activists involves persuading others to accept *this* rather than *that* representation of abortion, *these* rather than *those* definitions and terms.

The mainstream press is a particularly crucial site of contestation for abortion politics. Because abortion activists want to persuade others of their views, and because the media form part of our cultural repertoire or "tool kit" (Swidler, 1986) through which individuals construct meaning and make sense of the world, the media are a powerful force over which movement activists—of any sort—vie for control (see Molotch, 1979; Gitlin, 1980; Gamson and Modigliani, 1989; Condit, 1990). Consequently, the struggle over abortion takes place increasingly on mass-mediated terms; once a back-page "women's issue" rarely discussed, today abortion gets frequent play in the front pages of the mainstream press. Surprisingly, however, very little of the existing abortion literature looks at the relationship between abortion and the mass media and the ways in which media practices help shape the contours of the current controversy.

Abortion is well suited to media research both because it serves as a condensing symbol around which groups with conflicting morals, values, and cultures tend to oppose one another and hence is readily characterized in the press as an issue with an inherently dramatic structure (a structure the press exaggerates by highlighting and playing against one another the more extreme positions voiced by either side), and because the abortion debate is an ongoing one that evolves and changes over time. In the years since *Roe v. Wade*, differences around the issue have heightened public interest and spurred activists to struggle on a variety of fronts, including courts, legislatures, hospitals, clinics, schools, churches, and the mass me-

dia, over the ideological meanings of abortion and the material consequences that occur when certain meanings are granted institutional legitimacy through law and government policy. Consequently, laws and bills
regulating informed consent, parental and spousal notification, and public
funding of abortions for indigent women have been passed and vetoed,
ruled and overruled in what Eva Rubin (1987) calls a "ritual dance" between the courts and legislatures, and what one *Los Angeles Times* reporter calls a "legislative ping-pong game" (Tumulty, 1989a:A1)

In this chapter I explore how the competing rhetorics of prolife and
prochoice get played out in the popular press, focusing on coverage in
the *Los Angeles Times,* the *New York Times,* and the *Washington Post*
surrounding two key Supreme Court decisions: *Roe v. Wade,* which legalized abortion in 1973 and set parameters for state policy, and *Webster v.
Reproductive Health Services,* a 1989 ruling that upheld a Missouri statute
restricting access to abortion for poor women who rely on public funds
for their health care. The statute upheld in *Webster* also requires doctors
to perform viability tests at twenty weeks of gestation, and contains a
preamble stating that the fetus is a person with protectable interests under
the law. These two decisions constitute what journalists call "pegs"—critical moments in the ongoing social narrative of abortion that serve as a
kind of handle on which to hang stories, providing the opportunity for
further commentary.[2]

Employing content analysis and what is variously called textual analysis
or discourse analysis, I map changes and shifts in media representation of
abortion over time. More specifically, I examine the framing of abortion:
what the issues are, how they are represented, and who represents them.
Following Stuart Hall (1984) and others of the cultural studies tradition,
my primary aim is not to distinguish true/correct from biased/distorted
interpretations of events or to expose the relationship of signification to
"the real" (to determine what the abortion debate is "really" about and
how the media "gets it wrong"); rather, it is to explore the relationship
between competing strategies of representation in the press. That the discourses of prolife and prochoice are mediated by the press does not make
them any less real; it simply means they have been subjected to systematic
methods of framing. Media discourse selects what is news from an infinite
variety of daily problems, issues, and events, and organizes them into
meaningful stories.[3] The power involved here is the ideological power first
to name events and then to frame and signify them in a particular way;
the media selectively interpret what is important to know about the world,
making some meanings publicly available and not others. At the same
time, because media texts actively constitute society as a shared social phenomenon rather than passively reflect an objective reality "out there," it is
possible to ask about the silences in the text, the things left unsaid. Thus
to some extent I am interested not only in what the media allow, but in

Figure 4.1
Number of Abortion Articles Sampled, 1973 and 1989 Compared

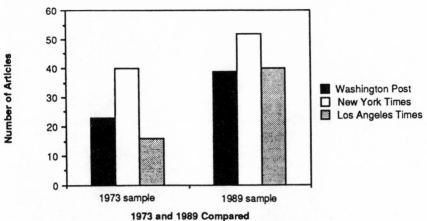

what they disavow—those issues and concerns that lie outside the frame. Chief among these are the feminist critique of "rights" discourse as it applies to the abortion context and the isolation of abortion from other reproductive issues such as sexual violence, job discrimination, inadequate housing, health care, day care, and effective birth control.

To summarize, my own story about the representation of the abortion conflict in the mainstream press consists of two main parts. The first is about the issues associated with the debate, the ways in which they are framed by journalists and their sources, and how and why those framings have changed (or not) over time. In the second section I discuss the feminist issues and concerns that remain marginal in media accounts of abortion and how the privacy framing of abortion rights constrains the rhetoric of choice in specific ways, with important consequences for feminism and the reproductive rights movement.

FRAMING THE DEBATE: *ROE* AND *WEBSTER* COMPARED

Without a doubt, the abortion debate has assumed an increasingly important position in U.S. politics in the years since abortion was legalized by the Supreme Court in *Roe. v. Wade,* reflecting both a shift in the status of women and the institutionalization of the abortion conflict. Perhaps the most obvious indicator of abortion's changing significance as a media issue is the growth in coverage over time: in 1989 there are roughly twice as many articles published on abortion as in 1973 (see Figure 4.1); they are longer and appear more frequently in the "A" section of the paper (see

Figure 4.2
Sample of Articles by Location in Paper, 1973 and 1989 Compared

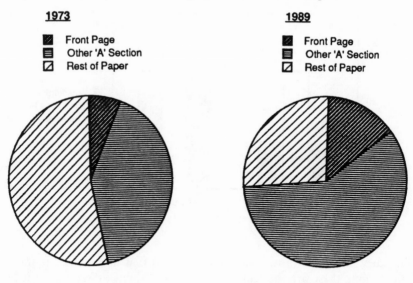

Table 4.1
1973 Experts on Abortion, All Papers Combined

Experts	Male (%)	Female (%)	Total (%)
Politicians	83	17	22
Religious	100	0	18
Supreme Court	100	0	14
Medical	86	14	13
Population Control/Family Planning	92	8	8
Legal	64	36	7
Other	64	36	7
Feminist/Abortion Rights	13	88	5
Right-to-Life	71	29	4
Academic	100	0	2
Total (n=160)	83	17	100

Figure 4.2). There is also an increase in the percentage of opinion pieces, political and legal analyses, and editorial cartoons generated by *Webster* compared to *Roe*—further evidence that abortion has "hardened" since 1973—as well as an increase in number of experts commenting on the abortion issue. Table 4.1 shows the breakdown of abortion experts by

Table 4.2
1989 Experts on Abortion, All Papers Combined

Experts	Male (%)	Female (%)	Total (%)
Politicians	91	9	33
Supreme Court	76	24	13
Prolife	66	34	12
Other	45	55	11
Feminist/Prochoice	0	100	9
Legal	67	33	7
Media	62	38	4
Medical	67	33	4
Family Planning	20	80	3
Academic	82	18	3
Religious	85	15	2
Total (n=587)	61	39	100

both category and gender in 1973, while Table 4.2 provides the same information for 1989.[4]

Although the status of abortion politics in the media has changed considerably over the years, the terms and framing of the debate have in many respects remained the same. While "abortion rights" has become "prochoice" and "right-to-life" has become "prolife"—and both sides have become bigger, more organized, and increasingly institutionalized—many of the same discourses invoked in 1973 are reproduced in 1989. This consistency of framing over time illustrates, among other things, that professional news values and the very organization of media practices continue to ensure that issues are presented and discussed following established conventions, conventions that help determine what counts as news in the first place. It also illustrates the extent to which early portrayals of a social problem or issue shape future ones. The abortion controversy is characterized by ongoing conflict, or what Snow and Benford (1988) describe as a "cycle of protest." In these terms, the legalization of abortion with *Roe* occurred very early in the cycle; indeed, it was one of the principle catalysts. Because social movements and political activism that surface early in a cycle of protest are likely to produce "master frames" that provide the ideational anchoring points and discursive boundaries for later movement activity, activists and experts who emerge later in the cycle will typically find their framing efforts constrained by previously elaborated master frames (Snow and Benford, 1988). *Roe v. Wade* established abortion as a constitutional question involving a woman's right to choose abortion based on privacy grounds and, for all kinds of social, political, legal, medical, religious, and moral reasons, set into motion an entire single-issue political machinery devoted to either reversing that decision or preserving it.

The Terrain of the Debate: The Courts and Legislatures

In both time periods, the question of whether abortion is properly the business of the courts or the legislatures is raised by voices in the press. Specifically, experts are concerned with the implications and consequences of judicial activism. Just as *Roe v. Wade* was condemned by right-to-life critics in 1973 as, in Justice Byron White's words, a flagrant misuse of "raw judicial power" (quoted in Farrell, 1973:1), *Webster* is similarly characterized by prochoice experts in 1989. Even many conservatives who were pleased with the decision felt the Court had once again overstepped its bounds. Justice Antonin Scalia, for example, says the Court "has needlessly prolonged [its] self-awarded sovereignty over a field where it has little proper business, since the answers to most of the cruel questions posed are political, not juridical" (quoted in *Los Angeles Times* 1989:A24). The lesson of *Webster* according to experts in the press is that what the Court gives, the Court can take away, and the continued willingness of the Supreme Court to restrict abortion rights has led prochoice activists to increasingly target politicians in their efforts to preserve *Roe*. Hence much of the media discourse on abortion centers around the legislative process, and abortion as an issue best fought out at the polls, despite the reluctance of politicians to take sides. Perhaps it is not surprising, then, that in 1989 politicians appear less concerned about the moral rights and wrongs of abortion than with the votes they will win or lose by taking a side—indeed, it is striking how much more sensitive to image and public opinion politicians seem to be.

Discussed frequently in the context of single-issue politics, abortion is said to serve as a kind of litmus test for re-election and is characterized as a particularly "hot" political issue after *Webster* because 1990 was an election year for state governors and all 211 state legislators. Dozens of articles in the 1989 sample are devoted to the then upcoming gubernatorial races and the positions of candidates, past and present, concerning abortion. Consequently, a fair amount of coverage reports the results of various public opinion surveys on abortion in 1989, a sizeable increase over the three Gallup poll articles published in 1973. Experts on both sides of the debate use poll results to claim support for their views and threaten politicians with electoral defeat; however, Republicans are said be particularly vulnerable to public disapproval if the Court goes beyond the "permit but discourage" stand taken in the *Webster* case to actually recriminalize abortion outright. As George Will warns, "the GOP could get crushed if the 1973 ruling is overturned and the party finds itself committed flatly against a right that a substantial number of Americans endorses" (Will, 1989:B7).

While many experts feel abortion is fundamentally a political question to be decided by elected politicians, many others see abortion as very much within the purview of the Supreme Court and frame the debate primarily as a constitutional question involving either a woman's right to choose abortion or the fetus's right to life. Indeed, the right to life and the right to choose are unequivocally the master frames employed by journalists and their sources in press accounts during both time periods sampled, though the ways in which these rights get articulated has changed somewhat over time.

Prolife Politics: The Fetal Right to Life

For opponents of abortion speaking and writing in the press, any right to abortion is superseded by the fetal right to life, a right that should be protected first and foremost under the Constitution. Employing a rhetorical strategy known as "overweighing" (Condit, 1990) or a "rhetoric of hierarchy" (Stewart, Smith, and Denton, 1984), prolife advocates place the right to life at the pinnacle of the human rights hierarchy, and claim abortion violates this most basic and fundamental right. Accordingly, abortion is murder, doctors who perform abortions are unscrupulous criminals, and women who get abortions are selfish and irresponsible, as the following quote from the dissenting opinion reveals: "During the period prior to the time the fetus becomes viable, the Constitution of the United States values the convenience, whim, or caprice of the putative mother more than the life or the potential life of the fetus" (quoted in Mathews, 1973:A1; see also MacKenzie, 1973). The "convenience, whim, or caprice of the putative mother" became a key phrase appropriated by right-to-life spokespersons and reproduced elsewhere in the press.

Right-to-life advocates also tend to invoke what Condit (1990) refers to as the "prolife heritage tale" by framing *Roe v. Wade* as an abrupt reversal of a long-standing cultural tradition that upholds the sanctity of life ethic. Called "pernicious," "horrifying," an "unspeakable tragedy," and a "monstrous injustice" (see *New York Times*, 1973; Van Gelder, 1973; Krol, 1973), *Roe* is said to "disenfranchise a whole segment of our society, namely those who are still in a prenatal state of development," and eliminate legal support for those seeking to protect the unborn (Stenson, 1973:A19). According to right-to-life sources, legalized abortion will encourage increasingly permissive sexual standards, subvert traditional sex roles, and encourage selfish and irresponsible behavior, especially among young women. More important, because of the decision "respect for life in the U.S. has been exposed to erosion from all sides," and "the general reverences for life" are seriously jeopardized (quoted in Dart, 1973b:B1).

For Cardinal Krol, the ruling "sets in motion developments which are terrifying to contemplate. . . . It is hard to think of any decision in the last 200 years of our history which has had more disastrous implications for our stability as a civilized society" (Krol, 1973:20).

Roe thus stands as a powerful symbol of moral corruption and decay, the first step down a slippery slope from abortion to infanticide to genocide and eugenics. In describing the decline of traditional values signified by legal abortion, right-to-life experts invoke a variety of metaphors, the most common of which compare abortion to the Nazi extermination of Jews and the right to life of fetuses with the civil rights of blacks:

It was legal for Herod to kill the innocent infants of his time. It was legal, according to Nazi standards, for Hitler to kill Jews and others of unwanted ethnic strains. And now our Supreme Court has legalized the killing of unborn babies. Our descendents will look back with horror at us and call us the legalized murder generation. (Cima, 1973:B6)

In 1857 the Court ruled that a Negro slave could claim none of the rights and privileges of the Constitution. Now the Court says the word "person" as used in the 14th Amendment does not include the unborn. Then the Court declared that freeing slaves would unconstitutionally violate the owner's right of property. Now it claims that forbidding abortions violates the mother's right of privacy. (Helgesen, 1973:28)[5]

Because the right to life is seen as absolute beginning from the moment of conception, antiabortion experts in 1973 are critical of the viability framework established by the *Roe* ruling. Although based on scientific and medical research, viability is not unlike the old notion of "quickening," the point at which the pregnant woman feels the fetus move within her. Justice Blackmun estimated viability at between 24 and 28 weeks of pregnancy, or the beginning of the third trimester. This is the point of compelling state interest, because until then fewer women die of abortion than of normal childbirth and because only then is the fetus capable of "meaningful life" outside the womb. Blackmun thus insisted that the extent of state controls must vary with the stage of pregnancy, and most abortion rights experts quoted in the press see this as a wise and reasonable attempt to balance the competing interests involved in the abortion controversy. However, right-to-life experts feel otherwise, and themselves draw upon scientific and medical research to contest the viability standard:

A simple examination with ultrasound equipment discloses a fetal heartbeat well in advance of the arbitrary standard of "fetal viability." Indeed, that standard is at best speculation; we have at present one youngster in our intensive care nursery born at five and a half months, which the Supreme Court holds as before viability.

Had the Court's standard prevailed, this youngster would have been permitted to die. (Sister Christine, 1973:B6)[6]

Sixteen years later, in 1989, the characterization of abortion by prolife voices has in some ways changed very little. *Roe v. Wade* is still mourned and condemned, legal abortion is still described as a violation of the con- stitutional right to life, the viability framework is still said to be based on "a completely arbitrary synthesis between medical opinion, law and theology" (Thomas, 1989:B7), and abortion itself is still compared to mur- der, slavery, genocide, and infanticide. Not surprisingly, then, the *Webster* decision restricting abortion rights is hailed repeatedly by prolife experts in the 1989 coverage as a historic victory for the constitutional rights of the unborn and an inspiration to prolife activism. Although they would have preferred an outright reversal of *Roe*, antiabortion advocates say they are eager to pass new restrictions on abortion and will pursue any legal means possible, including the re-introduction of a Human Life Amend- ment that states that legal personhood begins at conception.[7]

Many prolife activists in 1989 are eager to pursue illegal means as well—and herein lies the first major difference in the 1989 representation of antiabortion politics compared to that of 1973. Roughly 10 percent of the 1989 press sample is devoted to antiabortion violence, in particular to Operation Rescue and its leader Randall Terry. According to the *Los Angeles Times*, Norma "Jane Roe" McCorvey has had eggs thrown at her house, baby clothes strewn on her front lawn, and shotgun blasts fired at her house and car (Treadwell, 1989), while the *New York Times* reports that hospitals in several states have stopped performing abortions because of antiabortion pressure (Barringer, 1989). Close to thirty thousand pro- testors have been arrested at various clinic "rescues" nationwide in the year prior to the *Webster* ruling (Smothers, 1989), with the result that clinics are now characterized by journalists as a kind of "third battle- ground," after the courts and legislatures. For some prolife activists, mili- tancy is a welcome sign of political commitment: "We want polarization, we want people who are willing to pay the price" (quoted in Egan, 1989:A6). For other prolife sources, however, protesters who are militant or extreme are hurting the right-to-life cause. In general, the prolife move- ment is characterized in 1989 in much the same way as the abortion rights movement was portrayed in 1973: as a well-organized, well-financed, and militant minority.

Another difference in 1989 compared to 1973 is the subtle use of femi- nist principles to defend a prolife stance. Antiabortion experts in the press claim abortion is an excuse for sex-selection, which discriminates against female fetuses and devalues women (see Edsall and Dewar, 1989) and that the abortion procedure itself is psychologically damaging: "[The *Roe*] de- cision has led to the deaths of more than 24 million babies and the emotional scarring of millions of women" (Thomas, 1989:B7). Although women who get abortions are still characterized as selfish, irresponsible, and promiscuous, in a number of articles they are also positioned as "victims" of a manipulative and male-dominated abortion industry, as the following passage from the *New York Times* illustrates:

Olivia Gans . . . is 30 years old and frequently appears on television as head of American Victims of Abortion, a project of the NRLC. She was 22 years old, eager to please her boyfriend and desperate to hide her pregnancy from her family when she decided to undergo the procedure, she says. "I was being a good little girl. . . . I was going through with the abortion to solve everybody else's problems." She describes herself as a victim of abortion and says she has regretted it ever since. (Toner, 1989:A17)

"Prolife feminism" can be read as a development that partly reflects the incorporation of certain feminist principles into mainstream culture and partly serves as a rejoinder to accusations that prolife advocates care more about fetuses than women. As such it is a particularly good illustration of what Snow and his colleagues (1986) call "frame extension," whereby movement members extend the boundaries of their primary framework in the hopes of widening its appeal. From this perspective, the new frame signals an attempt on the part of antiabortion activists in the press to move beyond the narrow focus on fetal rights to include a concern for women by appealing to a certain female constituency that may have prolife sympathies but is also concerned about women's welfare and rights.[8] I found one prolife source who also warned against conflating "prolife" with "antiabortion," noting that the single-minded focus on abortion has prevented prolife committees from fighting for improved child care, improved working conditions for women who bear children, and father accountability (cited in Wilkerson, 1989). Similarly, Senator Mark Hatfield (R-Ore.) admits that in our "quick fix," materialist society, abortion may be the most humane option a woman has: "You can't replace something with nothing. An end to abortion will only come the hard way, when society can offer the pregnant mother a viable alternative to a life of deprivation for a baby born into poverty. . . . Those of us dedicated to the prolife cause should endeavor to give pregnant mothers a choice that is not one among evils but rather one among goods" (Hatfield, 1989:C7).

If prolife experts have appropriated feminist concerns and broadened the meaning of "life" in an attempt to widen their appeal, it is possible they have dropped virtually all overt references to religion for the same reason. Indeed, the absence of a religious presence in the 1989 sample of press accounts is striking and perhaps the single greatest change in prolife discourse over time. In 1973, religious arguments figure prominently, with officials of the Roman Catholic church comprising the second largest category of experts cited (see Table 4.1). As a religious issue, abortion tends to get framed in one of two ways: by abortion rights advocates as an attempt on the part of the Catholic church to impose its beliefs and morals on the rest of society, thereby undermining the separation of church and state, and by the Catholic clergy and other right-to-life advocates as a matter of God's law and God's will, which form the foundation of civilized society. Cardinal Patrick O'Boyle, Archbishop of Washington, D.C., reportedly asked pastors to devote the first post-*Roe* Sunday sermon to reminding people that abortion is morally evil (Hyer, 1973; *Los Angeles Times*, 1973), while Catholic lay organizations called on the nation's bishops to excommunicate Supreme Court Justice William Brennan, Jr., "as a symbolic gesture of protest against the Court decision" (*Washington Post*, 1973:A12).

In 1989, however, religious arguments have all but disappeared. It appears that abortion as a religious issue—specifically a *Catholic* issue—was a "misframing" (Snow et al., 1986) prolife experts discarded for the more persuasive language of constitutional rights. This shift does not necessarily deny the centrality of religion or religiosity in prolife politics, only its centrality in the framing of prolife discourse by experts in the press. That religious arguments are less visible in antiabortion rhetoric in recent years compared to the early 1970s is a finding consistent with the work of Paige (1983), Stewart, Smith, and Denton (1984), Sheeran (1987), Spitzer (1987), and Ginsburg (1989).[9]

Prochoice Politics: A Woman's Right to Choose

Turning now to the media discourse that upholds a woman's right to choose, there are important differences as well as similarities over time in the way abortion rights arguments are framed and packaged for public consumption. While a few feminist voices in the 1973 press sample insist abortion must be legal because women have the right to total control over their own bodies "without legal or socially imposed impunity" (Oehme, 1973:A15), most abortion rights advocates during this period follow the lead of Chief Justice Harry Blackmun and defend abortion on the basis of the privacy right, arguing that it is broad enough to encompass a woman's decision to terminate her pregnancy.

Consequently, although *Roe* is repeatedly hailed as a landmark victory for women's rights, this new freedom is framed almost exclusively as a negative right—the right to be free from state interference in the early stages of pregnancy—rather than the positive right to reproductive autonomy in the context of women's liberation. As the *Los Angeles Times* editorial states, the real contribution of *Roe* is its commitment to privacy doctrine, "which surely must include protection from unreasonable intrusions by government in private matters" (*Los Angeles Times* 1973:A4). Such a stance is, of course, "completely true to the principles of conservatism in this country," as conservative (and antiabortion) columnist Joseph Kraft notes (Kraft, 1973:A15). Moreover, on several occasions in 1973 Blackmun and other abortion rights spokespersons are careful to qualify more liberal interpretations of the ruling by pointing out that *Roe* in no way authorizes abortion on demand: specifically, a woman's right to privacy in the matter of abortion is not absolute because she needs the consent of a physician and because the state's interest in protecting potential life becomes compelling at viability.

Abortion rights are defended more frequently on medical than on feminist grounds in 1973, with physicians comprising the fourth largest category of experts, after politicians, religious officials, and Supreme Court justices (see Table 4.1). Doctors frame abortion as a matter of maternal health and professional autonomy, arguing that physicians have a right not to have their professional judgment subject to the dictates of politicians and lawmakers.[10] Given the primacy of the medical framing in 1973, it is perhaps not surprising that the anticipated consequences of the *Roe* decision are also defined largely in medical terms. According to abortion rights experts in the press, *Roe* is expected to equalize access to abortion across the country, stimulate an abortion clinic industry, lower infant mortality rates, and reduce population growth.

The larger impetus behind liberalized abortion as voiced in the media, however, concerns the health and safety of the pregnant woman. Justice Blackmun and other abortion rights sources point out that abortion will save women's lives by making back-alley abortions a thing of the past. As Alan Guttmacher of Planned Parenthood puts it, "Hundreds of thousands of women will be spared the medical risks and emotional horrors of backstreet and self-induced abortions" (quoted in Dart, 1973a:A12). Most accounts reproduce Blackmun's conclusion in the majority opinion of *Roe* that abortion was first criminalized in the 1800s because it was a dangerous procedure; since it is no longer dangerous—and in fact is many times safer than childbirth—the ruling serves to move the law out of the nineteenth century and into step with contemporary medical practice. A number of experts also note that women will get abortions no matter what, so why force them to do so under inhumane conditions? As one woman writing to the *Washington Post* puts it, "Abortions do occur and it is better to obtain one through a knowledgeable physician than a street quack. Better still to avoid the pregnancy" (Tordella, 1973:A19).

Closely linked to the medical discourse on abortion is the framing of abortion within the context of family planning and population control measures. Family planning and population control officials tend to characterize abortion as an issue of public as well as personal health, the former emphasizing the burden on society generally and women especially of "unwanted children" and "problem pregnancies," while the latter frame abortion as a means for managing national and international fertility rates. Overall, however, population control arguments appear relatively infrequently, and by 1989 they have all but disappeared. Indeed, this is the one abortion rights perspective from 1973 markedly absent in the 1989 accounts, likely because of its eugenic implications and the historic association of population control policies with race- and class-based sterilization abuse. Although prochoice arguments are voiced frequently in 1989 by spokespersons for Planned Parenthood—in particular by then-President Faye Wattleton—Planned Parenthood is not in theory or practice a population control organization. Thus, while Planned Parenthood is well represented in the press in both 1973 and 1989, only in 1973 is support for abortion rights linked to population concerns expressed by experts from groups such as Zero Population Growth or the World Population Institute.

Prochoice rhetoric in the media has changed in other ways over the years as well. As in the 1973 sample of accounts, the vast majority of arguments in 1989 focus on a woman's constitutional right to choose abortion. However, in 1989 this right is framed more strongly in feminist terms. Some sources in the press express disbelief that we still have to argue what a woman can or can't do with her body, since the right to individual autonomy is a basic right, and one *Roe v. Wade* seemed to secure. "We won't go back" is therefore a frequent prochoice rallying cry, and atrocity tales of illegal abortion and back-alley "carnage" surface again and again to remind readers that if history tells us anything, it's that "you can't stop abortion by outlawing it, you can only make it more dangerous and expensive for those who can least afford it" (Cohen, 1989:A17). "One has only to remember the carnage that existed before 1973," writes columnist Judy Mann, "when women showed up in emergency rooms across the country bleeding to death from botched illegal abortions to know what will happen if those sanctimonious bullies are not stopped" (Mann, 1989b:C3). This is an idea powerfully symbolized in a *Los Angeles Times* cartoon depicting the Scales of Justice holding aloft three interlocked coat hangers.

That restrictions on abortion discriminate against women on the basis of race and class plays a more prominent part in the prochoice discourse of 1989 compared to 1973. Class in particular becomes a salient issue in the 1989 articles because *Webster,* like the Hyde Amendment of 1977, restricts access to abortion for women who rely on public funds and facilities for their health care. The general consensus is that restrictions on abortion of the sort upheld in *Webster* apply to one class of women only, the poor. "Access to abortion has been narrowed, threatened, transformed into a maze," writes Ellen Goodman, to the point where "only those women with the proper maps or money have the right to their rights" (Goodman, 1989b:A23).

Yet the vocabulary most prochoice experts use to defend the right to abortion is that of privacy rights, which is not particularly useful when making an appeal for public monies for poor women's abortions. This is not to suggest the privacy right necessarily or inevitably precludes government financing for abortion. In California, for example, the privacy provision of the state constitution is used to safeguard rather than prohibit Medi-Cal funding for abortion. But just as often prolife politicians and lawmakers will interpret privacy narrowly (in economic terms) when challenging abortion rights claims, typically to justify the denial of public funding for abortion in the manner illustrated by Chief Justice William Rehnquist writing for the majority in *Webster*. According to Rehnquist, "Nothing in the Constitution requires states to enter or remain in the business of performing abortions. Nor do private physicians and their patients have some kind of constitutional right of access to public facilities for the performance of abortions" (quoted in *Washington Post,* 1989:A8; see also *New York Times,* 1989b). Thus privacy discourse has the double-edged potential to simultaneously safeguard women's "choice" in the abstract legal sense while foreclosing real choices for women who cannot obtain an abortion through private means—a serious contradiction rarely (if ever) discussed by experts in the media.[11]

While prochoice advocates in 1989 do not rely exclusively on the privacy framework, it remains central to prochoice discourse, and privacy is the principal prochoice issue, according to Kate Michelman, head of the National Abortion Rights Action League (NARAL). As Michelman puts it, "We are going to elect politicians who believe [the abortion] choice is ours, not theirs" (quoted in Mann, 1989a:D3), a sentiment echoed by prochoice demonstrators chanting, "Not the church, not the state, women must decide their fate!" (Johnston, 1989:A10) and in various editorial cartoons. Over and over again when discussing *Webster,* prochoice experts in the press re-articulate that the fundamental right to abortion established by *Roe* is based on the right to privacy and that *Webster* violates that fundamental right.

According to Michelman, the increasing reliance on appeals to privacy reflects a deliberate tactical decision made by the abortion rights coalition to shift the terms of the debate from the question "Whose rights will prevail, the woman's or the fetus's?" to "Who will decide, women or the government?" primarily because the slogan "Women have a right to control their own bodies" didn't gain the prochoice movement a lot of sympathy, whereas appeals to privacy did (cited in Shaw, 1990a:A1). Apparently "Who will decide?" emerged when prochoice advocates discovered the essential contradiction that public opinion surveys have consistently shown: most Americans are simultaneously prolife and prochoice. They dislike abortion and even consider it immoral, but most also think the abortion choice is one the individual woman should make (Shaw, 1990a). Thus, just as abortion as a religious issue was a misframing that prolife advocates in the press decided to reframe as a question of constitutional rights, "a woman's right to reproductive autonomy" was a misframing that also had to change. The new frame—"the right to choose"—was consistent with the liberal ideology of privacy rights and refocused the central issue around the person or institution making the abortion choice rather than the nature of the choice itself.[12]

Another shift in prochoice discourse is the relative insignificance of medical arguments made in defense of abortion rights in 1989 compared to 1973. Although the actual number of medical experts writing articles or quoted by reporters is the same (see Table 4.2), these experts tend to frame their arguments in feminist rather than medical or health terms. Former Chief Justice Harry Blackmun is a case in point. A man with close ties to the medical community, Blackmun authored *Roe v. Wade* using medical rather than feminist discourse, and was quick to point out that a woman's abortion right is qualified, contingent on proper medical authorization. In 1989, however, he emphasizes that "the decision to carry a fetus to term is quintessentially intimate, personal, and life directing. . . . The right to reproductive choice has become vital to the full participation of women in the economic and political walks of American life" (*Los Angeles Times,* 1989:A24). He calls *Webster* "chilling" and "ominous," and says he fears for the future of women's rights (quoted in Marcus, 1989).[13]

The medical discourse that does circulate in the press around the time of *Webster* focuses primarily on the issue of fetal viability, since one of the clauses in the Missouri statute upheld in the *Webster* case requires doctors to perform viability tests on fetuses twenty weeks old, fully four weeks earlier than the point of viability established by *Roe*. As in 1973, scientific "findings" about fetal development are used occasionally in 1989 to support a prolife position. The claim is made by columnist William Raspberry, for example, that prolife sentiment runs parallel to scientific inquiries into fetal viability and that as the fetus is gradually discovered as a developing human being, more people will disapprove of abortion (Raspberry, 1989).

But by far the most common discussions of viability center on the legal soundness of the viability concept and the practical implications of the testing requirement upheld by the *Webster* decision. Medical sources quoted all agree that twenty weeks is a very conservative estimate of viability, as no fetus can survive outside the womb before lung maturity, and the lungs do not develop before about twenty-three or twenty-four weeks. Thus while the point of viability may be creeping forward legally, medically it is not. Doctors call the viability testing a moot point and a nonissue inflated to false significance, not only because the onset of viability remains unchanged, but because so few abortions (less than 1 percent) are performed after the twentieth week (See Janny Scott, 1989; Rolata, 1989; Dellinger, 1989). Nevertheless, a *Los Angeles Times* poll published the day after *Webster* found that while more people disapproved the ruling than approved it (49 percent compared to 40 percent), a strong majority (57 percent compared to 32 percent) was in favor of the mandatory viability testing to determine whether the fetus could survive outside the womb (Boyarski, 1989). This finding is good evidence that neonatal medicine and science (including fetal therapy, ultrasound, and the new reproductive technologies) are redefining the abortion debate, not by lowering the actual age of viability but by helping to foster a popular conception of the fetus as an individual, a tiny patient, an entity separate and distinct from the pregnant woman—a trend many feminist scholars find disturbing but which goes unexplored in the press at the time of the *Webster* decision.[14]

Besides mandating expensive viability tests, *Webster* is predicted to have a number of other important consequences. According to press accounts, the decision will make abortion impossible to get in either a publicly financed medical unit or in a private unit on public land, and all but impossible to obtain in a hospital, since hospital abortions are generally performed in the late second or the third trimester—past the revised point of viability. For most experts commenting on *Webster,* however, the real significance of the decision is not so much its immediate impact but what it portends for future abortion cases. Consequently, there is a great deal of speculation in the press as to which states will be the next battlegrounds for future abortion legislation, and which aspects of abortion law will be its targets (fully 90 percent of all accounts sampled in 1989 deal with these questions). The consensus among experts on both sides of the issue is that *Webster* provides a green light to state courts and legislatures to further regulate abortion, perhaps overturn *Roe* altogether, and that many of the restrictions on abortion law and policy struck down in past years may now pass constitutional muster because *Webster* provides the requisite legal precedent. For opponents of abortion, the decision partly redresses the improper display of judicial activism that characterized *Roe v. Wade.* Those who defend *Roe,* however, say dealing with abortion on a state-by-state basis is dangerous because it creates a patchwork quilt of abortion laws that discriminate against poor women and women living in restrictive states.

Conflict and Compromise

In both time periods, experts predict increased polarization around the issue as a result of the Supreme Court rulings. As columnist Mary McGrory puts it, "There is a total inability to come to terms even on the terms. An 'unwanted baby' to one is an 'unwanted pregnancy' to another. Is the baby a soul or an inconvenience? Each side feels the other is unspeakably arrogant" (McGrory, 1989:A2). Only in 1989, however, do journalists and their sources consistently employ metaphors of warfare when describing the abortion conflict. The general perception is that the abortion debate has grown "increasingly bitter and agitated," the two sides "unbridgeably divided and bent on jihad" (Krauthammer, 1989:A17). Even a cursory glance at the headlines of abortion stories in 1989 confirms the centrality of the war metaphor.[15]

Virtually all experts agree that *Webster* will inflame an already incendiary situation and provide the catalyst for nationwide rallies and demonstrations, an observation supported by numerous photographs of angry protesters in hostile confrontation. *Webster* is characterized variously as the start of a full-scale "abortion war" (Balzar, 1989:A1), the beginning of a "snarling battle" (*New York Times,* 1989f:A28), and the spark that will set off a "political firestorm" throughout America (Dionne, 1989:A1). According to one reporter, "Abortion will grow to dwarf all single-issue political battles of the past, as an aroused electorate battles over life, death, and liberty" (Balzar, 1989:A1). Political analyst William Schneider agrees that the issue "will tear the country apart," and even compares the abortion conflict to the Vietnam war: "Abortion may be the Vietnam of the 1990s. For women of childbearing age, the abortion issue is as personal and as life-threatening as the draft was for young men in the 1960s. Last week's Supreme Court decision was the Gulf of Tonkin resolution. For millions of Americans, this means war" (Schneider, 1989:E1).

Because of the severity of the new restrictions, both journalists and their sources predicted *Webster* would galvanize in particular a lethargic prochoice movement grown somewhat complacent about the status of abortion rights in the years since *Roe.* According to Kate Michelman, "We have awakened the sleeping giant, and today we begin mobilizing that giant for the battles that lie ahead" (quoted in Tumulty, 1989b:A23). Prochoice spokespersons describe themselves as "rabid" and ready to wage an all-out war. They claim to represent the true majority opinion on abortion and will retaliate at the polls. "The anti-choice forces won't know what hit them when the prochoice majority starts to flex its muscle," Michelman warns (quoted in Yost, 1989:A10), while Robin Schneider of the California National Abortion Rights Action League insists, "You're going to see single-issue prochoice voting like something you've never seen before" (quoted in Balzar, 1989:A1). This of course was very much the response of right-to-life activists in the wake of *Roe,* and at least one reporter comments on the irony of the reversal when she notes that in their efforts to target individual legislators and launch a massive media campaign, prochoice groups of the 1990s may be using as their political model the prolife movement of the 1970s and 1980s (Barringer, 1989).

Amid the representations of the abortion debate as an increasingly fierce and polarizing conflict, now and again there is a voice in the press that speaks of compromise—yet another significant difference between the 1973 media discourse on abortion and that of 1989. At one level the appeal to compromise serves to further emphasize conflict and polarity, for only when the sides of an issue are unbridgeably divided does compromise become a serious issue; it is also, however, a recognition that no matter how long and hard the activists of "life" and "choice" struggle to alter abortion policy and persuade others of their views, neither side is likely to win total political dominance.

Most experts in the press who touch on the subject of compromise argue that in any competition of rights—in the case of abortion, the fetus's and the pregnant woman's—lawmakers must negotiate an acceptable balance between them. The results of public opinion polls published in the press seem to back this view, a majority of respondents not wanting unlimited abortion rights but not wanting a total ban either. Of course, what is considered an acceptable compromise is itself a matter of contention. Some sources see fetal viability as the ultimate point of political compromise. Others recognize that even if viability remains a workable concept, the issue of abortion funding and access remains. In general, just as courts and legislatures have tended to compromise on abortion around the issue of public funding, funding tends to be the target of compromise positions articulated by experts (both prolife and prochoice) in the press. Consider the version of compromise offered by David Broder of the *Washington Post:*

The decision on abortion is a matter for individual choice, within the family, by the person or persons directly involved. The state should neither inhibit nor facilitate that option. It should not assist or finance abortion, but neither should it stand in the way of women deciding on that option. Such a "neutrality doctrine" would not satisfy partisans of either side. . . . But when there is no consensus in the society, it is more sensible to step back from futile attempts to impose one view over another than to pick constantly at the scar this issue has become. (Broder, 1989:B7)

Discussions of compromise have become even more central to media discourse on abortion since the 1992 Supreme Court abortion ruling *Planned Parenthood of Southeastern Pennsylvania v. Casey,* which upheld a woman's constitutional right to an abortion within limits and with certain qualifications. Of course, allowing abortions while making them more difficult to attain—the "permit but discourage" strategy espoused by both *Webster* and *Casey*—is a narrow vision of what compromise on abortion might look like.[16]

The Influence of the Media

The last aspect of the 1989 press coverage I want to discuss is the transformation of the abortion conflict into a major mass media phenomenon.

Indeed, aside from the increase in sheer number of accounts and the shift in the definition of abortion from a "soft" to a "hard" issue, perhaps the single greatest difference in newspaper coverage of the *Webster* decision compared to that of *Roe* is in the representation of the abortion controversy itself. That is, the 1989 coverage devotes almost as much space to the representation of the debate—how each side perceives the other, how polarized the issue is, how one side has appropriated the rhetorical strategies of the other, how the debate is largely about language, imagery, and framing—as it does to the substantive issues being debated. In many of these accounts, *Webster* is described as a media spectacle the scope of which goes far beyond anything yet seen in the history of the U.S. abortion controversy, and the media are acknowledged as a powerful force over which both sides of the debate vie for control. Anticipated in Europe as well as in the United States, the ruling is characterized as "the most closely-watched abortion decision in a decade" (Savage, 1989a:A4), and the Supreme Court's "cliffhanging finale" (Greenhouse, 1989:A10). For nearly a month all the major television networks were on special events standby status, ready to break into regular programming with news of the decision, and for the last four days preceding it "hundreds of people, most of them intensely interested in the outcome of the abortion case, converged on the Court," some having waited all night in line to get a seat in the public gallery (*New York Times* 1989c:A8). The following passage describes the scene in Washington on the morning the *Webster* ruling was finally handed down:

If James Madison imagined democracy as a kind of outdoor flea market of competing groups peddling their wares in a wearying, blurry cacophony, the steps of the U.S. Supreme Court on the morning of the Court's decision came close to realization of the metaphor. Part of what the sellers at this flea market were selling was "spin"—the most advantageous interpretation on the decision from a particular point of view. For both sides, it seemed to be to make the decision as apocalyptic as possible. (Rosenstiel, 1989:A27)

What is revealed here is not only the heightened intensity of the pro-choice/prolife conflict, but the critical role of the media as its purveyors. To paraphrase the reporter cited above, the very machinery of modern democracy is now inevitably connected to the end of a microphone and linked by cables to satellite microwave trucks. Indeed, in his opinion the most remarkable aspect of *Webster* was not the ruling itself but the media's coverage of it, as well as the response of activists to the presence of the cameras. Ultimately, the media's self-reflexivity is further evidence of abortion's shifting public significance, for if an issue is big and controversial enough, at some point the amount and intensity of coverage itself becomes part of what Gamson and Modigliani (1989) call the "issue culture."[17] In the case of abortion, the issue culture is very much bound up in the struggle over discourse, a contest that plays itself out increasingly on mass-mediated terrain.

These, then, are the principal themes and narratives associated with the contemporary abortion controversy as represented by news accounts in the mainstream daily press. In some respects, abortion is the "perfect" media issue because it is a long-standing one with inherent drama and conflict and well-rehearsed slogans and catchphrases. Yet it is precisely because of these qualities that it becomes difficult to represent the abortion debate without reducing it to a two-dimensional caricature of high political warfare (a criticism one could make of abortion activists as well). Given the proclivity of the media to decontextualize events and simplify complexity, it is hardly surprising that press accounts of abortion are limited to a consistently narrow range of themes and experts, thereby neglecting important concerns of many on both sides of the debate. Perhaps most disturbing from a feminist perspective are the narrow framing of compromise, the failure of journalists and their sources to discuss the implications of the new reproductive technologies for abortion law and policy, and the increasing reliance of prochoice officials on appeals to privacy to justify a woman's right to choose.

Media discourse also tends to exaggerate and pit against one another the most extreme positions voiced by opposing spokespersons, a strategy that not only privileges conflict but also reproduces a structured "discourse/counterdiscourse" dialectic (see Terdiman, 1985). It is perhaps an obvious point that both sides of an issue like abortion expend considerable effort refuting competing claims in order to legitimate their own; less obvious is the fact that a counterargument, what Foucault (1981) calls a "reverse discourse," while making an opposite case, invariably reproduces the very position it is attempting to discredit. As Terdiman (1985:65) notes, it is a fundamental and paradoxical construction in which the contesters discover that the authority they sought to undermine is reinforced by the very fact of its having been chosen for opposition. The result is a "dispute paradigm" (Trew, 1979:135), a set of competing rhetorical options available for use in a given situation, each of which marks an alternative ideological position. In the case of abortion, the dispute paradigm takes the form of "right to life" versus "right to choose," a dialectic that locks the argument within the dominant framework of liberal legalism and validates that framework for the general public as well as the activists themselves.

RIGHTS, CHOICE, AND CULTURAL RESONANCE

The particular contours of the dispute paradigm reproduced in the abortion debate are shaped not only by media practices but by the larger cultural framework in which both media professionals and abortion activists

are embedded. In any public controversy at any point in history, the dominant ideology limits which narratives are considered persuasive. Those accounts that have "narrative fidelity" (Fisher, 1984), "frame resonance"
(Snow and Benford, 1988), or "cultural resonance" (Gamson and Modigliani, 1989) have a natural advantage because they resonate with larger cultural themes, values, and beliefs. The abortion controversy is no exception.
Because most Americans subscribe to strong cultural myths about privacy,
liberty, and individual rights (including the right to life), these are the
framings both prochoice and prolife experts in the press use to argue for
or against abortion. In the abortion context, then, the metanarrative that
has structured the abortion debate in the media since the late 1960s is the
discourse of individualism and the construction of abortion as a question
of individual rights.[18]

The underlying assumption here—no less significant because of its
taken-for-grantedness—is that the abortion issue is properly characterized
this way. Yet for many feminist scholars (whose critiques are not voiced
in the press), the language of individual rights is misguided and inappro-
priate in the abortion context because pregnancy involves an ongoing dependency relationship, not a conflict between two autonomous persons.
Framing the abortion issue as an abstract clash of rights ignores the biological, social, and practical realities of pregnancy, and perpetuates the
fundamental fallacy that fetal and maternal rights can be considered in
isolation (Hubbard, 1984; Brown, 1983; Smith, 1983; Willis, 1983; Johnsen, 1986). Consequently, some feminists would prefer to drop "rights"
altogether and simply work toward women's reproductive freedom and
equality on different terms without recourse to legal norms, standards, and
strictures (see Johnston, 1989). The "do-it-yourself" approach to abortion
is precisely the philosophy behind the pre-Roe underground abortion network known as "Jane," recently resurrected in the wake of the Webster
ruling (see Japenga and Venant, 1989).

Rights discourse is additionally problematic for many feminist scholars
because a woman's right to reproductive choice is framed largely in privacy terms. Privacy was a master frame employed by most abortion rights
experts in the media in 1973 because, for various reasons, this was how
the right was formulated in Roe v. Wade. The Court majority said the
right to privacy was broad enough to encompass reproductive decisions; it
did not say that childbearing disadvantaged women in the workplace, or
that abortion was a necessary backstop to failed contraception, or that
control over reproduction was essential to women's struggle for equality
with men. Privacy was chosen because, although not expressly guaranteed
in the Constitution, it has a long line of judicial precedents. As Condit
(1990:102) points out, the privacy frame thus enabled Justice Blackmun,
when writing the majority opinion in Roe, to work within a closed legal
vocabulary and avoid introducing any new, substantive rights (such as the

right to reproductive autonomy), which would have implied the Court was not dealing infallibly with universal, timeless truths.

In 1989 privacy still seems to be the paramount justificatory vocabulary used by prochoice experts, not only because the master frame of privacy constrained the efforts of future activists to articulate abortion rights otherwise but because this frame remained compelling to many people. Privacy is a persuasive cultural narrative that resonates with the cherished belief that people should be left alone to make decisions that affect them personally, and the prochoice movement has benefited from its strategic application. Unfortunately, not only has the right to privacy tended to justify the denial of public funding for abortion (as in the *Webster* decision) but it undermines the feminist insight that the personal is political and reinforces a public/private split that has historically disadvantaged women. More important, privacy discourse obscures the fact that it is specifically *women* who suffer most when abortion is strictly regulated, and thus fails to situate abortion in a political/legal context where restrictions of any kind on access to abortion can be seen as sex discriminatory.[19]

The primacy of "rights discourse" and the privacy framing of the right to choose are two of three major shortcomings in prochoice rhetoric identified by feminist scholars. The third is the isolation of abortion itself from larger reproductive concerns and the narrow focus of "choice" on the abortion right rather than, or in addition to, the right to bear children under humane conditions. Of course, the rhetoric of "life" is similarly narrow. Looking at the framing of abortion by both sides of the current controversy, abortion is clearly a synecdoche for reproductive rights more generally. For Sprague (1991), Joyner (1990), Davis (1983), and others, the opposition of "life" and "choice" in the prolife/prochoice debate emerges from the material interests associated with the specific race, class, and gender position of the major activists in the debate. In other words, the reason why the feminist discourse in the public controversy fails to offer an alternative to hegemonic ideological categories is that it has been dominated by straight, middle-class, white women, whose social location as participants within the dominant culture prompts them to construct the issue as a matter of the one personal choice they do not have: the right to choose abortion. Consequently, prochoice activists have not pushed to develop an alternative discourse. "The source of that challenge can be expected, rather, to come from the standpoints of those who have been more completely excluded" (Sprague, 1991:19). Indeed, it has been primarily working class feminists and feminists of color who emphasize a broader reproductive rights agenda that includes freedom from sterilization abuse and forced obstetrical interventions, access to adequate prenatal care, affordable housing and day care, safe workplaces, sex education, birth control, drug treatment, and socialized medicine (see Joseph, 1981; Davis, 1983; Nsiah-Jefferson, 1989; Avery, 1990; Smith, 1990).

Extending the meaning of choice by framing abortion as a constitutive part of a broader health and reproductive rights agenda is a positive move that will strengthen both the prochoice coalition and the institutional alliance between black and white feminists. Leaders of the prochoice movement have acknowledged as much to reporters (see Behrens, 1989; Fulwood, 1989). How it might affect the rhetorics of "life" and "choice" in the media remains to be seen. As Condit (1990) observes, a more rational approach to abortion might have tried from the very beginning to preserve life *through* choice by emphasizing the kinds of positive alternatives listed above, therefore reducing the need for abortion in the first place. Unless the value of "life" ends at birth, this expansion of choice should find support among prolife advocates as well as prochoice ones.

CONCLUSION

At the same time, situating abortion within a broader framework of choice does not argue against independent abortion rights organizing. Collectively we can reduce the need for abortion; however, we cannot eliminate it entirely. Birth control is not 100 percent safe or effective, and women do not always control the conditions under which they have sex; thus abortion gives women choices they otherwise would not have. The questions then remain, how to best frame the abortion right so that women are not forced to bear children they do not want, and how to translate the socially determined need for abortion into public discourse.

It is true that, so far, the contemporary prochoice movement has helped to formulate reproductive freedom narrowly as a contest of rights between the fetus's life and a woman's choice. It is also true that by focusing exclusively on one aspect of the total reproductive process (abortion) and by framing abortion as a privacy right, activists in the debate collude with the establishment in isolating abortion from related issues of gender, race, and class. But I agree with Celeste Condit (1990) when she insists that blaming the activists exclusively fails to situate abortion in a legal and political context where abortion law and policy are the outcomes of various competing interests, of which feminists are but one. As Pollitt (1992) and others point out, it is generally not prochoice advocates who need to be convinced of the merits of sex education, widely available contraception, access to medical services for poor women, day care, parental leave, tough enforcement of child support payments, and so on. Prochoice people routinely support these aims; the problem is, many prolife people do not. Indeed, many oppose sex education, contraception, and welfare rights as vehemently as they oppose abortion (see also Granberg, 1981; Willis, 1990; Petchesky, 1990; Peters, 1990; Faludi, 1991). My own analysis of the abortion debate in the press supports this observation.[20]

Condit (1990) suggests that originally the feminist demand for reproductive choice was rooted in the needs and wants of women across economic lines; however, the transference of those needs into public discourse was incomplete, so that choice was translated "from a substantive demand for real choices in one's life to a permissive liberal demand to prevent active government interference in whatever choices one might economically, socially and personally have" (p. 116). This incompleteness of transference is not necessarily the result of inherent limitations in liberal legalism and the right to privacy or a narrow vision of reproductive autonomy, but it is also—even primarily—the outcome of a compelling counterposition on abortion offered by a strong prolife opposition. Once a radical demand for reproductive freedom for all women, "choice" was reduced to a simple permission because of continuing disagreements about the standing of abortion (p. 116). For Condit, such compromise is the inevitable result of the process of public persuasion, and reflects the differential permeability of public discourse to private interests.

Because of our particular historical and cultural legacy, the right to privacy is seen as fundamental in law and popular opinion, whereas the right of women to reproductive autonomy and the right of women and men to a decent standard of living are not. The Bill of Rights secures the individual's freedom from governmental intrusions, not the individual's entitlement to governmental support. There is no guarantee that by framing abortion differently feminists could have prevented the outcome of *Maher v. Roe, Harris v. McRae,* or *Webster v. Missouri Reproductive Services,* Supreme Court rulings that allow states to withhold public funds for abortion. The meaning of a particular frame or discourse does not inhere in the frame itself but derives from the social context in which it is embedded. As C. Wright Mills (1963) pointed out long ago, "vocabularies of motive" have no fixed referent in particular values or systems of morality. This is perhaps best illustrated by the justices deciding *Planned Parenthood of Southeastern Pennsylvania v. Casey,* who did not emphasize privacy discourse as in their affirmation of *Roe v. Wade,* but instead declared a woman's right to abortion constitutional and fundamental using the language of sex equality—the very framing feminist scholars prefer. Yet the equality framework did not stop the majority from upholding the right of states to require informed consent, 24-hour waiting periods, parental notification, and detailed record keeping of abortion services subject to public disclosure—restrictions ruled unconstitutional in two previous Supreme Court cases operating under the old privacy framework. Nor did *Casey* change the status of public funding for abortion.[21]

Both prochoice and prolife groups vie for legitimacy and public support within the same social, legal, and political institutions, including the mass media. As we have seen, the abortion controversy is characterized for the most part in the media as volatile and uncompromising, as a battle of "life" versus "choice" waged between radical extremists. While the media did not create the abortion controversy, they have undoubtedly influenced its content and form by making some narratives available and not others, and by emphasizing those aspects of the debate consistent with the needs and values of professional news writing. As a result, the abortion debate is not only a clash of worldviews or a contest of underlying ideologies about the place and meaning of motherhood; it is a rhetorical struggle over discourse, over the language and imagery used to inscribe those worldviews in public consciousness. As Condit (1990) observes, the rhetorical process is itself a creative contributor to the distribution of power and resources through law, government policy, and other social practices. A critical analysis of rhetoric and framing is therefore vital in the abortion context, not for exposing the "truth" behind the words, but for understanding how negotiations among competing viewpoints generate new narratives on abortion and reframe old narratives in new ways; only by understanding how the struggle over discourse works, how meaning is made, can we begin to envision alternative articulations. By concentrating on how the camera works in addition to the pictures that it takes, perhaps we can begin to see the possibility of a space, and a discourse, beyond the frame.

NOTES

1. It should be noted that despite the contemporary framing of the abortion issue as a competition between legal rights, historically the decision to legalize or criminalize abortion was more an issue of medical control by physicians, and to some extent an issue of population control, than of women's or fetal rights (see Mohr, 1978). In fact, neither feminist nor right-to-life arguments entered the abortion debate in a serious way until the 1970s, with the *Roe v. Wade* decision. Even then, *Roe* was largely a victory for physicians, who lobbied on behalf of their own "right" not to have the state interfere with their medical judgment and practice (Mohr, 1978; Paige, 1983; Rubin, 1987; Petchesky, 1990).

2. More specifically, I focus on coverage two weeks before and two weeks after each Supreme Court ruling. The total number of articles published during these periods is 210 (79 in 1973, 131 in 1989), and comprise what I consider to be my primary data set. Any topically relevant newspaper content (hard news, features, editorials, letters to the editor, etc.) regardless of which section of the paper it appeared in became part of my base. Likewise, I did not distinguish between information derived from quoted sources, paraphrased experts, or the opinions of reporters, columnists, and editors. In addition to my primary data, I collected another 200 or so articles exclusively from the *Los Angeles Times* spanning roughly the year following *Webster* (i.e., August 1989 to August 1990), in order to better trace developments and changes in abortion policy subsequent to the decision. To ensure that the topics covered by the *Los Angeles Times* were not unique to that paper, I also examined the newspaper indexes of the *New York Times* and the *Washington Post* from August 1989 to August 1990, which contain both headlines and article summaries. Looking at all three papers together, roughly

950 abortion stories were published in the year after the *Webster* ruling came down.

3. In doing so, media discourse privileges official voices and elite definitions of reality; maintains "objectivity" by balancing opposing viewpoints; relies on spot news and news pegs, giving events a truncated, episodic character that masks the underlying social and historical conditions that give rise to them; hierarchically arranges information into discrete categories, some of which are "hard" (masculine, important) and others "soft" (feminine, unimportant); emphasizes conflict and violence over "normal" consensual relations; and personalizes issues and events, another framing strategy that tends to divorce issues from their sociohistorical context and thus denies the situated character of social interaction (in general, see Cohen and Young, 1973; Sigal, 1973; Tuchman, 1978; Hall et al., 1978; Gans, 1979; Gitlin, 1980; Hartley, 1982).

4. As noted earlier, journalists rely heavily for the content of their stories on "official" sources, or "experts"—over 90 percent of all spokespersons quoted in my sample. Although I tend to use "official" and "expert" interchangeably, strictly speaking, an official is the head of a recognized organization or institution or the spokesperson for such an organization, whereas an expert is anyone—official or otherwise—whose opinions or comments are solicited by news professionals. In the 1973 press sample, I counted 160 experts; in 1989 that figure had more than tripled to 587, as had the number of organizations cited in connection with these experts.

5. Such metaphors are common in prolife literature as well (see Noonan, 1970; Trinkhaus, 1975; Nathanson, 1979, 1983; Hentoff, 1989; Koop, 1984; Reagan, 1984; Neuhaus, 1988).

6. The letter submitted by Sister Christine is interesting because it relies for its persuasive power on the rare circumstance when a child is born before the twenty-fourth week of pregnancy and lives. It is thus a good example of what Joel Best (1987) in another context calls an "atrocity tale"—a compelling narrative, selected for its extreme nature, that attests to the frightening, harmful dimensions of a social problem (in this case, abortion).

7. For various reasons, U.S. lawmakers have never formally bestowed upon fetuses the rights of legal personhood. Westfall (1982) speculates that legislation attempting to do so is doomed to failure, not because the state has no interest in potential life, but because the impact of such legislation would extend far beyond abortion to affect, for example, the apportionment of congressional representatives, federal income tax expenditures, the drinking age, the driving age, insurance policies, the availability of certain types of birth control, strict maternal liability during pregnancy, fetal protection policies in the workplace, and so on. Nevertheless, courts have recently begun ruling in favor of the fetus in certain cases when the interests of the pregnant woman and her fetus (as represented by the state) conflict over medical treatment or prenatal care. The number of forced cesareans is increasing (Annas, 1982; Nsiah-Jefferson, 1989), and it is not uncommon for courts to prosecute pregnant substance abusers under child abuse or fetal neglect statutes originally intended to protect both the pregnant woman and her fetus from third-party injury (Johnston, 1986; Gallagher, 1987; Terry, 1989; Faludi, 1991).

8. Faludi (1991:406) cites other instances where prolife rhetoric has coopted prochoice language and imagery, using the feminist credo that a woman has a right to control her own body and applying it to female fetuses, or chanting at

demonstrations, "The baby has to have a choice." I found the prolife appropriation of "choice" in the press most pronounced not in the *Webster* coverage but in discussions of abortion following the most recent relevant Supreme Court decision, *Planned Parenthood of Southeastern Pennsylvania v. Casey,* decided on June 29, 1992. Much of this discourse focuses on choice in relation to birth control. For example, one woman writing to the *Los Angeles Times* states, "I applaud the Supreme Court justices who are working to make abortion harder to attain. Why is the obvious solution of birth control always omitted from these heated debates? Everyone should be prolife, but the choice is to get pregnant or not to get pregnant" (Hibbard, 1992:B6). "You have a choice," another woman writes, "you can choose whether or not to have a baby before you engage in sexual activities. Abortion is not birth control; it is murder" (Mayer, 1992:B6). A prolife television commercial aired on CNN in 1993 using the slogan, "Life, what a beautiful choice." This appropriation of quasi-feminist rhetoric in the service of antiabortion politics has proven successful precisely because feminism has gained a certain institutional legitimacy in the United States, and thus, as Willis (1983) has pointed out, can be read as a kind of perverse tribute to the women's movement.

9. According to both Sheeran (1987) and Stewart and his colleagues (1984), most prolife advocates not directly affiliated with the Roman Catholic church insist that abortion is not a religious issue but a "human issue." They say the concern for fetal life transcends theological and religious denominations, and they rely instead on medical, scientific, and philosophic sources to support their stand against abortion. Nonetheless, the claim that religion plays no role in antiabortion politics runs contrary to most demographic profiles of abortion activists, which consistently reveal the importance of religion in the lives of antiabortion activists—many of whom are Catholic. Paige (1983) suggests that the NRLC has made a conscious effort to avoid religious language and imagery and to place non-Catholics in leadership positions in order to alter its public profile (for example, the last three out of four NRLC presidents—Mildred Jefferson, Judie Brown, and Jack Wilke—are all Protestant). Sheeran's (1987) study of abortion activists supports this interpretation. Judging from the growing number of fundamentalist Christians involved in prolife politics today, I suspect religion still plays a central role even though spokespersons may not necessarily frame their arguments explicitly in religious terms. There is also greater religious diversity among antiabortion activists and thus less evidence today than in the past for specifically Catholic involvement in the prolife movement. This indicates that an antiabortion stance may be more a question of religiosity than religion per se, as Alice Rossi (1966) suggested in her work on abortion and public opinion over twenty-five years ago.

10. The emphasis on medical and scientific justifications for abortion makes sense, since physicians played a key role in bringing abortion to public consciousness in the early 1960s and in backing the various state abortion reform bills subsequently introduced. Condit (1990) suggests that this support was crucial to the success of abortion reform and legalization because medical and scientific discourses are more compelling and authoritative than those limited strictly to women's rights. In sociological terms, it seems medical arguments have a certain "cultural resonance" (Gamson and Modigliani, 1989) because they ring true with larger cultural narratives about rationality and objectivity, a quality lacking in both women's rights and fetal rights arguments in 1973.

11. The privacy framing is also problematic for many prolife advocates who oppose abortion but otherwise subscribe to a hands-off approach to political governance. This tension is the focus of at least one account published in the *Los Angeles Times* after the *Casey* case. "It's a challenge," the author writes, "to find the logic in the conservative position that believes in getting government off the backs of people, except for the backs of those who choose to have an abortion" (Daniels, 1992:B6). In general, however, there is little or no discussion in the press on the shortcomings of privacy discourse and its implications for either side of the debate.

12. Snow and his colleagues (1986) call this reframing process "frame transformation," a process in which the objective contours of a given problem or situation do not change so much as the way the situation is defined and promoted.

13. The change in Blackmun's vocabulary is rather striking, and is partly strategic. In 1973 Blackmun was trying to "sell" *Roe v. Wade* to as wide a public as possible, while in 1989 he was trying to preserve what little was left of it. But another reason has to do with the successful institutionalization of mainstream feminism. Liberal feminism has become a more legitimate and persuasive cultural narrative since the 1970s; whereas then the right to an abortion needed the authority of medical discourse, by 1989 it did not. Moreover, as Condit (1990) notes, medical issues were always less central to the legal doctrine of choice; they were related more to the conditions that made the legal doctrine relevant in the first place. "This is evident," she notes, "in the fact that the medicalization content has gradually withered away, leaving the much more substantive part of the decision to stand" (Condit 1990:102).

14. See Hubbard, 1982; Lynn, 1982; Callahan, 1986; Petchesky, 1987; Terry, 1989. The belief that technology is reframing the abortion debate is no idle concern. According to Callahan (1986), the main cumulative effect of medical and scientific developments has been to focus greater attention, both public and professional, on the status of the fetus as a moral claimant in the abortion conflict. This focal shift seems to have affected public opinion on abortion as well as generated new challenges to abortion law. For example, a *Newsweek* survey found that 18 percent of those polled said they were less in favor of abortion today than in the past because of "new scientific evidence" (cited in Callahan 1986:39). It is surprising, therefore, that there is no mention in the press of such matters. Nor do experts discuss the preamble contained in the Missouri statute upheld by *Webster*, which states that "life begins at conception," and that "unborn children have protectable interests in life, health, and well-being." According to Chief Justice Rehnquist, the preamble is a "harmless philosophical statement" that merely expresses the state's preference for childbirth over abortion (Savage, 1989b:A1; see also *New York Times* 1989b; Apple, 1989; Kamen, 1989). I found only one account that speculates on the possible impact of this "harmless" statement. In a legal analysis, University of Southern California law professor Michael Shapiro notes that because of the preamble, *Webster* will affect "the regulation of pregnancy in order to protect fetuses, the fate of stored embryos and germ cells, fetal therapy, genetic control— a universe of technologies and social and personal arrangements that affect our most intimate interests and indeed our very identities" (Shapiro, 1989:B1).

15. This observation is consistent with the findings of Mumby and Spitzack (1985), who studied TV news on three U.S. networks and discovered war to be the most commonly used metaphor in political coverage.

16. The 5–4 ruling in *Casey* essentially upheld the constitutional right of a woman to obtain an abortion before fetal viability (and thus invalidated abortion law in Louisiana, Utah, and Guam), while at the same time upholding most of Pennsylvania's abortion statute, including laws mandating informed consent, a 24-hour waiting period, parental notification, and public record keeping of abortion services. The Court struck down a spousal notification requirement. According to press accounts, *Casey* is most notable for the compromising centrist position taken by Justices O'Connor, Kennedy, and Souter, all of whom were expected to join the more conservative justices (Rehnquist, White, Scalia, and Thomas) in overruling *Roe v. Wade*. Experts say the fact that the three centrist judges did not reverse *Roe* and instead sought middle ground by affirming it with qualifications is symbolic of a new state in the abortion controversy, one aimed at truce and compromise. Indeed, judging from the coverage of *Casey* in the *Los Angeles Times* and the *New York Times,* compromise is the fastest-growing framing of the debate.

17. Note also the difference between Tables 4.1 and 4.2 with respect to the "media" category. When I first started classifying experts based on the frequency with which they appeared in the newspapers I sampled, no such category existed, because in 1973 not a single reporter or other media spokesperson was asked to speak on the issue. But in 1989, twenty-one such individuals were cited or quoted, most of them reporters or producers from the three major television networks: ABC, NBC, and CBS.

18. Two points need to be made here. The first is that journalists, politicians, lawyers, and activists all help perpetuate the primacy of "rights discourse" by becoming interested in abortion chiefly when the Supreme Court hands down a decision. This is not to suggest Supreme Court rulings are the only media "pegs" for abortion. But even legislative attempts to amend abortion laws, acts of antiabortion violence, and marches, demonstrations, and rallies—events that also draw media attention—tend to be organized in response to Court decisions (see Ginsburg, 1989; Condit, 1990). The second point is that when abortion reform arguments first entered public discourse in the early 1960s, the range of acceptable frames for "choice" was in some ways more restricted than it is today, not less. As Condit (1990) observes, most appeals to legalized abortion at this early stage did not rely on notions of privacy or reproductive freedom and autonomy, nor did they contest dominant conceptions of "womanhood" or "motherhood" or the conflation between the two. Instead, women seeking abortions were portrayed as essentially good people caught in evil circumstances—victims of rape, incest, eugenics, or extreme youth. Thus, although the national abortion debate has been locked within a legal framework since *Roe v. Wade,* this framework in fact widened the existing terms of the debate for women in significant ways.

19. With the exception of *Planned Parenthood of Southeastern Pennsylvania v. Casey,* abortion has rarely been argued as a matter of sex equality before the courts or in the media despite decades of feminist scholarship supporting this position, primarily because the law has adopted an essentially assimilationist vision of sex equality: men and women must be similarly situated (that is, women must be similar to men) in order to receive equal treatment. This is known as the "sameness doctrine," and is problematic in that it cannot, by very definition, reconcile the idea of equality with the reality of biological differences (see Law, 1984).

20. In general, there is very little discussion in the press about how to reduce the need for abortions by focusing on pregnancy prevention and improved social

benefits for mothers and children. When it does appear, however, this version of compromise is typically voiced by prochoice sympathizers in the press who are angry at (1) the hypocrisy of a position that believes in the dignity of human life up to the point of birth but not beyond and (2) the diversion of energy and resources away from these broader issues to a narrow prochoice/prolife conflict (see Hagner, 1973; Oehme, 1973; Teck, 1973; Cutler, 1989; Ferraro, 1989; *Time*, 1992).

21. The *Casey* decision reads, "An entire generation has come of age free to assume *Roe*'s concept of liberty in defining the capacity of women to act in society, and to make reproductive decisions . . . the societal costs of overruling *Roe* at this late date would be enormous. *Roe* is an integral part of a correct understanding of both the concept of liberty and the basic equality of men and women" (*New York Times*, 1992, A8; see also *Los Angeles Times*, 1992). Consequently, all state regulations that impose an "undue burden" on women seeking abortions may be held unconstitutional (the "undue burden" standard replaces the old "strict scrutiny" standard previously used). Yet what does unduly burdensome mean? The fact that most state governments refuse to finance abortions for low-income women is not considered an undue burden by the Court; thus even the equality framing of the abortion right does not mandate government financing for abortions, nor does it necessarily invalidate other state regulations on abortion.

5 "Where's the Land of Happy?" Individual Meaning and Collective Antiabortion Activism

Carol J. C. Maxwell

This chapter explores the narratives of several people who practiced pro-life direct action between 1978 and 1991. (I would like to emphasize that my study refers only to those prolifers who practiced direct action, a small segment of the much larger group of people who identified themselves as prolifers.) Two salient themes emerged when prolifers narrated their direct action experiences. On the one hand, such activists generally described a linear process beginning with abortion disapproval and at some point reaching the conclusion that the most appropriate response to legalized abortion was direct action. These accounts were punctuated by understandings and attitudes generally shared by their companions. Through these accounts, direct activists told how they came to sit in, or "rescue." On the other hand, each individual's activism usually had a very specific, personal meaning. These particular subjective understandings played a crucial role in radicalizing activism, that is, in moving it away from conventional forms of political action and toward illegal and more deeply symbolic actions.

Implicit in my analysis is the assumption that self-identities are complex and dynamic. Individuals' self-concepts change throughout their life spans as new information about themselves and others is gained and as experience and cognitive development provide new ways to process these data (Kegan, 1985; Hart and Damon, 1985). Change does not occur in a thoroughgoing, across-the-board manner. As the individual is inclined and equipped to deal with the various domains of life differently, so the individual's self-definition tends to vary from one domain to another, and within each domain over time (Leahy, 1985; Hart and Damon, 1985). Rescue played a crucial role in reconfiguring the self-identities of the people introduced in this chapter. The relationship between the different "selves" in three key areas appears crucial to individuals' participation in prolife direct action. Shifts in the relationships between individuals' ideology regarding abortion, their material circumstances, and their internal, psychological needs formed the contexts that promoted changes in the idiosyncratic meanings of rescue. These personal meanings of rescue featured prominently in narratives explaining why individuals decided to rescue or to stop rescuing.

For many rescuers spiritual growth and activism were linked in their own particular "walk with God"; that is, rescue fit into a certain point in their material, emotional, and intellectual lives. At such times, rescue satisfied specific needs more pressing than the risks rescue entailed. In this sense, rescue was more than a logical response to abortion disapproval (as its practitioners publicly framed it and genuinely perceived it); it was also a response to God and to oneself—to one's own needs.

Through diverse media, rescue promoters persistently presented a distinct set of arguments intended to persuade other prolifers to join them; I argue that while prolife rhetoric expounded a perspective rescuers shared, it was not necessarily relevant to the factors actually impelling their activism. There was often a disjunction between the modeling, assurances, and warnings conveyed through prolife rhetoric and the personal experiences rescuers articulated when telling why they became direct activists (cf. Rapp, 1990). This tension may explain why rhetoric sometimes failed to inspire civil disobedience, even among "true believers."

The decision to rescue depended upon particular issues intimately entwined with the self-identity and previously established ethics of individual listeners. However, both would-be recruits' and practicing activists' self-identities and ethics were influenced by factors that varied over time. Through the narratives of three direct activists, I will explore shifts in the balance of influence accorded by activists to their own emotional needs, ideology, and the practical constraints on their activism. The interplay of these factors created distinct understandings and motivations that frustrated the efforts of rescue organizers, whose rhetoric addressed the common concerns of an audience the organizers apparently conceived of as a collective.

The individuals discussed in this chapter were among the prolife direct activists I observed and interviewed in a large midwestern city between February 1989 and December 1991. Their narratives described activism beginning in 1978 and continuing beyond the end of my research period. During 1990 and 1991, I tape-recorded in-depth open-ended interviews with a sample of eighty activists. Quotations in this chapter were taken from transcripts of those interviews.

The three people discussed in this chapter were active in local rescue groups in the same city; however, their experiences were not concurrent.

The man I call Dylan joined rescue shortly after its local inception in 1978; in 1984 he founded the organization that the woman I call Jan joined later that year. (This organization hosted an early regional rescue gathering where Randall Terry, who later founded Operation Rescue, was trained to sit in.) Jan stopped sitting in shortly before Dylan withdrew from rescue in 1987. At that time Jan had been arrested around ten times and Dylan had had more than four hundred arrests. Both were lifelong Catholics. Two years later, in 1989, the man I call Rick sat in for his first and only time. Rick rescued with his fellow nondenominational congregants, and they were led by the local Operation Rescue affiliate, an offshoot of the group Dylan founded.

The historical roles and social characteristics of these three individuals differed substantially, but they were not atypical within the sample as a whole. These three people earned moderate incomes and had attained typical educational levels compared to their companions in the sample, and all were married with children, like more than half of the sample. Several people in the sample had more arrests than Dylan, and many were only arrested once, like Rick. Most long-term rescuers were arrested around ten times, like Jan. Some in the sample founded larger organizations than Dylan's; others were never leaders. The time elapsed between the beginning of Dylan's activism and the end of Rick's covered most of the modern history of prolife direct action (which began in 1975 in Maryland). Rick subscribed to a different religious tradition than Jan and Dylan; together, they were affiliated with all three rescue organizations in their locale, and they held disparate roles in the rescue movement.

As was true for the other people I interviewed, the personal meanings these three individuals attributed to their activism allowed them to pursue highly idiosyncratic purposes through rescue. Although a clear pattern of shared understandings and attitudes accompanied these particular motives to rescue, personal interpretations of rescue were evident in the narratives of all eighty people interviewed. The roles these differences played in moving individuals to adopt or reject direct action are the topic of this chapter.

Through these differences, I will explore the diversity of individual paths into and out of rescue. Common threads ran through the narratives of the activists I call Rick, Jan, and Dylan. Each of their narratives illustrated a different configuration of the shifting relationships between ideology, material circumstances, and personal needs that preceded entrance into and exit from direct action. Variance within and among these dynamic domains altered activists' self-identities, and rescue played a crucial role in reconfiguring the self-identities of these three people.

RICK

Rick's experience of rescue was pivotal in resolving the seventeen-year-long struggle between his resistance to God-as-an-authority and his desire to feel connected to God. By reshaping his relationship to God, the alchemy worked by his rescue decision also changed Rick's perspective on other people and how he related to them. Rick described his conversion to direct action as a significant shift from a state of conflict, tension, and need to a sense of security, calm, and achievement. It paralleled and extended his previous religious rebirth in its nature and in its effects on him. Rick used a metaphor to describe the role rescue played in his life:

And you always see these pictures of airplanes that try to break the sound barrier, you know, it kind of builds up the tension, at the point, and then when it breaks through there's a big sonic boom, and then it goes real clearly. And all of a sudden the turbulence is gone and it's free to fly faster. And I think the rescue movement was what God used in my life to kind of break that barrier.

As a teenager Rick had decided that "God wasn't too smart if he made a bunch of rules that people couldn't follow . . . and he's pretty stupid because he did't create us properly." Rick had rejected the model of God "with a big stick," ever ready to punish His own creatures for breaking His own rules—rules God had made them unable to follow. This paradigm struck Rick as illogical and unbelievable, but feeling disconnected from God frustrated and pained him. At times Rick physically "beat up" Christians because "it seemed too easy to say I got a relationship with God when I had spent a lot of time trying to find what that relationship was." Rick spent six or seven years looking "for what I thought God should be," taking drugs, or, like many people in my sample, studying Eastern religions.

During his search for spirituality, Rick received a letter from a friend that answered his objections to Christianity. In the letter, Rick's friend argued that "God existed . . . and that man wasn't capable of living the life he was created to do," both beliefs Rick already held. But the friend continued to argue that God knew about "man's fallen nature . . . and God didn't expect us to live the rules." This made sense to Rick, but what "clicked" was the idea of a link between himself and God. He remembered,

But the link between the two was salvation through Jesus Christ. That's what clicked. And that God was concerned about me enough. He knew I couldn't keep the rules but he would make a way for me anyway, whether I could follow the rules or not. I'd been trying to link myself to God whether it was through drugs or whatever we were doin'.

Rick accepted Christianity when he was presented with a model of God who also wanted a relationship with him and who had indeed made such a connection possible. This new concept of God resolved Rick's intellectual need for a God who made sense and his emotional need for a God who cared about him and would make possible a personal relationship to him.

In Rick's rescue decision, God completely lost his "big stick" and Rick stood free-willed and autonomous. God merely proffered a question without threatening to punish Rick for failure or commanding him to follow a rule. God asked him, "Would you be willing to be inconvenienced for one person even if you never knew that one person for the rest of your life? Would you be willing to be inconvenienced to the point of going to jail for 30 *years?!*" Rick saw his relationship to God reestablished on a basis of freely given obedience rather than compliance. During his original conversion, Rick said, he was "finally just surrendering to God. Just saying, 'OK God, I accept this for me, if this is what you want. I'll do whatever you want me to do. Just give me my life.' " In his second watershed experience, Rick redefined himself as empowered through caring and self-sacrifice. He chose to accept a sense of inherent connection to others and reconceived those others as valuable. He chose to care as God cares, in a sense choosing to be like God. Rick explained,

Because I did say yes and go ahead with it, I've had a deeper understanding of God in my life and a deeper understanding of what he requires of me and a deeper understanding of what his concept of the world is. Because *now* because of the one time, and that one point, when God asked me that one question, and I responded "Yes" to it . . . it's almost like, I see God's heart a little clearer now. And that people are really precious and life is really precious to him. And that he is willing to sacrifice for just one person.

Rick's enhanced sense of the inherent value of others reworked his experience of interpersonal relations and everyday interactions. In rescuing, Rick agreed that he should and did choose to care for an unknown individual (that is, a fetus he potentially deflected from abortion). Afterward he recognized this commitment as a continuing admission and choice and extended it to people in general, regardless of any connection to abortion. His exposure to prolife rhetoric heightened his awareness of the inherent value of others, and his rescue experience marked his commitment to act on that valuation (that is, he adopted an ethic of extensivity and response). He explained,

I think before, I honestly say, I didn't view people's lives as important as I do now because of the abortion and because I was willing to put my life on the line, not knowing what was going to happen, jeopardizing my job, jeopardizing everything in all honesty. . . . And it's a lot easier for me to talk to other people, to do other things for other people, because it's kinda like I took that step. I took that step and God responded to that step. . . . It's easier for me to go to work and do something I don't really want to do because I'm doing it for my children than I did before. It's easier for me to take the time to do something with someone else because I see their worth now, that they have worth, because God sees the fact that they have worth.

Rick understood his rescue as an altruistic act that subsequently increased his sense of connection to people in general; these feelings sharply contrasted with the attitudes and actions that arose from his earlier anti-abortion stance. In college Rick adopted an intellectual opposition to abortion after viewing Frances Schaefer's film series, *What Ever Happened to the Human Race?*. This opposition was a dispassionate opinion that prompted no action on Rick's part. Later, in a position of responsibility at a large metropolitan hospital, Rick observed a politically imposed shift in the terminology used to refer to abortion. First the term "abortion" was officially changed to "interruption of pregnancy," then to "IOP." Soon "baby" was changed to "uterine contents," and then to "products of conception." At that point, the hospital that employed Rick "had a really big meeting and standing up and saying and being real emphatic about it and people were disciplined if they didn't write it that way." Rick remembered, "That's when I started thinking this is really not good"; he reacted to this imposition with increasing resistance.

When the hospital began disciplining people who failed to implement the new terminology, Rick exerted autonomy by refusing to help set up the rooms or relieve nurses involved in abortion procedures. Independent, justice-oriented (cf. Gilligan, 1982) reasoning dominated his approach to those cooperating with hospital authority. He concluded that "if they're in there workin' that's their problem. They're goin' to have to take the consequences."

Once he had taken a stand, Rick's opposition to abortion increased and he began to see a pattern of "culpable" behavior associated with abortion practice in his hospital. He explained,

There seemed to be a stigma tied to abortion. And I didn't want to be tied to it. I wanted to be away from it. It didn't seem right. The doctors were rougher and gruffer and complained a lot more. They were rougher with the patients. They were rougher with the nurses. And I didn't like that. They always wanted to seem to cover up and change the terminology. And there was this big hush hush when they do 'em. They wouldn't tell people. It was kind of like they push them off in the corner. And it just didn't seem like a normal surgery. I could sense that they weren't dealing with it that way. There was something dirty goin' on. Something wicked was goin' on.

As Rick's opposition grew, his need to respond grew. When he and his wife heard about St. Louis's annual prolife picket, he told her, "I think we need to do something about it and we need to take the stand, we need to say something."

When Rick's antiabortion stance was linked to his religiosity, an important element of communion was introduced into his activism. This element grew until it dominated his prolife activities and reconfigured his worldview. Rick and his wife joined a large nondenominational church that became a leader in local antiabortion activism. There, in addition to reading books on abortion, they became regularly involved in prolife activities and met like-minded people. He recalled, "It seemed like we teamed up, we met a few other people in the church that felt real strong about it [and] it seemed like there was a likeness of hearts."

Rick's youthful rebellion had ended with the conversion that returned him to mainstream society; he returned to college, became a professional, married, and began raising a family. His conversion also planted him in an evangelical Christian community. Through direct action, he found a way to remain within that community, revive his former independent self, and stand once again in rebellion against an externally imposed authority. His increased rebelliousness was authorized by God. He recalled, "It kinda clicked that this is something that in my heart I really felt God wanted me to do and get involved with." Rick's return to activism and defiance of authority were authorized by God, and so legitimated. He explained, "I think God was in there sayin', 'You as a Christian, have a responsibility to step in and do something.' It seemed like something that I *could* get involved with and I did want to do it also. Somebody has to take a stand." His activism fed on itself. He recalled, "It seemed like the more I picketed, the more I said things, the more I wanted to do it more."

Rick's activism became further radicalized when his church began to more aggressively promote antiabortion rhetoric and rescue. Then his brother was arrested for sitting in, and Rick searched the scriptures for a rebuke; instead, he found support for being arrested as a consequence of carrying out one's Christian duties and, in particular, for proclaiming the gospel.

When Rick conceived of God as caring for him in a personal, believable manner, he yielded to a sense of connectedness with God. His conversion fulfilled his need to commune with God. The need for connection was also important in his commitment to prolife direct action. His church invited the local Operation Rescue affiliate to show antiabortion videos. These graphic images of both healthy developing fetuses in utero and the tangled remains of aborted fetuses heightened Rick's awareness of fetuses' concreteness and stimulated his sense of responsibility toward them. When his brother's arrest triggered the scriptural search in which he found authorization for radical actions, Rick began to take his Christianity as an injunction to act. Rescue became an appropriate response to God's demands and a necessary response to the needs of others.

Rescue was crucial to reformulating Rick's understandings and relationships, but it was not an end in itself. Through rescue he discovered and developed an ethic of obedience that integrated his conflicting personal needs. He sat in once, agreeing to accept God's challenge and be inconvenienced for an unknown other. But that one rescue landed almost all of his church's leaders in jail for most of a week and caused considerable contention within the congregation over the appropriateness of this response to abortion. As the sole income earner in his household, Rick feared rescue would blacklist him in his profession and ruin him financially. Unemployment also would have threatened important aspects of his self-identity, such as his roles of husband, father, and provider. Rick retained his commitment to be "inconvenienced" by continued legal antiabortion activism, which he considered to be, literally, proclamation of the gospel. By proclaiming God's will, Rick's activism aligned him with God in an ultimately dominant position. This gave him security and a sense of rightness and power, or, in his own words, "arrogance." This legal but very public activism provided Rick a leadership position and continuous interactions within his congregation. His standard of obedience to God balanced his desire for fellowship against his need for a sense of independence. He concluded that both the choice to rescue and the choice to not rescue could be made in obedience to God and independent of others' arguments for rescue.

Rick explained that as a youth, he protested the Vietnam War to prove the war was wrong and to impose his own will. His early conventional antiabortion activism was based on his opposition to abortion and his general resistance to authority. In both cases his own will was central. Rick's rescue was based on a qualitative shift in his concepts of God, his fellow beings, and his relationship to them. Rick's prolife activism began as resistance to authority and a willingness to alienate himself from others. Through rescue, his activism became an assumption of authority in unity with God and his peers and an acceptance of his connectedness to other people. Rescue decentered his will. He understood himself to be setting his fears aside to do something for other people, and he did this because someone else (that is, God) wanted him to. As Rick put it, rescue was a turning point in his maturity. Rescue integrated Rick's urges both to dominate and to be in communion and tailored them to his new paradigm of partnership with God.

JAN

Jan's religiosity provided the moral context within which she struggled to reconcile her tendency to become violent and the standards she set for personal interactions. Like Rick, Jan rescued to integrate a personal conflict. Unlike Rick, Jan approached rescue with a well-developed sense of connection to other people and a desire to conform to God's standards as she understood them. It was dismay at her own disobedience that motivated her to rescue, not a need to overcome resistance to authority.

Jan explained her involvement in prolife direct action on two levels. She gave a chronological recounting of external influences that prompted her to engage in activism and steered her toward rescue (and then out of it). Separate from that account, she explained her personal need to rescue because of what rescue meant to her.

Woven through Jan's narrative was a tale of conflicting demands on an ethic of care and response (cf. Gilligan, 1982). Jan rescued, in part, in response to the needs of "the babies." When relating how she became an activist she explained that, "if you had anything at all to do with saving the baby and later you saw the baby, and you were holding the baby! What a miracle that is to know that if you hadn't been there that very day and placed yourself between this person and that, this baby wouldn't be there." Jan also described her struggle to reconcile conflicting feelings of connectedness and urges to respond.

That's real hard to measure, too, when you should pull back and when you should work. Because you're talking about lives of babies. . . . So it's really hard. You think, "I've gotta be there, I've gotta, I might save a baby!" But then, is your family falling apart back here, too? It's really a hard decision to make.

Jan's withdrawal from rescue reaffirmed her moral commitment to care and response and appears to illustrate a maturing of her ethical reasoning that alleviated the need for self-sacrificing (and self-destructive) behavior.

However, when relating why she became involved in rescue and what it meant to her, Jan explained that she had rescued to solace a personal need that had less to do with "the babies" than with her own self-identity. Jan rescued to redeem what she described as a "deficiency" in herself. She reflected,

I was talking to you about how people have disrespect for life, and people. And I'm talking about myself! See? [laughs] . . . [stammers] Our family, we grew up thinking the way to solve problems was to have fights, physical fights, fistfights. I'm really prone to hitting people. It's terrible to say! . . . I thought to myself, I see a deficiency in myself, and I think, "This is awful! Why am I like this?" And so I wanted to do something positive . . . to counteract that. . . . That's one of the primary reasons I got involved in it. . . . I'm a certain kind of person and I see how I am and I want to change that. And I got involved in prolife because I want to change it, yet I got involved in direct action because I'm that kind of person and that kind of confrontation just doesn't bother me. . . . If I go to one of these things and some clinic personnel threatens me, that's not going to scare me! I take advantage of that. I think I'm the kind of person that should be there because it doesn't bother me. . . . I kind of feed on it. . . . I'm trying to make something good out of something to me that's really a deficiency on my part. It's hard.

The disparity between her real self-image (her current view of herself) and her ideal self-image (the ideal person she would like to be) (cf. Glick and Zigler, 1985: 1, 2, 36) impelled her to "improve" herself, and rescue provided a means to reconcile these two aspects of her self-understanding. In her own understanding, Jan turned around her proclivity for violence and so saw herself as able to go out and face violence in order to stop abortion, which she considered to be violence.

Jan's interest in activism was triggered by her church's call to become involved in a social issue, but the form her activism eventually took was shaped largely by her personal needs. Her proximity to a newly opened abortion clinic was important in determining the cause she would address; also due to this proximity, Jan was exposed to both committee work and direct action. She found chairing a committee unsatisfying, frustrating, and personally distasteful (because she prefered to do whatever seemed necessary herself rather than asking others to participate or contribute). Picketing showed Jan the potential satisfaction, greater personal involvement, and risk taking offered. She was tantalized by the potential for confrontation with police during pickets and excited by strident confrontations with the abortionist as he left his clinic. Just when Jan began to explore activism and found herself unsatisfied with conventional practices, Dylan (described by followers and observers as a charismatic leader) began to organize sit-ins near her home. Dylan provided the organizational structure that made Jan's direct action possible. Rescue, in turn, fulfilled Jan's need to make something good out of what she saw as a deficiency in herself. Clearly, Jan's path into rescue was inspired and made possible by the organizational contexts available to her, but just as clearly, Jan chose rescue because of its unique meaning to her.

After several years' involvement, Jan's "little support system" broke down. Her husband left his teaching position and took on a variety of jobs; his hours became erratic and she could no longer rely on him to care for their six children while she was in jail. Other babysitting arrangements proved short-lived. When one of Jan's arrests was televised on the evening news, her mother-in-law disowned Jan's family and refused to accept calls from her own son, Jan's husband.

As rescue became increasingly impractical for Jan, one stressful event precipitated her withdrawal from direct action. She reminisced,

I'll tell you I did have one really bad experience when I was in jail when I was nursing my baby. . . . I was in real pain. . . . I remember trying to express my milk into this dirty sink and I was sick, I was just sick thinking, "I gotta get outta here! I gotta get outta here! You don't understand!" . . . At the time I was getting a lot of breast infections and they can really hit ya, really get ya down. And I said to myself I just can't do this when I'm nursing anymore.

Jan did not conceive of this changed attitude as a decision not to rescue or a rejection of rescuing; she reassessed the moral value of conflicting claims on her time and commitment. These demands had changed over the period of time she rescued (because three of her children were born after she became a direct activist and because of her husband's career change). Immediately following her frightening experience in jail, Jan assessed each call to rescue in light of her other responsibilities and concluded that she would have to defer until the next call came. As she found herself consistently "unable" to rescue, she began babysitting the children of other rescuers. Finally, Jan became critical of these women for leaving their children in her care for weeks at a time, and determined that her family responsibilities precluded babysitting. These decisions effectively extricated her from active involvement with the rescue movement without ending her ideological commitment to it.

When Jan's method of atoning for her "deficiency" became destructive to her, and possibly when her activism had served its purpose, she was able to relinquish rescue as a responsibility while retaining the ethic of care and response that had underlain her activism. This shift was described in the language of self-sacrifice and family obligation. The new mediating ethic was "balance," which required self-preservation but allowed nurturance. Jan reasoned,

You've got to have a balance in your life. . . . [I]f you let even a good issue get in the way of living a normal life, that's not right either. . . . You've got to take care of yourself, you've got to take care of your family or you're not going to be much good to anyone, anyway, in the long run.

Jan participated in rescue to reconcile conflicting aspects of her self-identity, and she withdrew from rescue when this pursuit became a threat to her physical and emotional well-being. The historical account of her rescue experience is suggestive of Carol Gilligan's model of care-oriented moral development. That is, first Jan's exposure to the practice of abortion concretized for her the loss of the fetus, a prominent theme in the prolife rhetoric surrounding her. Her care-oriented moral reasoning impelled her to respond to the needs of others, although this response entailed self-sacrifice. Then, when this sacrifice became self-destructive, Jan's ethic of care was extended to include her own well-being, and her response to abortion changed. Read in this manner, Jan's history illustrates the second and third stages of Gilligan's model. However, Jan's explanation of the significance of rescue for her suggests self-inclusion was a constant factor in her activism, not an innovation in response to stress and maturation.

Jan's life was integrated into diverse contexts, and her self-identity altered as those contexts changed (cf. Ginsburg and Tsing, 1990). With the closely spaced births of her last three children, Jan found herself caring for infants once again just when her husband's work schedule became erratic. These changes created a new set of practical constraints on Jan's self-expression, and so provided her a new configuration of moral considerations. Jan adjusted her behavior in response to the new constraints and the reasoning they generated; she was impelled to do so in order to avoid conflicts that threatened to harm her. Jan entered rescue to bring her self-identity, her moral principles, and her lived experience into accord, and she left rescue for the same purpose. She stopped rescuing because conflicts in her lived experience caused her to reassess and reorganize the principles that guided her decisions and to adjust her behavior accordingly. However, the sense of conflict that drove Jan out of direct activism derived in part from the moral values she held; that is, her strong feelings about family, motherhood, and the need to care made her rescue activities seem damaging.

Rather than the linear progression described by Gilligan (1982)—or perhaps subsequent to such development—Jan's narrative suggests an ongoing reassessment and reinterpretation of moral values and of circumstances. This reworking appears aimed at attaining a balance between (1) practical, external circumstances; (2) internal, personal needs; and (3) existing moral beliefs. Jan's narrative suggests a continual revision of moral beliefs in response to circumstances conducted in pursuit of a consistent moral philosophy. Her narrative further suggests that such revision can guide behavior in opposite directions over time. Jan rescued to bring about consistency between her values, her self-concept, and her behavior, and she left rescue for the same purpose.

Jan was conscious of this self-healing project, but her actions were expressed to others in the language of self-sacrifice. (That is, she rescued to "save the babies"; she left rescue to attend to the needs of her family.) The need to provide such socially acceptable explanations for her actions was externally reinforced, and this may explain Jan's tendency to keep the two accounts of her experience of activism separate in her narrative. When Jan hinted to her prolife friends of the violent side of her nature they quieted her with, "Oh, little Janny, you wouldn't do that! Oh, little Janny, you're not like that!" Jan gave up trying to introduce her "dark side" to her friends. Rescue allowed it to emerge in what was for Jan a self-affirming manner, but her friendships would not admit that part of her, so it remained private, unacknowledged.

Jan's religiosity encouraged her self-criticism and her desire to live a morally consistent life, that is, to address that aspect of her identity that made her "NOT as prolife as I should be." Religion underlay her activism in that it constructed a moral context within which she employed her own style of moral reasoning and made her own choices.

DYLAN

While rescue was the vehicle that allowed Jan to redefine a troublesome aspect of her self-identity, deepened Rick's human attachments, and redefined his relationship to God, it played a damaging role in Dylan's life. For him, rescue began as a vehicle for self-expression but became a trap that had to be escaped.

Dylan remembered evenings in his parents' home dominated by his father's dinner-table lectures on social justice. As a child, Dylan longed to join the civil rights marchers in the South; as a young man, he followed his father into antiabortion political action. Dylan, the silent shadow, learned as he watched the older man perform publicly. When Dylan's father died, he was "left with the legacy of living out his idealism. . . . It was like the throne was vacated and I sort of slipped right in there." While the translation of his father's ideals into activism was tempered by his family and other responsibilities, Dylan was unencumbered. His activism became an unmoderated implementation of his ideals, modeled more on what he had heard his father say than on what he had seen his father do. Dylan first rescued shortly after his father died, and he continued to rescue at least once a week for just under eight years. The antiabortion ideology Dylan embraced dominated his decisions and overrode his other personal needs. He explained, "I think it was because I never had modeled for me how you live in the real world with ideals. And then I was left with, 'Well, you just *do 'em!*' And the consequences start filtering down later and it's like, 'Oh, my gosh, now what do I do?' And you just keep doin' it some more."

Involvement in rescue reinforced Dylan's conviction that direct action was necessary. Before he began to rescue, Dylan studied prolife literature and felt inundated by "the gory details about abortion." This exposure gave him a concrete concept of fetuses that convinced him of "the humanity of the unborn child" and his duty to "do something" about it. Later, after becoming involved in rescue, he found fetal remains in an abortion clinic's dumpster. This direct exposure solidified Dylan's concept of abortion as a means of death, and this understanding strengthened his sense of personal responsibility to stop imminent abortions and the guilt he felt for failing to do so. He recalled, "Things like that really emphasized the commitment. I was shocked; even though I knew it [intellectually], seeing it and knowing that was a baby who was alive that day, when I was at that [abortion] mill, who had died that day at that mill was just devastating."

Dylan accepted a logical need and a moral obligation to rescue, but the whole project terrified him. He described the dichotomy between his intellectual and emotional responses by saying, "I was scared to death . . . but my drive and my belief system was in a way almost apart from that. . . . It flowed from the Catholic and the antiabortion." As he continued to respond to his ideology and to external demands, these considerations came to outweigh other, internal needs. He remembered, "As the years went on . . . I became more and more aware of the emptiness inside. I'd be saying these things; I'd believe 'em. I'm doing them. Where's the land of happy? How come inside I'm empty?"

For eight years Dylan-the-person was increasingly displaced by Dylan-the-activist-and-leader. All of his close personal relationships revolved around rescue, but in rescue Dylan lived out a role based on an ideal model of what to do and say that denied his actual feelings. His real self-image (the way he knew himself to be) languished in the shadow of his ideal self-image (the person he would have liked to be). Dylan recalled that because he presented himself to others through an assumed role, he needed to be "on a pedestal" that distanced him from people and made him feel safe.

Dylan's radical activism was impelled by a juridical concept of God as "somebody up there kinda lookin' at me and goin', 'Well, you didn't do too hot today!' Makin' check marks on a list." He understood God to have prescribed right and wrong, but, as he put it, all he had were the rules. And they put him in continual conflict with his own inclination to avoid confrontations.

Eventually the conflict between his ideology, the lived experience it generated, and his own emotional needs led Dylan into a severe depression. He recalled, "I was personally empty; there was nothing there. I had . . . to rebuild from square one. . . . I was naked with nothing . . . and I had to put my life back together piece by piece." Dylan's actions just prior to the depression caused his followers to reject him both as a leader and as a person. Many refused even to speak to him. His marriage fell apart.

Dylan retreated to the countryside, where he reconstructed his understanding of himself and his relationships on a model of connectedness and balance. To do this he had to increase the importance of his personal feelings and practical needs so that they moderated the role antiabortion ideology played in his life. He explained, "What I've learned after all this experience is that we do not live in an ideal world. We do need to have ideals as such, but they need to be in their proper place. . . . I was able to sustain myself in that ideal world for quite awhile. I was terrified."

The strong emphasis on social responsibility and neglect of close personal ties in his family of origin inclined Dylan toward an idealistic pursuit of social justice. With few mediating constraints, his activism intensified until he had created a heroic persona through which he related to others. While seeking to care for unknown, unseen others, Dylan denied his own need for nurturance, protection, and acceptance. In attempting to do what was "right" according to the external standards he had adopted, Dylan neglected what was needed to meet the internal demands that he repressed. When the conflict between his internal and external needs overwhelmed him, Dylan withdrew from all social contacts, relinquished all responsibility toward others, and addressed his own needs.

Dylan understood his activism to be in accord with God's rules (to be right), but his actions prior to leaving rescue were a distinct breach of those rules. They made his moral status ambiguous (if not villainous) and severely disrupted his social ties. In essence, Dylan created a crisis in the two areas he had neglected. He acted on his own needs in a way which abrogated his ideals and radically restructured his material circumstances. This crisis forced him out of rescue and toward self-healing.

Dylan made the transition from an unrestrained pursuit of externally rewarding goals to a moderated search for internally satisfying goals by means of a core religious experience (cf. Kaiser, 1991). Through this experience Dylan replaced his earlier juridical notion of divinity with a concept of God as a companion who would walk "every step along the way and . . . was a buddy." This was a "personal relationship" he could "tap into." Working outward from this new perspective based on connectedness, Dylan redefined his relationships and responsibilities to others. His new understanding recognized equal moral value in diverse demands, rather than the single, formerly undeniable demand of "the unborn children."

Dylan's activism was deeply rooted in a morality that merged justice and care reasoning (cf. Rogers, 1987). His intense sense of attachment to "the preborn" was tied to rulelike moral imperatives that superseded his own feelings and guided his decisions. Dylan emerged from his social withdrawal with his attitudes toward abortion and rescue intact; however, his moral imperative to care and respond was moderated by an ethic of balance that precluded destructive self-sacrifice (cf. Gilligan, 1982). His new conception of God as collaborator (cf. Kaiser, 1991) supported this morality of self-inclusion.

SUMMARY

Rick left rescue when his own inner conflicts were eased and when he felt his other interests would have been threatened had he continued. Through rescue he came to terms with God's authority and enriched his capacity to engage with other people. When his own inner conflict was unaddressed, he accepted the risks entailed in rescue to bring about change in himself. Once this was accomplished, he regained a balance between his internal needs and the external demands he allowed to become his own. When continued activism threatened this balance, he withdrew from rescue. Rick's activism served his religious experience by reconciling him to God and strengthening his relationships with other people.

Through rescue Jan expiated that part of her she saw as contradicting her prolife ideals; she transformed her "deficiency" into an ability to be at the core of something she believed in. By enabling Jan to attain her own goal (of being more prolife), rescue helped restore the self-esteem her proclivity for violence damaged (cf. Harter, 1985). When rescue threatened the peace she had obtained through it, she withdrew from direct action to pursue "balance" in her life and returned to her preferred role as mother and homemaker.

Through rescue Dylan enacted an altruistic notion of social service and pursued his own need to establish an individual identity and relationships based on it. However, his unrestrained commitment to rescue organized Dylan's self-identity around his pious antiabortion ideology and based his relationships on this partial and distorting expression of himself. Eventually Dylan wanted more satisfaction than a self tailored to rescue afforded. He retained his antiabortion ideology but moderated it with a new understanding of God as collaborator that enriched his personal relationships, enlarged his self-concept, and removed the jarring conflicts rescue had introduced into his life. Like Rick and Jan, he experienced a qualitative change in the way he viewed himself. No longer the lonely, heroic leader living mainly through public projections of one aspect of his identity, he became a more private, whole, and integrated person.

Each activist approached rescue with a self-identity in conflict and solaced that conflict, to some degree, through activism. Jan's conflict stemmed from actions that belied beliefs and created a personal need to find consistency. Dylan's conflict grew out of the need to learn how to put certain beliefs into action (and in so doing, address certain needs) without trammeling others. Rick's conflict resulted from simultaneously held but contradictory needs. The personal meanings given to rescue made it a vehicle for either reducing or aggravating these internal conflicts.

CONCLUSION

Rescue organizers attempted to create a "window of opportunity" by bringing together a sufficient number of willing people in an appropriate setting. They hoped for a legal, community, and media response that would allow them to succeed. However, individuals considering rescue also needed "windows of opportunity" within their own material circumstances, intellectual orientations to abortion, and psychological and emotional needs. People rescued when the relationship between these three spheres of influence provided a reason to rescue, made rescue practical, and promoted a desire to rescue that was strong enough to overcome their resistance to the risks rescue entailed.

One evening during Operation Rescue's Summer of Mercy '91, Joseph Foreman (one of the organization's leaders) entreated an audience of around five hundred men and women to take advantage of the "window of opportunity" then open in Wichita to "count the cost" and join him in rescue. In a wave of emotion (prefaced by the comment that he hadn't "intended to get into this"), he asked, "If you can't set your house in order now, the things that hold us hostage, your debts, your children, your houses, your jobs, when can you? Because the time is getting short!" (The thinly veiled threat of imminent judgment was a frequent enjoinder to rescue.) Foreman climaxed his appeal by asking, "Will all those who'll walk across a street to save a child stand up now?" The atmosphere was electric, qualitatively different from other prerescue rallies I had attended in the preceding two years. I expected the entire assembly to stand, leaving me the only one seated. But it didn't happen.

The evening's speakers had constructed links between rescuing and "rightness" based on patriotism, Biblical example, religious ardor and responsibility, and social acceptance. Rescue was linked to heroic examples of currently acclaimed civil disobedience (such as popular resistance to the 1991 coup in the Soviet Union) and to biblical "civil disobedience" (such as that of Shadrack, Meshack, and Abednego). Rescuers were likened to Jesus persecuted by people who manipulated the law, and rescue was defined as the individual's simple obedience to God. Speakers reassured the audience that friends would support and opponents would respect the decision to rescue. They were warned that the spiritual narcotic of euphoric emotion they were experiencing was insufficient to meet their obligation to God and that only real action and personal suffering would suffice (however pale that sacrifice would be compared to Jesus's). Finally, speakers assured listeners that even opponents unknowingly or unadmittedly hold to prolife values and objectives. Despite the audience's tremendously approving and supportive response to these points, those assembled did not stand up en masse. Fervent religious devotion coupled with disapproval of abortion, supported by metaphoric validations and implied peer approval, was insufficient to inspire rescue. Although religiosity was usually a crucial element in the impulse to rescue, something more was needed to bring one to stand.

Arguments about abortion sufficient to trigger a commitment to rescue in a particular person at one time would be insufficient another time. Foreman's appeal failed because his rhetoric, correct and pertinent to the group as a whole, was not sufficient, or even necessarily appropriate, to align the different spheres of influence on each individual so that the urge to rescue overcame resistance to the risks rescue entailed.

Many of the people who came to Wichita's Summer of Mercy did so intending to rescue. Most who planned to risk arrest had also decided in advance approximately how many times and which days they would do so. These decisions were private and individual, not a mass response to incendiary rhetoric. While rhetoric played a key role in many individuals' decisions to rescue, it did so as part of a complex process that was contingent on many aspects of the individuals' life circumstances and self-identities. While the familiar patterns of "moral sensibility" that people used to confer meaning on daily events were employed in such significant moral decisions (Oliner and Oliner, 1988: 222), at the moment of choice, interlaced, idiosyncratic factors came to bear and gave the various options their meanings. For most people, rhetoric was either a catalyst or a facilitator, not a cause of rescue.

Activists' narratives included historical accounts of their progressive disapproval of abortion and increasingly radicalized response to it. These accounts provided chronological descriptions that suggested linear causality. However, like the people discussed in this chapter, most activists indicated the importance of shifting spheres of influence in their lives that converged at times so that ideological conviction, personal need, and practical opportunity coincided. These convergences leant meaning to events and to the options available to the individual, and so were crucial to involvement in rescue. They wove together individuals' emotions, social backgrounds, personal experiences, and moral understandings to produce their behavior.

6 Cut from the Whole Cloth: Antiabortion Mobilization among Religious Activists

James L. Guth,
Lyman A. Kellstedt,
Corwin E. Smidt, and
John C. Green

Few issues have elicited as much political mobilization as abortion. Although we have many studies comparing prolife and prochoice activists (Granberg, 1981), we have little evidence about why activists cast their lot with one movement organization and not others. Options for prolife activists are especially numerous. As many observers have noted, the antiabortion camp has never been monolithic, but includes several organizations that differ in shade of opinion, religious base, and political strategy (Paige, 1983; Ginsburg, 1989). Recently the spread of direct action tactics has further complicated matters. Operation Rescue (OR), inspired by Randall Terry, has pleaded with potential mothers to forego abortions, demonstrated outside clinics, and, as a last resort, committed civil disobedience. More mainstream prolife groups, such as the National Right to Life Committee (NRLC), have disavowed these tactics, preferring to stay with more prosaic electoral, legislative, and judicial approaches.

This chapter seeks to answer a simple question: Why do activists support one antiabortion group and not another? What are the attitudinal, religious, political, and demographic characteristics of the constituencies for conventional and unconventional action? To address this issue, we consider the way religious activists evaluate the two exemplars of traditional and direct action strategies: the National Right to Life Committee and Operation Rescue. In so doing, we will draw on observations of journalists and scholars, extend generalizations from studies of both the mass public and political elites, and develop other hypotheses from more limited clues. And, although our study is frankly exploratory, we show that activists' evaluations of the two best-known antiabortion groups are clearly predictable from their own religious, political, and demographic traits.

Our findings can be summarized quite easily: support for antiabortion groups is accounted for by staunch political conservatism, religious fundamentalism, firm commitment to Christian political action, and deep concern for traditional social values. Activists scoring highest on all these variables are most likely to accept the direct action fostered by Operation Rescue, while those less extreme prefer the more conventional organization. Rather than a "seamless garment" of concern for many "life" issues or a "coat of many colors" bringing together activists of varying ideological hues, antiabortion mobilization among religious activists is cut from the whole cloth of moral, religious, and political conservatism.

THE STUDY

This study is based on a mail survey of 4,995 members of eight interest groups with strong religious ties, ranging roughly from left to right on the ideological spectrum: Bread for the World, JustLife, Evangelicals for Social Action, the National Association of Evangelicals, Prison Fellowship, Focus on the Family, Americans for the Republic, and Concerned Women for America. These groups were chosen because they represent a significant mass base and because their leaders offered some degree of cooperation. The groups vary from single- to multiple-issue in focus and from explicitly to tangentially political. The sample is particularly appropriate for this inquiry, representing just the sort of conservative religious constituency that supports the antiabortion movement. Although dominated by evangelical Protestants, the sample also contains other religious activists, as these voluntary associations are open to anyone sharing their policy goals. Consequently, mainline Protestants from every major denominational and doctrinal tradition are present in force, along with many Catholics and even a few secular respondents. (See the Appendix for details of the survey.)

As part of a battery of questions on prominent organizations and leaders, we asked respondents how close they felt to the National Right to Life Committee and to Operation Rescue, two prominent antiabortion groups with dramatically diverging political strategies. The NRLC is the nation's leading prolife organization. Reorganized as a mass membership group in response to the 1973 Supreme Court decision of *Roe v. Wade,* NRLC has focused on legislative efforts to proscribe or limit abortion, whether through a national constitutional amendment, limitations on public funding, or state legislative restrictions. NRLC's conventional political operation boasts a large Washington lobbying staff, professional representatives in many state capitals, and thousands of citizen volunteers. To pave the way for its lobbying, NRLC has also supported prolife candidates for pub-

Table 6.1
Evaluations of Antiabortion Groups by Religious Activists

	OPERATION RESCUE (OR)	NATIONAL RIGHT TO LIFE (NRTL)
PROXIMITY		
Very close	14.4%	32.6%
Close	27.5%	36.1%
Neutral	29.7%	13.2%
Far	12.0%	8.1%
Very Far	16.4%	10.1%

lic office (Rubin, 1991). On the other hand, Operation Rescue, founded in 1988 by Randall Terry, has shunned conventional politics in favor of direct action: members block entrances to abortion clinics, harrass clinic personnel, and attempt to persuade clients against having abortions. Such activities usually entail civil disobedience and result in mass arrests, jail terms, and fines for OR members; Operation Rescue itself has been successfully sued in federal court and, indeed, destroyed as a national organization. Local activists continue the protests, however, and the movement still spreads (Wills, 1989). Despite their common goal of ending abortion, there is little cooperation between the two groups. The NRLC refuses to work with Operation Rescue, whose activists often reciprocate with scarcely veiled contempt for NRLC.

Given our sample's dominant prolife orientation (Guth et al., 1993), we were not surprised that both groups evoked much sympathy. As Table 6.1 shows, NRLC has massive support, with over two-thirds of the respondents feeling either very close or close to the organization, while Operation Rescue draws more lukewarm approval, along with many neutral and negative assessments. Obviously, the two antiabortion groups elicit different reactions. In this chapter, we compare four sets of respondents: (1) those close to both OR and NRLC (41.7 percent), (2) those close only to NRLC (29.5 percent), (3) those who profess neutrality toward both (6.9 percent), and (4) those distant from both antiabortion groups (21.9 percent). Approximately 19 percent of the respondents did not rate one or both groups and have been excluded. Interestingly, only a few reported feeling close to Operation Rescue but *not* to National Right to Life. They were also excluded, because analysis revealed that this very small category was largely the product of measurement error.

In the following pages, we explore several hypotheses about why many conservative activists approve both groups, some support only NRLC, and yet others are neutral or hostile to both. We consider the following possibilities:

1. That differences stem primarily from attitudes about abortion itself: those who support both groups—and presumably approve both conventional and direct action tactics—have extreme positions on abortion or perceive it as a more critical national issue.
2. That differences derive from religious perspectives, with fundamentalists and charismatics sympathizing with both the proponents of direct action and groups persisting in more conventional activities, while less sectarian evangelicals repudiate organizations engaging in disruptive or unconventional tactics.
3. That differences are rooted in conceptions of the role that Christians play in society and politics, with proponents of aggressive activism backing both organizational expressions of antiabortion activity.
4. That differences result from ideology, with Operation Rescue attracting support from militant conservatives and NRLC from more centrist elements.
5. That differences stem from social and demographic characteristics: those traits that have been found conducive to antiabortion opinion in the mass public, such as limited education, age, and rural origins, also influence group evaluations among activists.

Of course, all these explanations may have some validity. After examining each possibility, we use multivariate analysis to determine which variables contribute most to determining activists' organizational sympathies.

ABORTION ATTITUDES, NATIONAL PRIORITIES, AND MORAL TRADITIONALISM

Perhaps organizational assessment, like activism itself, reflects above all the intensity of an individual's antiabortion sentiments (Scott and Schuman, 1988). Table 6.2 reports answers to two abortion questions, the first a modified version of General Social Survey items asking under what circumstances abortion should be permitted (Guth et al., 1993) and the second a five-point Likert query on whether the "government should stay out of the private decision of a woman to have an abortion." Those who sympathize with both groups are, in fact, tougher on abortion: they are more likely to limit exceptions to a rule against all abortions and to have fewer doubts about government intervention. Those supporting only NRLC are somewhat less adamant, while opponents of both groups favor more exceptions, freedom of choice, or at least think that government should stay out of the issue. The differences are consistent and quite strong, which is especially significant given the high level of religiosity in our sample.

Table 6.2
Abortion Views of Religious Activists by Proximity to Antiabortion Groups

	CLOSE TO BOTH	CLOSE TO NRTL	NEUTRAL TO BOTH	FAR FROM BOTH	
(N=)	(1657)	(1231)	(285)	(909)	
CIRCUMSTANCES FOR ABORTION					gamma
Never	28%	21%	12%	6%	.56**
Mother's Life	57	47	33	18	
ML+ Rape and Incest	12	24	29	23	
ML,R&I,Birth Defects	3	7	15	19	
ML,R&I,BD,Poverty	0	0	4	6	
Woman's choice	0	0	7	28	
GOVERNMENT SHOULD STAY OUT OF WOMAN'S DECISION					
Strongly Disagree	70%	49%	20%	11%	.63**
Disagree	22	37	36	16	
Not Sure	3	5	20	16	
Agree	3	6	18	24	
Strong Agree	3	3	7	23	
MOST IMPORTANT PROBLEM					
Percent of respondents listing abortion as one of the most important problems facing the country	33%	19%	9%	3%	.56**

**Significant at .001.

We expect similar patterns on the priority that each group places on abortion. We asked respondents a standard Gallup poll question about "the two or three most important problems facing the country today." The results are as expected: a third of those supporting both groups cite abortion as one of the nation's most critical problems, compared to a fifth of NRLC supporters and, of course, only a tenth of those supporting neither group. In addition, some respondents mentioned abortion more than once. Fully 20 percent of the OR/NRLC partisans offered *only* abortion-related problems, twice as many as the NRLC backers (data not shown). Not surprisingly, the issue was not at all salient for most abortion group opponents.

The evidence thus far is quite suggestive: those favoring Operation Rescue and NRLC have more extreme opinions on abortion and see the issue as a top priority. Direct action, then, may be the outgrowth of passionate conviction frustrated by the inability of conventional politics to stamp out this social evil. But these perceptions are also rooted in a much deeper vision of national purpose. Here Ronald Inglehart's pioneering work on political culture is helpful. Inglehart argues that conflict in contemporary Western societies is rooted in a "culture shift" from a Materialist value orientation, based on desires for economic security and social order, to a Postmaterialist emphasis on self-fulfillment, personal freedom, and quality of life. The possibility that citizens might regard protection of social morality as a major function of politics was ignored in Inglehart's early work, but later was grafted on (somewhat awkwardly) as part of Materialist political culture. Inglehart claims that views on abortion are grounded in these larger cultural systems, which envision different functions and priorities for government (1990:195). A prochoice attitude is a natural concomitant of Postmaterialist preoccupation with individual autonomy, while a prolife stance fits better with Materialist concerns (cf. Cook, Jelen, and Wilcox, 1992:32).

We tapped these priorities in two ways: first, by collapsing the "most important national problems" responses into categories reflecting Inglehart's cultural orientations, and second, by asking respondents to rate government functions using Inglehart's own categories, but adding a choice on "maintaining moral standards." Table 6.3 reports the results. Note that the first two groups are quite likely to cite a moral issue as one of the most important problems confronting the country. Indeed, half of all mentions by those who support both OR and NRLC concern social issues, with the proportion declining for each successive category. On the other hand, the further a respondent feels from both groups, the more frequent the references to economic, social welfare, environmental, foreign policy, and rights problems. Overall, the largest intergroup differences appear on moral issues and environmental problems. This pattern is replicated in striking fashion by the modified Inglehart items, with the strongest anti-abortion group stressing morality but unconcerned with the environment. They are also somewhat more likely to rate the maintenance of order as an important function of government. Surprisingly, no group is preoccupied with economic growth; none of these religious activists really fit the Materialist mode.

Table 6.3
National Priorities by Abortion Group

	CLOSE TO BOTH	CLOSE TO NRTL	NEUTRAL TO BOTH	FAR FROM BOTH	
(N=)	(1657)	(1231)	(285)	(909)	
TOP PRIORITY+					eta
Maintaining moral standards	1.32	1.52	2.05	2.66	.39**
Maintaining order in society	3.20	3.21	3.48	4.02	.22*
Protecting free speech	3.41	3.51	3.45	3.01	.13**
Giving people more say	3.80	3.93	3.90	3.70	.06*
Preserving the environment	4.37	3.85	3.19	2.52	.42**
Maintaining economic growth	4.67	4.72	4.65	4.86	.06*
MOST IMPORTANT PROBLEMS++					
Moral problems	1.49	1.18	.81	.58	.39**
Economic problems	.36	.44	.50	.52	.12**
Public order	.29	.33	.27	.31	.04
Social welfare problems	.25	.31	.39	.49	.16**
Political process	.20	.19	.18	.18	.02
Environmental problems	.09	.15	.29	.38	.29**
Foreign policy problems	.08	.10	.16	.19	.14**
Rights issues	.03	.06	.07	.11	.13**
MORAL TRADITIONALISM+++					
High Score on Traditionalism	79%	62%	34%	19%	.66**

+ Mean rank of priority among six items: 1 = Highest, 6 = Lowest.
+ + Number of mentions out of three possible falling into each category.
+ + + Percent above mean on factor score in each category.
** Significant at .001.

This stress on the priority of morality is corroborated by a moral traditionalism scale developed by the National Election Study. The six scale
items measure support for traditional morality, the importance of family
values, discomfort with modernity, and disapproval of moral diversity (see
Conover and Feldman, 1986). Note the wide range of the scores and the
gap between the complete antiabortion activists and the NRLC contingent.
This evidence certainly underscores the primacy of moral issues for the
most thoroughgoing prolifers and confirms that this preference is
grounded in deeply seated values, which these activists perceive to be under attack—the traditional family, conventional moral standards, and
community moral homogeneity.

RELIGIOUS TRAITS AND SUPPORT
FOR ANTIABORTION GROUPS

Moral traditionalism, of course, is often grounded in religiosity. And scholars have consistently found religious commitment to be highly correlated with abortion attitudes in both the mass public and among elites (Legge, 1983; Himmelstein, 1986). Although most studies of public opinion on abortion have utilized church attendance or religious salience to measure religiosity, these have little discriminating power in this observant sample. Consequently, we employed more powerful measures, tapping specific denominational traditions, doctrinal perspectives, religious worldviews, spiritual experiences, and ritual practices. (See the Appendix for details on the measurement of these variables.) As we have demonstrated elsewhere, even in uniformly religious samples, such detailed religious measures can explain shadings in activists' views on abortion (Guth et al., 1993). Here we extend the analysis to their evaluations of movement organizations.

Casual perusal of the press suggests that antiabortion groups have dissimilar religious constituencies. Although Operation Rescue early on recruited some clergy and laity from Protestant, Catholic, and even Jewish traditions, it now relies heavily on various types of evangelical Protestants (Wills, 1989; cf. Ginsburg, 1989). NRLC, on the other hand, started as a Catholic project and gradually drew in some mainline and conservative Protestants (McKeegan, 1992:23). In Table 6.4, we examine the religious affiliations of our four groups. These activists do vary in religious tradition (based on denominational affiliation), but not markedly. Those supporting both OR and NRLC are overwhelmingly evangelical Protestants, while those endorsing only NRLC are marginally more mainline and Catholic. Opponents are drawn about equally from among mainline and evangelical Protestants and include the largest percentage of Catholics.

These very modest differences in religious tradition prompt us to turn to other measures. First, we consider religious self-identification. We asked respondents whether several common religious terms accurately described their views (they could choose as many labels as appropriate). The results are quite revealing: those supporting both antiabortion groups more often embrace sectarian identities such as "fundamentalist," "charismatic," or "Pentecostal" (fundamentalists are the Evangelicals who are most adamant on the inerrancy of Scripture and separation from "worldly" people and practices, while charismatics and Pentecostals emphasize the "gifts of the Spirit," such as speaking in tongues and faith healing). This comports nicely with data on fundamentalists and Pentecostals in the mass public (Cook, Jelen, and Wilcox, 1992:100). The two antiabortion categories differ little in choice of "conservative" or "evangelical," however. Opponents of both organizations are much more likely to accept "ecumenical,"

Table 6.4
Religious Characteristics of Religious Activists by Abortion Groups

	CLOSE TO BOTH	CLOSE TO NRTL	NEUTRAL TO BOTH	FAR FROM BOTH	
(N=)	(1657)	(1231)	(285)	(909)	
RELIGIOUS TRADITION+					eta
Evangelical	74	69	53	43	.27**
Mainline	13	16	33	40	.27**
Catholic	11	13	13	15	.03
SELF-IDENTIFICATION+					
Evangelical	73	72	58	53	.18**
Conservative	67	60	39	23	.33**
Fundamentalist	48	36	20	9	.32**
Charismatic	38	21	25	11	.24**
Pentecostal	21	13	10	5	.17**
Ecumenical	14	18	30	44	.29**
Mainline	9	12	23	32	.24**
Liberal	5	8	19	39	.38**
Christian Orthodoxy	84	77	61	44	.39**
Fundamentalism	79	63	39	22	.52**
Individualism/ Communalism	69	59	43	21	.44**
Revivalism	68	51	39	21	.43**
Involvement	65	65	57	55	.14**
Spiritual Experience	58	52	46	39	.20**

+ Percentage of respondents in each group scoring above the sample mean on each religious factor score. See Appendix for items and deviation of scores.
** Significant at .001.

"mainline," or "liberal." Across all four groups, however, "conservative," "fundamentalist," and "liberal" self-identifications discriminate best.

Of course, these labels may be shorthand for more specific religious beliefs, attitudes, and behaviors. As the last section of Table 6.4 shows, a number of other religious variables distinguish systematically among the activists. Although the four groups differ somewhat on traditional Christian orthodoxy (such as belief in Jesus as the only way to salvation, the Virgin birth, and the Resurrection), the best discriminator is a factor score summarizing ten items that measure core elements of historic Protestant fundamentalism: biblical literalism, ecclesiastical separatism, and premillennial or dispensationalist theology (Marsden, 1980). Activists who support both OR and NRLC are more firmly orthodox and fundamentalist than those who approve only NRLC. The other two groups are noticeably less orthodox and much less fundamentalist.

Two other religious measures are also especially helpful. Religious individualism is a good predictor (Benson and Williams, 1982). Individualists are those whose religious orientations are primarily focused on a person's relationship with God, salvation in the next life, and the self. Communalists, on the other hand, see religion in a social context, as binding individuals together in a just society. Supporters of both antiabortion organizations are religious individualists, while foes lean toward religious communalist perspectives. Although individualism is usually associated with aversion to government action on social ills, individualists are often willing to undertake corporate action when they perceive an evil so great or intractable that personal moral reform—their preferred form of social action—cannot cope with it. In any case, abortion represents an instance in which they see the state as a legitimate agent of individual moral tutelage. Revivalism (participation in charismatic practices, such as speaking in tongues, attending revival meetings, and using religious media) also reveals large gaps between the four groups (although most of the discriminating power is provided by the speaking-in-tongues component). A four-item scale of religious involvement and a measure of religious experience, incorporating reports on the frequency of answers to prayer, closeness to God, and receiving spiritual insights (cf. Poloma and Gallup, 1991), are not as useful, but conform to the same pattern.

Thus, we see the payoff from using nuanced and specific religious measures. Even in this observant and otherwise homogeneous sample, we can draw important inferences about the religious constituency for the two major antiabortion organizations: those approving both groups come from the fundamentalist and charismatic wings of evangelicalism, espouse the most orthodox and fundamentalist theological perspectives, undergo the most intense religious and spiritual experiences, and regard faith as a matter between the individual and God.

ORIENTATIONS TOWARD SOCIAL AND POLITICAL ACTION

An irony of Christian Right politics is the activism of people who by virtue of their theology should be passive, otherworldly, and nonpolitical (Wilcox, Linzey, and Jelen, 1991). Fundamentalism historically stressed separation of believers from the world, the hopelessness of human reform, and the evils of politics. Similarly, the Pentecostal and charismatic movements have usually been politically quiescent, concentrating on spirituality and internal growth (Kellstedt and Noll, 1990:372). But these traditional attitudes may not preclude political activism; we have already observed the seeming political contradiction of religious individualists supporting corporate action to constrain behavior by law. These findings suggest that the attitudes toward social and political activism held by our respondents might be instructive. In Table 6.5 we report answers to questions about their understandings of the appropriate form of Christian political activism as well as their actual patterns of involvement.

The most ardent prolife activists clearly possess a philosophy that links Christian belief to militant political action. They see religious characteristics as relevant to political activities and attitudes, think there is only one correct Christian view on most contemporary issues, insist that the faithful should not compromise just to be effective in politics, fear that American Christians need special protection, believe ministers and congregations should address social and political issues aggressively (inside and outside the church), and argue that people of different theological views should unite for political purposes—perhaps even in an explicitly Christian political party. These findings are buttressed by data from another battery of questions asking about pastoral activism (see Appendix). Those close to both groups not only report more engagement by their pastors on conservative issues (including abortion) but wish their ministers were even more active! Opponents, on the other hand, are much more desirous of pastoral action on homelessness, hunger, and peace.

All these convictions help explain why some Christians from purportedly apolitical traditions have become involved: they see the faithful as a persecuted minority, think that religious leaders and institutions should address national politics, are willing to apply the most important criteria in their own lives—religious ones—to political choices, and are reluctant to concede or compromise on what they take to be Christian positions. After more than a decade of Christian Right politics, these perspectives no longer come as much of a surprise, but they do help explain why some activists and not others are enticed by the militancy of Operation Rescue.

And actions reflect attitudes. Table 6.5 also reports on the frequency of political acts among respondents. Although these citizens are by definition more politically attentive and active than most Americans (Verba and Nie, 1972), those who endorse both antiabortion groups are by far the most energetic. Not only do they have the highest mean level of political interest, but they excel in all types of conventional activities as well as more unconventional ones. They vote at the highest rate, work in campaigns, attend rallies, sign petitions, contact public officials, write letters to the editor, demonstrate, boycott, give money to candidates, and run for party

Table 6.5
Christian Militancy by Abortion Groups

	CLOSE TO BOTH (1657)	CLOSE TO NRTL (1231)	NEUTRAL TO BOTH (285)	FAR FROM BOTH (909)	
(N=)					
CHRISTIAN MILITANCY+					eta
Only one Christian view on most issues	2.57	2.99	3.47	3.91	.43**
Candidate's religious views important	2.20	2.44	3.03	3.65	.42**
Religious need protection in US today	2.31	2.65	3.00	3.23	.33**
Conversion cures social ills	2.28	2.57	2.81	3.34	.33**
U.S. needs a Christian political party	2.92	3.22	3.54	4.02	.33**
My religion influences my politics	1.43	1.70	2.06	2.09	.25**
Christians must compromise for impact	4.03	3.85	3.64	3.42	.22**
Clergy influence people's views	1.86	2.12	2.21	2.29	.21**
Clergy in political campaigning OK	2.19	2.53	2.53	2.46	.14**
Churches/clergy shouldn't lobby	3.77	3.52	3.46	3.61	.11**
Must cooperate despite varying beliefs	1.77	1.89	1.97	1.86	.08**
SUMMARY: Christian Militancy	17.41	19.85	22.40	25.16	.54**
PASTORAL ACTION					gamma
Pastor speaks out on abortion	82%	79%	56%	54%	.40**
Pastor should speak out on abortion	92%	89%	71%	68%	.51**
Approve pastor on moral issues++	85%	80%	62%	52%	.48**
Approve pastor on liberal issues++	61%	61%	66%	79%	.22**
PERCENT PARTICIPATING					
Voted in a primary	89	84	82	84	.14**
Circulated/signed petition	88	83	78	82	.17**
Boycotted to protest policy	61	45	35	40	.28**
Contacted a public official	54	44	35	46	.12**
Donated money to campaign	50	41	39	45	.18**
Demonstrated to protest	40	21	15	27	.09**
Wrote letter to editor	34	25	17	28	.12**
Attended campaign rally	30	20	16	21	.18**

Worked in political					
campaign	15	8	3	9	.24**
Held party office	8	4	2	4	.29**
Ran for public office	3	1	1	2	.23**

SUMMARY:Total Activism					
(means acts)	4.71	3.78	3.22	3.88	.19**

+ Mean score on five point scale: 1 = Strongly agree; 5 = Strongly disagree.
+ + Based on factor score combining five and four issues, respectively (see appendix for details).
** Significant at .001.

and public office more often than other groups. Their summary mean activism score exceeds the next busiest group—the foes of both organizations—by a substantial margin. That this group has some educational and other social disadvantages (see later discussion) makes their activism level even more impressive.

To summarize, those supporting both prominent antiabortion organizations are distinguished by greater Christian militancy and by more actual participation, especially in unconventional activities such as demonstrating and boycotting. Quite obviously, Operation Rescue's tactics are most attractive to Christians who see involvement as imperative and are willing to engage in vigorous activism, although not necessarily in the forms of civil disobedience practiced by the organization.

IDEOLOGY, PARTISANSHIP, AND POLITICAL ALLIANCES

We have now ascertained that Christian activists with diverging opinions of antiabortion groups vary in the stringency of their views on abortion, on the political urgency of this and other moral issues, in their religious views and affiliations, and in their understanding of the appropriate political role for Christians. The next query is this: What ideological and political traits distinguish these activists? Are militant prolifers pure single-issue activists who are otherwise politically diverse (Hershey, 1984)? Or are they ideologues who have simply fixed on abortion as the most egregious example of America's moral and political decay (Tesh, 1984)? Table 6.6 shows that they are not single-issue specialists: their abortion attitudes are part and parcel of a larger conservative worldview.

Those close to both antiabortion groups are the most conservative and the most Republican on every measure. They voted almost unanimously for George Bush in 1988, usually label themselves "extremely" or "very" conservative, and solidly identify with the GOP. (They also include the largest number switching from Democratic or independent preferences at age 21, showing the realigning power of the abortion issue.) The other

Table 6.6
Partisanship and Ideology by Abortion Groups

	CLOSE TO BOTH	CLOSE TO NRTL	NEUTRAL TO BOTH	FAR FROM BOTH	
(N=)	(1657)	(1231)	(285)	(909)	
PARTISANSHIP AND IDEOLOGY					gamma
Voted for Bush in 1988	90%	82%	63%	35%	.70**
Conservative (Extremely + very)	74%	56%	31%	14%	.55**
Republican ID (Strong + weak)	62%	49%	14%	7%	.46**
Moved toward GOP since age 21	50%	37%	28%	23%	.34%
POLITICAL ATTITUDE FACTORS+					eta
General policy conservatism	73%	64%	37%	20%	.63**
Social welfare conservatism	60%	50%	42%	29%	.35**
GROUP PROXIMITIES:++					
Liberals					
Gay rights movement	4.83	4.69	4.31	3.78	.43**
Planned Parenthood	4.80	4.61	3.87	3.37	.52**
Nat'l Organization for Women	4.74	4.50	3.95	3.53	.45**
ACLU	4.69	4.50	3.85	3.54	.44**
People for the American Way	4.35	4.18	3.71	3.83	.22**
AFL-CIO	4.33	4.21	3.84	3.78	.24**
Democratic Party	4.33	3.93	3.29	2.87	.46**
Jesse Jackson	4.25	3.99	3.46	3.15	.35**
National Council of Churches	4.19	4.06	3.42	3.28	.32**
NAACP	3.84	3.63	3.25	2.91	.29**
Conservatives					
Focus on the Family	1.46	1.82	2.31	3.15	.57**
James Dobson	1.50	1.89	2.41	3.25	.55**
Concerned Women for America	2.16	2.90	3.17	3.98	.52**
American Family Association	2.23	2.77	3.16	4.09	.55**
Pat Robertson	2.36	3.14	3.46	4.44	.55**
Ronald Reagan	2.45	3.90	3.50	4.28	.49**
SUMMARY FACTORY SCORES+					
Close to Conservatives	83%	62%	35%	7%	.67**
Far from Liberals	79%	68%	38%	32%	.48%

+ Percent of group above mean (conservative) on each factor score.
+ + Mean scores on five point scale with 1 = Very close, 5 = Very far.
** Significant at .001.

groups are progressively less conservative and Republican. Nor do findings on issue attitudes modify this picture. We used a principal components analysis with varimax rotation to produce two summary factor scores from our large battery of political issue items. (See the Appendix for the derivation of these measures.) For easy illustration, Table 6.6 reports the percentage of respondents scoring on the conservative side of the sample mean on each measure.

The most thoroughgoing supporters of antiabortion activism are not only moral traditionalists, as we observed above, but across-the-board policy conservatives. On our first score, general conservatism, which taps attitudes on social, economic, and foreign policy issues, the groups are quite distinct. The pattern is similar, but weaker, on the social welfare conservatism score, incorporating views on raising taxes to help the poor and hungry, to protect the environment, to balance the budget, and to finance a national health insurance system. Nevertheless, the differences are substantial enough to lend some credence to the charge that prolife activists fail to support public welfare programs that might discourage poverty-related abortions and enhance the quality of life for children after birth (Granberg, 1982).

Some analysts have argued that ideology is better measured by group symbols than by self-identification or issue positions, that "liberal" and "conservative" are really shorthand for positive and negative political reference groups (Conover and Feldman, 1981). Although this approach may be especially useful with the mass public, here the results merely reinforce our earlier findings. We asked respondents to tell us how close they felt to thirty-five prominent political groups and figures, including a number of religious organizations. A principal components analysis identified two factors—one liberal and one conservative—that account for the lion's share of the variance. Table 6.6 shows mean ratings of groups identified on each factor. As anticipated, the complete prolife activists feel furthest from the gay rights movement, Planned Parenthood, feminist organizations, and other liberal interests. Conservative symbols, ranging from Focus on the Family to Ronald Reagan, get the best ratings. The summary factor scores show that it is proximity to conservative leaders and groups, rather than opposition to liberals, that provides greater differentiation.

No matter what approach we take, then, the conclusions are the same: the most resolute prolife supporters, at least in this predominantly Protestant sample, are also hard-line conservatives. This fact certainly limits the movement's political flexibility; for better or worse, the prolife camp is constrained to work within the Republican party and primarily within its right wing, now out of power even at the White House. The data also explain why the originally "single-issue" movement has gravitated in a conservative direction. While there are antiabortion activists who promote social welfare programs, fight capital punishment, and champion international disarmament, they are few indeed among Operation Rescue sympathizers and not all that numerous in the ranks of those who support only NRLC. Protestant adherents of Cardinal Bernadin's "seamless garment of life"—such as the JustLife members in this sample—find little fabric to work with in the dominant ideology of their potential constituency. The prolife activists in this sample clearly prefer abbreviated garb.

SOCIODEMOGRAPHIC DIFFERENCES

Although earlier studies of elites show that sociodemographic factors pale in comparison with religious and political variables in accounting for abortion attitudes, we must note that there is clearly a social basis for evaluation of movement organizations, and one that confirms findings in the mass public that link antiabortion attitudes with limited education, age, rural origins, and traditional family status (Cook, Jelen, and Wilcox, 1992:chap. 2). Table 6.7 shows the social and economic background traits of our four activist groups.

Education is commonly the best demographic predictor, and this sample provides no exception. The extreme prolife contingent has the most limited schooling of the four categories, while opponents of both groups are the best educated, with over half having some training beyond college. The type of education also matters: opponents have degrees in the humanities, sciences, and social sciences—all of which are associated with less support for the prolife views (cf. Lipset and Ladd, 1975). On the other hand, when the most intense prolifers attend college, they usually study business or other applied disciplines (data not shown). So both extent and kind of education differentiate these groups.

The literature on abortion activists has uncovered the contrasting worldviews of the two sides, rooted in fundamentally opposed conceptions of women's role, the nature and the value of the traditional nuclear family, and the responsibilities of parenting (Luker, 1984). Although we have few items that measure such attitudes, the ideal family situation envisioned by prolifers is mirrored to a degree in the actual families of our activists. Those who endorse both antiabortion groups are mostly married and disproportionately female; a plurality of these women are homemakers and not in the work force. And a plurality of male supporters are married to a homemaker. This pattern stands in stark contrast to the employed female activists and spouses of male members on the other side. The antiabortion activists also have more children and are more likely to enroll their children in a religious school rather than a public institution. (Interestingly, there is no difference among the groups as to whether the respondents themselves attended religious school as children.)

Other demographic contrasts follow our expectations but are very modest: antiabortion activists are slightly more likely to live in nonurban areas, although the sample as a whole is quite rural in background. In fact, those who have lived in rural areas for their entire lives are most likely to favor Operation Rescue (data not shown). Similarly, they are slightly more southern and less northeastern in residence; once again, those who have

Table 6.7
Demographic Traits of Religious Activists by Abortion Groups

	CLOSE TO BOTH	CLOSE TO NRTL	NEUTRAL TO BOTH	FAR FROM BOTH	
(n=1)	(1657)	(1231)	(285)	(909)	
EDUCATION					gamma
Less than 12 years	13%	9%	8%	4%	.30**
High school graduate	26	21	16	13	
Some college	23	18	18	15	
College graduate	14	16	14	15	
Postgraduate work	24	36	43	54	
CURRENT REGION					
South	26%	20%	21%	16%	.10**
Midwest	31	35	32	32	
West	24	24	27	27	
Northeast	20	21	20	25	
FAMILY VARIABLES					
Female	55%	44%	40%	45%	.15**
Married	86%	84%	81%	77%	.16**
Homemaker (If female)	40%	34%	23%	14%	.34**
Spouse homemaker	41%	36%	31%	21%	.21**
NUMBER OF CHILDREN					
Four or more	24%	22%	18%	16%	.13**
Three	23	23	22	18	
Two	27	27	26	28	
One	9	8	9	10	
None	16	20	24	28	
Child in church school	41%	38%	30%	24%	.21**
INCOME					
Income under $25,000	27%	26%	28%	20%	.06**
RESIDENCE NOW					
Rural	28%	26%	29%	20%	.10**
Small City	40	41	39	40	
Suburbs	23	21	19	22	
Major Metro	9	12	13	17	

**Significant at .001.

lived exclusively in the South are most supportive of both antiabortion organizations. The groups do not differ significantly in age (data not shown), and although antiabortion activists are less affluent than their foes, class differences are not sharp. Clearly, social background factors do not match the power of ideological, political, and religious variables in distinguishing our four categories. Those who are more thoroughly prolife do fit traditional images of the life worlds of antiabortion activists, but the patterns are not particularly striking. Keep in mind, however, that the entire sample is quite conventional in life-styles and values and that we have few militant prochoice advocates here. If we did, some of the demographic contrasts would be much more dramatic.

CONCLUSION: MULTIVARIATE ANALYSIS

What progress have we made in explaining how religious activists evaluate antiabortion organizations? To recapitulate: those supportive of both Operation Rescue and NRLC are the most extreme in their opinion on abortion, hold traditionalist moral views and think government should enforce those views, put a lower priority on other governmental functions, are adherents of fundamentalist and charismatic religious beliefs, possess a militant perspective on Christian political involvement and participate at a high level, are conservative and Republican, and exhibit traditional social and family roles in their own lives. Interestingly, on virtually every one of the distinguishing traits, the four groups lie on a clear continuum, with monotonic movement across the continuum on almost every variable.

But which set of variables is the best discriminator? Answering this question is made more complex by the strong relationships between these independent variables. To give just one example, fundamentalism is strongly correlated with both moral traditionalism and political conservatism. To use fully the explanatory power of each set of variables, we employed discriminant analysis to differentiate among groups. Discriminant analysis is a technique that allows the researcher to use a number of variables simultaneously to predict which group a particular case falls into. One mark of a successful effort is correctly predicting the group location of respondents. In a four-group analysis, for example, we would expect to assign individuals to the right group 25 percent of the time by chance. Markedly better results reflect good discriminating variables. (For a good introduction to discriminant analysis, see Klecka, 1980).

We first used discriminant analysis with each set of variables and found that, with the exception of social and demographic items, all sets did quite well in this rather homogeneous sample. The proportion of cases correctly classified varied only slightly: abortion views and moral traditionalism (51 percent), religious attitudes and behaviors (51 percent), Christian activism (48 percent), ideological conservatism (56 percent), and social and demographic items (38 percent). To identify variables with the greatest discriminating power and to conserve cases, we ran stepwise discriminant analyses with each set of variables to eliminate items offering little discriminating power beyond that contained in other variables. We then employed the surviving items in a single discriminant analysis. Table 6.8 reports the final result of this process.

The findings are quite straightforward: one discriminant function ac-

Table 6.8
Discriminant Analysis of Variables Predicting Group Evaluations

	FUNCTION 1	FUNCTION 2	FUNCTION 3
MORALITY VARIABLES			
Abortion views	.668		-.279
Moral traditionalism	.566		
Environmental problem	-.273		
Abortion problem		.317	
Public order problems			.242
RELIGIOUS VARIABLES			
Fundamentalist beliefs	.502		
Conservative ID	.412		
Individualism/ Communalism	.385		
Revivalism	.372		
Mainline denomination	-.226		
Charismatic/ pentecostal ID		.293	-.295
Evangelical denomination	.200		
CHRISTIAN POLITICAL ACTION			
Christian militancy	.548		
Unconventional politics		.539	.325
Political interest		.335	.294
Approve pulpit politics		.299	-.269
Campaign politics		.272	
IDEOLOGICAL VARIABLES			
Close to conservatives	.775		
General conservatism	.519		
Bush vote 1988	.456		
Republican identification	.427		
Social welfare conservatism	.237		
Moved toward GOP	.221		
DEMOGRAPHIC VARIABLES			
Education	-.193		
Female		-.315	
Spouse housewife		-.218	
Born in West			.259

Canonical Discriminant Function Evaluated at Group Means

	FUNCTION 1	FUNCTION 2	FUNCTION 3
Percent of variance	91.12	6.60	2.28
Canonical correlation	.76	.30	.18
1 BOTH GROUPS	-1.00300	.28068	-.02206
2 NRTL ONLY	-.27342	-.41552	.10828
3 NEUTRAL ON BOTH	.84851	-.29799	-.64539
4 OPPOSE BOTH	2.13730	.21546	.08916

counts for the overwhelming amount of variance (91 percent), with a canonical correlation of .76, signifying excellent discriminating power. This
function consists primarily of the moral traditionalism, religious fundamentalism, Christian militancy, and political conservatism variables (cf.
Cook, Jelen, and Wilcox, 1992:154, 159). As the discriminant function
shows, this impact is almost linear. In other words, the combination of
extreme abortion attitudes, moral traditionalism, religious fundamentalism, and political conservatism accounts for the overwhelming amount of
discriminating power among all these variables. The second function might
be labeled activism, with strong correlations for disruptive politics, political interest, approval of conservative pulpit politics, and campaign involvement (see Appendix for these items). Note that charismatic and Pentecostal
identifications also correlate with this function, which assists in distinguishing the two extreme groups (those feeling close to both antiabortion
groups and those opposing both) from the NRLC and neutral respondents,
who score much lower. The third (and very minor) statistically significant
function has modest loadings for public order problems, noncharismatic
identification, disapproval of pulpit politics, and western origins. This
function provides a little help in distinguishing the neutrals from all other
groups.

The classification results confirm our success in distinguishing among
these activists. The reduced variable set classifies 61 percent of the sample
accurately. Correct placement is highest for the strong antiabortion group
and their opponents (68 percent and 69 percent respectively). Half (50
percent) of the NRLC supporters were put in the right group, with most
of the rest misclassified as supporters of both groups. Half (51 percent) of
the neutrals were put in the proper category, with equal numbers misclassified as NRLC supporters and opponents of both groups. Use of the functions to place respondents with missing data reduces classification success
only slightly (to 58 percent).

Perhaps these results should not be so surprising. The finding that activists who are most passionate about abortion undertake more strenuous
political activity or approve of those who do is intuitively satisfying. Like
other political groups, Christian activists pursue their objectives in instru-
mentally rational fashion (Green, Guth, and Hill, 1993). Nevertheless, we
also see both the limitations and the possibilities in the potential constituency for direct action. Those who oppose abortion but are not obsessed
with this issue, or do not share Operation Rescue's religious or political
militancy, or see the political world in different ideological terms are unlikely to be converted to direct action tactics. But the fact that the beliefs
and attitudes of OR sympathizers are common among fundamentalists,
Pentecostals, and charismatics suggests that the end of the abortion wars
is not yet near. That their most vigorous opponents possess vividly contrasting attitudes and values portends further escalation of the conflict.

NOTE

The authors wish to acknowledge major financial support from the Pew Charitable Trusts, which made this study possible. Additional assistance was provided by the Institute for the Study of American Evangelicals at Wheaton College, the Research and Professional Growth Committee and President's Fund of Furman University, the Ray C. Bliss Institute of Applied Politics at the University of Akron, and the Calvin Center for Christian Scholarship.

APPENDIX

The Religious Activist Survey

The Religious Activist Survey was conducted during 1990–1991 and studied a stratified random sample of members of eight organizations. Bread for the World, founded in 1973 and now claiming over 40,000 members, is an advocacy group on hunger issues. JustLife, created in 1986 with 5,000 financial supporters, is a political action committee promoting a "consistent life ethic" on abortion, economic justice, and the arms race. Evangelicals for Social Action, formed in 1978, fosters "a holistic discipleship which actively pursues peace, justice and liberty in society according to Biblical principles." The National Association of Evangelicals, founded in 1942, is the voice of the evangelical movement, the counterpart of the mainline National Council of Churches. The Prison Fellowship, with a staff of 277 and 44,000 volunteers in 1992, ministers to prison inmates, educates the public, and lobbies public officials on behalf of prison reform. Focus on the Family, led by radio psychologist James Dobson, has several hundred thousand members and is headquartered in Colorado Springs; its now-independent Washington lobbying arm is the Family Research Council, led by former Reagan White House staffer Gary Bauer. Concerned Women for America (CWA) dates from 1978 and has 300,000 members who seek to "preserve, protect, and promote traditional and Judeo-Christian values through education, legal defense, legislative programs, humanitarian aid and related activities." Americans for the Republic (formerly the Committee for Freedom) was part of Pat Robertson's 1988 presidential bid. The committee is now run by the Christian Coalition, which boasts some 300,000 members and was a visible presence at the 1992 Republican Convention.

Five organizations provided random membership samples and a cover letter from the executive director asking for respondents' cooperation. Focus on the Family cooperated to the extent of sending one wave of questionnaires to an anonymous random membership sample, but no follow-ups were possible. The CWA sample was drawn from local leadership lists printed in the monthly CWA magazine. Donors to Americans for the Republic were found in Federal Election Commission public records. As the number of respondents varied by organization, we used an identical weighted N for each group in the analysis to prevent any group from dominating the results. In fact, analyses using the unweighted sample produced almost identical results.

The questionnaire was ten pages long and included over 250 items. The survey elicited 4,995 completed questionnaires (a 56.9 percent response rate), providing the largest data set available on religious activists. Given the great variety of religious and political measures employed, we can provide a much more detailed picture of religious political activism than hitherto available.

Measures of Religiosity and Ideology

In this article, we use numerous multi-item measures of religiosity, ideology, and other variables. Most are factor scores isolated and derived by a series of principal components analyses with varimax rotations. The lowest theta reliability score was .69 for the revivalism variable; most thetas were .80 or above.

Fundamentalism. Belief in Biblical authority, in the historicity of Adam and Eve, in the rapture of the church, in original sin, that Paul's teaching on women is still valid, that women's ordination is not permitted by Scripture, that Christians must separate from the world, that U.S. laws should be based on the Old Testament law, that the prophets of Israel predicted the future, and that Christ will return to earth before the millennium.

Christian orthodoxy. Belief in the Virgin birth of Jesus, in the historicity of His Resurrection, that only Jesus provides salvation, and that He was both God and man.

Individualism/communalism. Individualists believe that only changing individual hearts changes society, that the church should concentrate on individual morality, and that individuals are poor because of personal inadequacies.

Revivalism. Frequency of watching religious TV, attending revivals, listening to religious radio, and speaking in tongues.

Spiritual experience. Frequency of feeling God's presence, having prayer answered, experiencing divine inspiration, receiving a biblical insight, and feeling deep peace.

Religious involvement. Levels of church attendance, activity level in church, having most friends attend same church, and holding formal church membership.

Religious tradition. Virtually all Christian respondents were classified as evangelical Protestants, mainline Protestants, or Roman Catholics, using a very detailed code modified from the new National Election Study denomination code.

Moral traditionalism. Should be more tolerant of people whose moral standards differ from our own, need more emphasis on traditional family, only one moral philosophy is correct, must adjust our view of morality with changes in world, newer life-styles breaking down society, diversity of moral views creates healthy society.

General conservatism. Approve the death penalty, distrusted the U.S.S.R. (which was existent at the time), agree that only free enterprise is Christian, oppose the Equal Rights Amendment, oppose gays teaching school, reject affirmative action, support scientific creationism, and oppose pornography.

Social welfare conservatism. Oppose higher taxes to solve problems of world hunger, poverty, the budget deficit, and the environment, and oppose national health insurance.

Approval of pastoral activism on moral issues. Approve pastor addressing prayer in schools, abortion, proper sexual behavior, and pornography.

Approval of pastoral activism on liberal issues. Approve pastor addressing homelessness, world hunger, peace, prison reform, sanctuary for refugees.

Unconventional politics. Contacting public officials, writing letters to the editor, boycotting to protest policy, participating in public demonstrations.

Campaign politics. Work in campaign, attend rally, party office, public office.

7 Abortion in the United States and Canada: A Comparative Study of Public Opinion

Marthe A. Chandler,
Elizabeth Adell Cook,
Ted G. Jelen, and
Clyde Wilcox

In recent years, political scientists have devoted increasing attention to comparisons between the United States and Canada (see especially Lipset, 1990, and Merelman, 1991). One's initial reaction to such a project might be to suppose that a U.S.–Canadian comparison is not likely to generate substantial cross-national differences. The similarities between the countries seem almost too numerous to contemplate. Both countries are liberal democracies that span an entire continent, with abundant natural resources. Both are former British colonies, which have within their territories areas formerly colonized by the French (Quebec and Louisiana). Each country has had to deal with a region that has or has had separatist aspirations (Quebec and the American Confederacy). Both countries are experiencing sustained, intense conflict based on demographic characteristics (region and language in Canada, race in the United States). In addition, both countries share access to the same (U.S.) electronic media. Thus, a plausible case can be made that both Canada and the United States are part of a common North American culture, which is (perhaps) dominated by the United States.

However, some analyses of North American cultural differences, based on accounts of the popular culture, suggest that U.S.–Canadian similarities should not be overstated. Recent studies have emphasized two important differences between the United States and Canada. First, there appear to be major differences between the countries with respect to individualism. Many analysts (Gans, 1988; Glendon, 1987, 1991; Lipset, 1990; Merelman, 1991) have suggested that what is unique about the United States is its pervasive "rights-based" culture. Most Americans appear to believe, at least implicitly, in John Stuart Mill's (1975) Very Simple Principle: to paraphrase, one can do as one pleases, as long as no one else is harmed. Indeed, many Americans appear to construe the concept of harm very narrowly, suggesting the existence of a very broad private sphere in which the individual is accountable to no one but herself. In an insightful work by Mary Ann Glendon (1991), it is suggested that the American concept of rights is used precisely to assert a claim of autonomy and to suggest the irrelevance of competing considerations (see also Cook, Jelen, and Wilcox, 1992).

By contrast, the Canadian political culture is thought to be much more communal and cooperative than that found south of the border. Canadians are generally regarded as less tolerant of egoism and more accepting of authority (Berton, 1982). Canadians appear more willing to regard government authority as legitimate than their American counterparts, and more willing to surrender individual prerogatives for the sake of the community (Merelman, 1991). In particular, some analysts of Canadian politics have suggested that Canadians trust democratic institutions to protect individual liberty and are less trustful of judicial decision making than are Americans. Canadians tend to regard Parliament as the most important political institution, and do not appear to regard judicial review as a settled part of the political life of the nation (Smithey, 1991; Schmeiser, 1973; Matkin, 1986).

Lipset (1990) traces these Canadian–U.S. differences to differences in the experience of colonialism and independence. The radical break of the United States with Britain in the late eighteenth century is thought to provide a sense of national autonomy that is extended to the individual. By contrast, Canadian independence came more gradually and was granted much more recently. One important facet of the individualist-communalist difference between the two countries is that the United States provided its citizens a Bill of Rights very early in its history. Indeed, many accounts of the adoption of the American Constitution suggest that the promise of a Bill of Rights was an essential precondition to the ratification of the Constitution. By contrast, Canada did not pass its Charter of Rights and Freedoms until 1982. Lipset (1990) goes so far as to assert that this difference between Canada and the United States is the difference between a "revolutionary" and a "counterrevolutionary" society.

A second contrast between the United States and Canada concerns differences in the acceptance and practice of religion. There are several important differences in religious affiliation and observance between the two countries:

1. In the first place, citizens of the United States are more religious than Canadians, or, for that matter, than citizens of most industrialized countries (Wald,

1987). Americans are more likely to call themselves religious, to belong to a particular congregation, and to engage in religious practice.

2. There are more religions practiced in the United States than in Canada (Swatos, 1991). Religious Canadians appear to place a much higher value on ecumenism than do religious Americans (Lipset, 1990) whose sense of religious particularism (Stark and Glock, 1968) has caused an enormous proliferation of churches and sects (Roof and McKinney, 1987). In the United States, an emphasis on the personal, voluntary nature of religion, as well as a focus on matters of doctrine, has occasioned a great deal of fragmentation. By contrast, religion in Canada often appears to be a source of social integration. For this reason, several analysts (Grant, 1973; Kollar, 1989) have argued that the U.S. tradition of Protestant fundamentalism, with its critical and otherworldly emphases, has no direct equivalent in Canada. While there certainly exist denominations that are doctrinally conservative in Canada, the notion of religious separatism (see Jelen, 1987) has not taken hold among Canadian Evangelicals.[1]

3. There is a strong tradition of church-state separation in the United States, while Canadian churches have historically been sources of governmental legitimation (Grant, 1973). Stark and Bainbridge (1985) have argued that the major churches in Canada have the "quality" of established churches. Religion in Canada is thought to enhance obedience to governmental authority. By contrast, the U.S. emphasis on the separation of church and state virtually assumes that there will be frequent conflicts between government authority and individual consciences, which will typically be resolved in favor of conscience (Lipset, 1990:77).

ABORTION LAW IN THE UNITED STATES AND CANADA

The purpose of this study is to compare public attitudes on the abortion issue in the United States and Canada and to determine the extent to which the national differences described affect national differences on abortion. As is often the case, there are many similarities between the two countries with respect to the abortion issue. In 1973, the U.S. Supreme Court declared that, under most circumstances, a woman has a right to terminate a pregnancy. The decision the Court rendered in *Roe v. Wade* places substantial limits on the ability of state governments to regulate the practice of abortion and, for practical purposes, permits virtually unrestricted abortion during the first trimester of a pregnancy. Similarly, the Canadian Supreme Court overturned a national statute limiting abortion, in the case of *Morgentaler v. Regina* (1988). Pending further legislation by Parliament, abortion is, for practical purposes, unrestricted in Canada (Wallace, 1991).

In both countries, then, the national Supreme Court invalidated acts of legislatures (Parliament in the Canadian case, state legislatures in the U.S. case) that had previously limited access to legal abortion. Judicial review of this sort is extremely common in the United States and is considerably more unusual in Canada. Indeed, in the United States, recourse to the courts seems natural, since U.S. courts are regarded as protectors of individual rights. In the United States, both sides of the abortion controversy invoke the language of rights ("right to life," "right to choose") in setting forth their agendas, and both sides have attempted to use the courts to advance their position on the abortion issue (Glendon, 1987; Cook, Jelen, and Wilcox, 1992; Tribe, 1990).

The centrality of the courts in abortion politics in the United States is illustrated most clearly in the case of *Webster v. Missouri Reproductive Services.* In this case, the U.S. Supreme Court did not overturn *Roe,* but upheld some restrictions that would limit a woman's access to a legal abortion. The importance of the Court's 1989 *Webster* decision seems to some to invite state legislatures to pass more restrictive abortion legislation. This points to a tendency in U.S. politics for legislatures to defer to the judicial branch and to operate within judicially imposed limits, since the Court (in both *Roe* and *Webster*) defined the political space within which the elected branches of state governments can operate.

By contrast, the response to *Morgentaler* by Canadian prolife activists was to go to Parliament to correct what they regarded as an unfortunate decision. Unlike *Roe, Morgentaler* does not establish a "right" to legal abortion, but merely invalidates a section of the 1861 Offenses against Person Act, which had been inherited from Britain. The ruling in *Morgentaler* was quite deferential to the legislature, and does not rule out the possibility that future antiabortion legislation in Canada may be consistent with the Charter of Rights and Freedoms (Tribe, 1990). In other words, the overturning of *Morgentaler* in Canada would not be nearly as important an event as the overturning of *Roe* by the U.S. Supreme Court. In 1989, Prime Minister Mulroney introduced a bill to the Canadian Parliament that would prohibit abortion without the approval of a doctor (Government Bill C-43), and it was defeated by a tie vote in the Canadian Senate in February of 1991 (Wallace, 1991).

This study will address the question of differences and similarities in abortion attitudes between the United States and Canada. We would expect that there are powerful social forces that pull public opinion in the United States in opposite directions: although the commitment of citizens of the United States to individual autonomy would seem to exert influence in a prochoice direction, the extent and style of religious observance in the United States might have the opposite effect. In Canada, the lack of concern for individual rights (relative to the United States) might provide legitimacy for antiabortion sentiment, but the legitimating, supportive aspects of Canadian religion might suppress prolife activity.

DATA AND METHOD

Data for this study were taken from the 1988 American National Election Study (ANES) and the 1988 Canadian National Election Study. The dependent variable in this study is, of course, the respondent's attitude toward legal abortion. In the ANES study, the abortion item was worded as follows:

There has been some discussion about abortion in recent years. Which of the opinions on this page best agrees with your view?

1. By law, abortion should never be permitted.
2. The law should permit abortion only in cases of rape, incest, or when the woman's life is in danger.
3. The law should permit abortion for reasons other than rape, incest, or danger to the woman's life, but only after the need for the abortion has been clearly established.
4. By law, a woman should always be able to obtain an abortion as a matter of personal choice.

The abortion item in the Canadian study was worded somewhat differently:

Now, we would like to get your views on abortion. We know that this is a sensitive question. Of the following three positions, which is closest to your own opinion?

1. Abortion should never be permitted.
2. Abortion should be permitted after the need has been established by a doctor.
3. Abortion should be a matter of a woman's personal choice.

In the Canadian study, a split half version of the abortion question was used, reversing the order in which the response categories were presented. Experimentation with the relationships between the two different orders and a number of other variables reveals no systematic differences between the versions. Therefore, the versions of the question have been combined.

Since the question asked in the United States contains four alternatives, while the Canadian abortion item contains only three, the United States version was recoded to combine response categories 2 and 3. Thus, in the analyses which follow, respondents from both countries are classified into "always prohibited," "it depends," and "always permitted" groups.

A variety of independent variables were used to explain variation in abortion attitudes in each country. Religious variables include denominational dummy variables for Roman Catholicism and evangelical Protestantism (with mainline Protestantism being the comparison category), the respondent's view of the Bible, frequency of church attendance, and the subjective importance of religion. Two items relating to the role of women in society were also included in the statistical models for both countries. One of these was a "feeling thermometer" for "feminists," which was con-

Table 7.1

Regression of Abortion Attitudes on Religious, Attitudinal, and Demographic Variables, Canada and United States

	Canada			United States		
	b	beta	r	b	beta	r
Catholic	-.19	-.14**	-.17	-.18	-.12**	-.07
Evangelical denom	-.18	-.07*	-.13	-.06	-.04	-.12
Church attendance	-.20	-.27**	-.41	-.16	-.21**	-.33
Bible view	-.19	-.14**	-.27	-.21	-.17**	-.30
Religion Important	-.13	-.08*	-.32	-.15	-.11**	-.29
Partisanship	.04	.05	.08	-.04	-.05*	-.06
Feminist temp.	.007	.03	.05	.001	.05	.12
Woman's role	-.10	-.12**	-.22	-.08	-.11**	-.23
Education	.008	.01	.09	.07	.08*	.14
Parent	-.10	-.07*	-.06	-.11	-.08**	-.09
Sex	-.004	-.003	-.04	.06	.05	-.03
Marital status	-.07	-.05	.001	-.07	-.05	-.09
Labor force	-.02	-.01	-.07	-.04	-.02	-.10
Income	.03	.04	.11	.04	.05	.10
Age	.004	.01	-.07	-.004	-.02	-.05

R2 = .25   N = 985   R2 = .23   N= 1129

* significant at .05.
** significant at .01.

tained in both the U.S. and Canadian surveys, while the other was a measure of the proper role of women in business or industry. The effects of partisan identification on abortion attitudes were also considered.[2]

Explanatory demographic variables included education, gender, marital status, labor force participation (for women), income, age, and parental status. All items were recoded to a common range, to facilitate comparison across countries (for details, contact the authors). In order to make the samples more directly comparable, the U.S. analyses were limited to white respondents.

CROSS-NATIONAL COMPARISONS

How different are abortion attitudes in the United States and Canada? Canadians are very slightly more supportive of legal abortion than are residents of the United States: On the three-point abortion item, the Canadian mean is 2.35, while the mean abortion attitude for the United States is 2.25. This result would appear at first glance to suggest that there are few important North American differences with respect to the issue of abortion.

The similarities between public abortion attitudes in Canada and the United States are also apparent when the religious, political, and demographic correlates of abortion attitudes are examined. Table 7.1 presents for both countries multiple regression equations in which the abortion item is the dependent variable. Since all independent regressors have been recoded to a common range, it is possible to compare the effects of each variable across countries by examining the unstandardized regression coefficients for each. This comparison suggests that few demographic variables are significantly related to abortion attitudes in these multivariate models. In both countries, being a parent is significantly related to a restrictive position on abortion, while education is related to support for legal abortion in the United States only. No other demographic variable achieves statistical significance in either multivariate model.

Partisanship is weakly, but significantly, related to abortion attitudes in the United States only, although this difference is entirely attributable to the larger U.S. sample. The magnitude of the regression coefficients relating party identification to abortion attitudes is identical across countries. In both countries, the women's role item is related to abortion attitudes, but the feminist feeling thermometer is not.

Both models in Table 7.1 are dominated by religious variables. In both countries, Roman Catholicism is related to opposition to legal abortion, while membership in an evangelical denomination is related to a conservative abortion attitude only in Canada. Although the zero-order correlations between membership in an evangelical denomination and abortion attitudes are virtually identical for both countries, the standardized regression coefficient for evangelical denominational affiliation retains its statistical significance in the multivariate model in Canada only. Public religiosity (as measured by church attendance) has a stronger effect on abortion attitudes in Canada, while the more private, subjective attitudes of biblical interpretation and religious salience are more important in the United States.

With the exception of the irrelevance of evangelical denominational preference in the United States, the U.S.–Canadian religious differences are not particularly large. In general, the effects of religious variables appear slightly stronger in Canada, although Canadians are more supportive of legal abortion than are respondents from the United States. This apparent anomaly becomes less puzzling when it is remembered that religious affiliation and observance are more widespread in the United States, as are beliefs in an inerrant Bible and the importance of religion in everyday life. In the United States, the effects of religious variables on abortion attitudes are weaker (perhaps owing to the higher level of individualism that exists south of the border) but are more widespread. Thus, it is possible that the effects of the higher levels of U.S. religiosity are offset by the pervasive individualism of U.S. political culture. Conversely, the relatively strong effects of religious variables in Canada may be suppressed by the rather low percentage of Canadians who are highly religious or who are members of evangelical denominations.

Table 7.2
Comparison of Observed and Expected Means with Substitution of Mean Religious Values, Canada and United States

	Mean
Simulated U.S. (a)	2.48
Observed Canadian	2.35
Observed United States	2.25
Simulated Canada (b)	2.19

This conjecture is tested in Table 7.2, which makes use of a simulated regression technique. Table 7.2 compares the observed mean values on the abortion items for the United States and Canada with estimates of the mean values that would be obtained if U.S. citizens were as religious as Canadians, and vice versa. These estimated means are computed by recomputing the expected abortion means from the models presented in Table 7.1, while reestimating the contributions of particular religious variables. The simulated Canadian mean value on the abortion item is computed by reestimating the Canadian equation presented in Table 7.1, substituting the means of the religious variables in the United States, while the simulated U.S. mean is computed by substituting the Canadian means for the religion variables in the U.S. equation.

Thus, the simulated Canadian mean abortion attitude essentially estimates the probable mean abortion attitude if Canadians were as religious as U.S. citizens. Conversely, the simulated United States mean addresses the issue of how prolife U.S. citizens would be if religious belief and practice were only as widespread as it is in Canada. If the effects of religion on abortion attitudes were as strong in the United States as they are in Canada, what would abortion attitudes look like in the United States?[3]

As Table 7.2 shows, the disparity between the simulated means with abortion attitudes is much greater than the observed difference between the two countries. The least restrictive estimate of national support for legal abortion is derived from the combination of Canadian levels of religious observance and membership combined with the effects of religion derived from the United States (as measured by the unstandardized regression coefficients associated with those variables in the United States). The strongest estimate of prolife sentiment is generated by the combination of U.S. levels of religiosity and Canadian religious effects. The actual observed levels of support for legal abortion in both countries fall between these simulated estimates.

This comparison suffers from the lack of a direct measure of individualism for both countries. The effects of individualism in the United States are inferred through the slightly reduced effects of most religious variables, rather than directly observed. Nevertheless, the data in Table 7.2 are quite suggestive. The close similarity between abortion attitudes in the United States and Canada appears to result from markedly different processes in the two countries. The United States is a highly religious country, but the effects of religion on abortion attitudes seem to be reduced by the pervasive individualism of the U.S. political culture. Citizens of the United States may be opposed to abortion as a result of their religious beliefs but reluctant to impose that opposition on others.[4] The traditional mistrust of government that characterizes the American political culture makes possible a distinction between personal opposition to abortion and a desire to use the coercive power of government to enforce that preference. By contrast, prolife sentiment in Canada appears to be enhanced by the relatively strong effects of religion on abortion attitudes. However, while antiabortion attitudes are not suppressed by individualistic values, such attitudes are inhibited by the relatively lack of religiosity among Canadians. Thus, abortion attitudes in the United States are shaped by powerful cultural forces, pulling public opinion in opposite directions. In Canada, by contrast, the effects of religion and individualism both appear to be relatively weak.

REGIONAL COMPARISONS: CANADA AND THE UNITED STATES

Of course, no discussion of any aspect of Canadian politics would be complete without considering the distinctiveness of Quebec. Quebec constitutes a unique, francophone, Catholic region that is a source of separatist sentiment. Indeed, the issue of whether or not Quebec constitutes a separate society animates many aspects of contemporary Canadian politics. Nevertheless, the existence of an anomalous, politically distinctive region is not unique to Canada. The American South is an unusual region in the politics of the United States in a number of respects. While the issue of southern separatism was settled over a century ago, the experience and historical memory of secession remains an important part of the region's political culture.

Both Quebec and the South are religiously distinctive as well, which might affect public attitudes toward abortion in each region. In particular, Quebec is a bastion of Roman Catholicism (an important source of antiabortion sentiment) in an otherwise Protestant country. Similarly, the South has a disproportionately high percentage of evangelical Protestants, who have recently been quite vocal and active in the abortion debate in the United States (see Cook, Jelen, and Wilcox, 1992).

The question of regional distinctiveness on the abortion issue is addressed in a very simple form in Table 7.3, which shows the mean values

Table 7.3
Comparison of Mean Abortion Attitudes by Region, Canada and United States

Canada:	Mean	Standard Deviation	N
Quebec	2.40	.625	325
Non-Quebec	2.34	.667	850
United States:	Mean	Standard Deviation	N
South	2.19	.646	368
Non-South	2.27	.631	761

on the abortion item for the regions of Canada and the United States. As might be anticipated, southerners are less supportive of access to legal abortion than are nonsoutherners in the United States. Perhaps surprisingly, residents of Quebec are more supportive of abortion rights than are respondents residing in the English-speaking provinces. This difference is largely attributable to the lower levels of church attendance that characterize Quebec. It should also be noted that regional differences do not account for differences between countries at all, since the least prochoice region in Canada is more supportive of legal abortion than the U.S. region most supportive of legal abortion.

To what extent do these regional distinctions represent U.S.–Canadian differences in political culture? Table 7.4 presents the same regression equations shown in Table 7.1, recomputed for residents of each broad region in each country. In the United States, certain demographic variables (income and education) have slightly greater effects in the South than elsewhere, while the experience of having one's own children affects abortion attitudes outside the South. Attitudes toward feminism are related to abortion attitudes outside the South only.

What is most interesting about the U.S. data is the effects of religious variables across regions. In general, comparison of the unstandardized regression coefficients across regions suggests that religion has its greatest effect on abortion attitudes in relatively inhospitable social environments. Thus, a Roman Catholic denominational affiliation has a stronger effect on attitudes toward legal abortion in the South, where Catholics are a minority. Conversely, church attendance, belief in an inerrant Bible, and subjective religiosity have their greatest effect in the North, where such attitudes are (relative to the South) moderately unusual. It is interesting to note that the zero-order correlation between membership in an evangelical denomination and abortion attitudes is a statistically significant −.15 in the North, but only −.06 in the South. Although some of the differences are not particularly large, they do exhibit a consistent pattern.

Table 7.4
Regression of Abortion Attitudes on Religious, Attitudinal, and Demographic Variables by Region

United States

	South			Non-South		
	b	beta	r	b	beta	r
Catholic	-.21	-.12**	-.07	-.16	-.12**	-.08
Evangelical denom	-.03	-.03	-.06	-.13	-.04	-.15
Church attendance	-.13	-.17**	-.21	-.17	-.22**	-.38
Bible	-.18	-.13**	-.26	-.23	-.18**	-.32
Religion imptant	-.06	-.04	-.20	-.20	-.15**	-.32
Feminist temp.	.00	-.002	-.05	.002	.09*	.16
Woman's role	-.11	-.14**	-.23	-.06	-.08*	-.23
Partisanship	-.08	-.12*	-.11	-.01	-.02	-.04
Education	.09	.10@	.20	.06	.07	.10
Parent	-.04	-.04	-.008	-.12	-.09*	-.13
Sex	.06	.04	.003	.04	.04	-.04
Marital status	-.05	-.04	-.04	-.09	-.06	-.11
Labor force	.03	.02	-.05	-.08	-.04	-.11
Income	.09	.11@	.17	.008	.01	.05
Age	-.001	-.03	-.10	-.00	-.001	.05

        R2 = .18   N = 368   R2 = .27   N = 761

**significant at .01.
*significant at .05.
@significant at .10.

Canada

	Quebec			Non-Quebec		
	b	beta	r	b	beta	r
Catholic	-.37	-.15**	-.17	-.24	-.17**	-.23
Evangelical	-.12	-.06	.05	-.23	-.09**	-.15
Church attendance	-.07	-.10	-.28	-.24	-.32**	-.46
Bible	-.33	-.25**	-.35	-.15	-.11**	-.24
Religion important	-.25	-.18**	-.33	-.08	-.05	-.31
Feminist temp	.007	.03	.006	.007	.04	.06
Woman's role	-.08	-.11@	-.24	-.09	-.11**	-.20
Partisanship	.05	.05	.07	.06	.03	.08
Education	-.01	-.02	.13	.02	.02	.08
Parent	-.007	-.006	.06	-.15	-.11**	-.10
Sex	-.02	-.01	.03	-.009	-.006	-.05
Marital status	-.01	-.02	.03	-.11	-.07*	-.01
Labor force	.27	.09	.07	-.05	-.02	-.10
Income	.03	.04	.05	-.03	.04	.14
Age	.001	.02	-.11	-.006	-.02	-.06

        R2 = .23   N = 257   R2 = .29   N = 728

**significant at .01.
*significant at .05.
@significant at .10.

By contrast, the public aspects of religion have their greatest effect on Canadian abortion attitudes in social environments in which particular religious characteristics are relatively common. Thus, antiabortion sentiment has a stronger relationship with Catholicism in Quebec than in the rest of Canada, while the effects of evangelicalism are much stronger in the English-speaking portions of the country. Interestingly, the more private aspects of religion (belief in the Bible and subjective religious intensity) display a pattern similar to that found in the United States. Both of these private, subjective variables have a greater effect on abortion attitudes within the province of Quebec.

Thus, this regional comparison of abortion attitudes in Canada and the United States suggests that religion affects political attitudes differently in the two countries. While it would be a mistake to exaggerate the importance of relatively small differences in regression coefficients, the pattern of relationships described in Table 7.4 is at least intriguing. In the United States, religion appears to affect political attitudes through the role of social critic. That is, religion has an independent effect on public attitudes toward political issues such as abortion when religious values stand outside the locally dominant political culture (see Jelen, 1982; Wilcox and Jelen, 1993). By contrast, the public aspects of religion in Canada have their greatest effect on public opinion when such attitudes reinforce (or at least do not oppose) the prevailing political climate. Religion in Canada appears to be a source of legitimation or accommodation rather than a source of political criticism and conflict.[5]

DISCUSSION

At this point, it seems appropriate to note that the contrast we have drawn between U.S. and Canadian attitudes toward abortion should not be exaggerated. There are important similarities between the politics of abortion in both countries, and our data show that these similarities extend to several aspects of public opinion on the abortion issue. The effects of feminism, partisanship, Roman Catholicism, and demographic variables on abortion attitudes are quite comparable across the two North American democracies.

Nevertheless, our data have shown that important differences between the two countries do exist. In particular, the role of evangelical Protestantism differs between the United States and Canada in interesting and counterintuitive ways. In Canada, membership in an evangelical denomination has the effect of producing prolife attitudes even when the effects of religious observance and doctrinal orthodoxy have been controlled. Despite the fact that there are relatively few evangelical Protestants in Canada, membership in such congregations appears to be a powerful source of political socialization. By contrast, the effects of evangelicalism are much weaker in the

United States. We interpret these differences to mean that the political consequences of a widespread evangelical movement are suppressed in the United
States by the pervasive individualism of the U.S. political culture. Lacking as
we do direct measures of individualism that can be applied in both countries,
this last point must remain conjectural. Nevertheless, this empirical study
bears out more ethnographic, impressionistic works concerning U.S.–
Canadian differences (Lipset, 1990; Merelman, 1991).

We have also shown that the role of religion in affecting political attitudes varies across countries by subnational political context. In the United
States, religion appears to be a more successful agent of political socialization in opposition. Minority religions appear to have the greatest independent effect on political attitudes. By contrast, religion in Canada affects
political attitudes most directly when it is supportive of (and supported
by) the local political culture. These empirical findings are also quite consistent with previous research.

Our findings thus suggest that there do exist important differences between the political cultures of Canada and the United States. The issue of
abortion has served to illustrate more general themes: Individualism and
religion operate differently in diverse cultural contexts. Apparent similarities between the two countries may conceal important cultural distinctions.

NOTES

A version of this paper was presented at the annual meeting of the Association
for Canadian Studies in the United States, Boston, November 1991.

1. Classification of Canadian denominations is as follows: Mainline = Angli-
can, United Church of Canada, Presbyterian, and Lutheran; Evangelical = Baptist,
Christian Reformed, Pentecostal.

2. In both countries, partisanship was trichotomized. In the United States, the
values for party identification were Democrat, Independent, and Republican, with
independent leaners classified as Independents. For Canada, the values were Conservative, Liberal, and New Democratic Party. Experimentation with different cod-
ing schemes (such as isolating one party in a dichotomous variable, eliminating
independents, or altering the classification of independents) does not alter substantially the results presented here.

3. This procedure holds constant the effects of all demographic variables reported in Table 7.1.

4. For example, a 1989 CBS/New York Times Survey shows that a substantial
number of prolife citizens agreed that "even in cases where I might think abortion
is the wrong thing to do, I don't think the government has any business preventing
a woman from having an abortion" (see Cook, Jelen, and Wilcox, 1992: 140–42.)

5. It is of some interest to note that state-level Catholicism appears to occasion
a prochoice countermobilization among non-Catholics in the United States, while
there is no equivalent phenomenon in Canada. The effects of religious variables
appear to operate exclusively at the individual level in Canada, with no measurable
contextual effects. See Cook, Jelen, and Wilcox, 1993a, for further details of non-
Catholic countermobilization in the United States.

8   The Structure of Attitudes toward Body Issues in the American and Canadian Populations: An Elementary Analysis

John H. Simpson

While abortion, pornography, the rights of gays and lesbians, and so-called family values have become objects of intense social and political conflict in recent times, many features of attitudes and beliefs toward those matters in the general population remain unexplored. In part, that is due to the entanglement of the issues with the politics of the New Religious Right in the United States. Since the election of Ronald Reagan in 1980, a literature that delves into the effects of sociomoral issues on political mobilization, electoral behavior, and public choices has appeared, for example, Liebman and Wuthnow, 1983; Bromley and Shupe, 1984; Hadden and Shupe, 1988; Moen, 1989; Jelen, 1989, 1991; and Wilcox, 1992. While that literature sheds much light on recent electoral outcomes and political trends, it tends to bypass what is, perhaps, a more fundamental and basic question: how should the capacity of societies for a politics of sociomoral, body-oriented issues be conceptualized, measured, and understood?

One approach to answering that question addresses the structure and population distributions of relevant beliefs and attitudes. Where such beliefs and attitudes are salient and mobilized, they can become resources in the social and political conflicts of the day. In this chapter a number of body-oriented attitude items from surveys of the American and Canadian populations are analyzed in order to establish a better understanding of the capacities of those two late capitalist societies for a politics of the body.

THE NATURE OF AN ELEMENTARY ANALYSIS

Where a polity provides for the expression and institutionalization of differing or opposed interests and those interests are factored (in some sense) into electoral and political decisions, the question arises regarding how interests and concomitant beliefs, attitudes, values, and policy orientations—that is, public opinion—should be measured and represented. As Back (1988) points out, public opinion is a relative notion. What counts as a legitimate source and voice for the expression of public opinion is both society-specific and historically variable. In contemporary advanced societies, sample surveys of individuals are the most important means for measuring and assessing public opinion. In those societies the major primary element of public opinion is an individual's answer to a survey question regarding his or her beliefs, attitudes, values, political views, and so on (Back, 1988).

Where adequate sampling and reliable measurement have occurred, an inspection of the distribution of respondents' answers to a question reveals the degree of polarization or division on the question in a population. In the hypothetical ideal case, no politics would occur where all respondents answered "yes" (as opposed to "no") or "agree" (as opposed to "disagree") in response to an item since there would be a perfect consensus in the population. On the other hand (and again, in the hypothetical ideal case), were the distribution of answers to an item split evenly between "yes" and "no" or "agree" and "disagree" and were the item focused on some highly salient public matter, one might expect a great deal of public action with much symbolic "pushing and shoving" in the media, an overlay of heavy and thick rhetoric on both sides of the issue, and even collective public disturbances.

Now suppose that instead of one highly salient item on which a population is evenly divided, there are two such items, each focused on a substantively different matter of public concern. Furthermore, suppose that respondents who answer "yes" (or "no") to one item also answer "yes" (or "no") to the other item. We would then have a population that is divided on two salient issues that are highly (indeed, perfectly) correlated. There of course may be no explanation for the observed association between the items apart from sampling variation. But if there is a stream of discourse— a narrative or story—that renders the correlation meaningful, we then have set of beliefs and attitudes that are formally associated and also rhetorically bound together. In other words, an ideology exists. The example of two numerically and rhetorically correlated items is, of course, merely illustrative. Ideologies may, and if well established, usually do contain a multitude of correlated items.

An elementary analysis in the sense in which the term is used in this chapter focuses on the distributions and associations of belief and attitude items that may be rhetorically bound together in ideological "packages." On the one hand, an elementary analysis deals with the formal modeling or representation of the elements or items in ideology packages. On the other hand, it focuses on the discourse, rhetoric, or substantive logic that binds those items together into a meaningful whole. In the broadest sense, an elementary analysis, then, deals with the interplay between the texts of political and social philosophies, the considered opinions and comments of experts and pundits, general public discourse on issues, and the measurement and representation of relevant attitudes and beliefs in a population. In this chapter we are particularly concerned with the latter, that is, with the measurement and representation of attitudes toward a set of body-oriented items in the American and Canadian populations and the extent to which patterns of attitudes, where they exist, provide insight into the nature of body politics in the political arenas of the two countries.

A TYPOLOGY OF POLITICAL ARENAS

Further elaboration and development of the notion of an ideology as defined here provides a range of possibilities for typifying political arenas. The notion that an ideology exists where a diverse set of items is empirically associated can be traced to Philip Converse's seminal article, "The Nature of Belief Systems in Mass Publics" (Converse, 1964). Among other things, Converse showed that *some* respondents in sample surveys of the American population had well-formed belief systems that encompassed a broad range of foreign and domestic issues. Converse characterized those belief systems as "configurations of ideas and attitudes in which the elements are bound together by some form of constraint or functional interdependence" (Converse, 1964:207). Converse's operational measure of constraint was the degree of correlation among a set of items. Large numbers of high correlations among diverse items indicate the presence of ideologically based belief systems, while weak correlations suggest their absence, according to Converse.

However—and here is an important point—Converse not only generated an empirical procedure for detecting the presence or absence of ideologies in a set of respondents. He also showed that ideologically based belief systems were not widely distributed in the American population. High interitem correlations indicative of significant constraint among items measuring orientations to a wide range of domestic and foreign issues occurred among less than 20 percent of the respondents in the samples examined by Converse. Converse concluded that it was very difficult to attribute the political choices and actions of most individuals in mass democratic publics—at least those individuals in the mass public that formed the American electorate thirty to forty years ago—to well-developed and ideologically consistent systems of ideas, beliefs, and attitudes, since relatively few persons provided empirical evidence that they held such systems.

A central feature of an ideology, according to Converse, is its power to bind together diverse elements or items that orient an actor to a wide range of institutional sectors and distinct types of policies and practices that are germane to each sector. A political ideology, in other words, provides a set of purposes and orienting principles that "cover off" all or most of the major problems and directions that are thematized in a public arena. In probing the nature of mass belief systems, Converse examined attitudes of Americans in 1958 toward guaranteed employment, federal aid to education and housing, the Fair Employment Practices Commission, and foreign economic and military aid. Had he been writing in the wake of the 1992 U.S. presidential election, he might have examined the relationships among attitudes and beliefs pertaining to the "rescue" of the education system, crime in the streets, health care, the environment, minority groups, poverty, America's role in a postcommunist world, and, of course, so-called family values.

Extending the argument further, the diversity and universal scope of an ideology as an operative philosophy in a political arena can be contrasted with so-called single-issue politics, where one belief, policy, or legislative goal energizes a subset of actors in a population and serves to mobilize their actions. Such politics are organized around the achievement of very specific outcomes and lack the diversity of ideologically oriented politics with its broad reach across the institutional sectors of a society. That is not to say, of course, that single-issue politics lacks reasons, justifications, orienting perspectives, and philosophical embellishment. Single-issue politics may be and frequently is justified by elaborate systems of thought and intellectual work. Nevertheless, such justifications tend be single-minded and narrowly focused. They do not "cover off" the universe, as it were. In other words, they are not ideologies in Converse's sense of the term.

Variations in terms of the diversity of salient items and the locations in a population where one would expect to find a high degree of association among such items suggest a general classification scheme or typology of political arenas. Thus, where a political arena is characterized by ideological politics, an analyst would expect to find a high degree of association in the general population among a diverse set of items ranging across many problems and policies. In the case of single-issue politics, one would expect a high degree of association among only a very limited range of items—essentially, different indicators of beliefs and attitudes toward a single issue or policy—in restricted population subgroups. Converse's mass politics would be characterized by high correlations among diverse items in population subgroups. High correlations, however, would not exist in samples of the general population. Finally, quasi-ideological politics would be found where high correlations occur in the general population among

Table 8.1
A Typology of Political Arenas

		Issue Diversity	
		High	Low
Location of High	Elites/ Subgroups	Mass Politics	Single Issue Politics
Constraint Among			
Beliefs and			
Attitudes Toward			
Issues	General Population	Ideological Politics	Quasi-Ideological Politics

items that are more diverse than is the case where single-issue politics holds sway. However, the items would lack the universal sweep characteristic of beliefs and attitudes implicated in ideological politics. Table 8.1 summarizes the typology.

As is the case with any typology, Table 8.1 defines logical possibilities and simplifies empirical realities. The cell entries in Table 8.1 obviously do not exhaust the complexities of actual existing politics. Nevertheless, they do provide a starting point that has both theoretical and practical value. A political theorist, for example, might wish to consider the conditions and forces that impel movement along the diagonals or marginals of the table. Under what conditions, for instance, would a political arena move from ideological politics to mass politics or single-issue politics? Again, a political strategist might advise different courses of action depending on the type of political arena she or he is operating in. For example, if a congressional district (U.S.) or a federal riding (Canada) were an ideological political arena and the set of salient items in the arena included both economic issues and more delicate family values or ethnic issues, a campaign strategist could focus attention on the economic issues and be reasonably certain that unspoken messages would get through regarding the more delicate issues. In ideological politics one issue tends to code another issue, since issues are bound together in ideological wholes. On the other hand, were the electoral unit best characterized as a single-issue political arena and were it deemed prudent to address some salient delicate issue, that issue would be best treated in a direct and manifest fashion in order for the message to get through. One issue, in that case, would not tend to code another issue.

In the remaining portion of this chapter, I will explore and analyze a set of body-oriented issues in the Canadian and American population with an eye on Table 8.1. Clearly, some body-oriented issues—pornography, abortion, and rights for gays and lesbians, for example—organize intense single-issue action in contemporary political arenas. But, it can be asked, is there a population base in either the United States or Canada for moving beyond single-issue politics and joining the aims and goals of the various movements associated with body issues in a quasi-ideological politics of the body? If there were such a base, a particular stance on abortion would, for example, code stances on pornography and rights for gays and lesbians and would suggest that the items could be rhetorically bound together in a general ideological package. The analysis that follows explores that possibility.

BODY ISSUES IN NORTH AMERICA: QUASI-IDEOLOGICAL POLITICS?

If a political arena is best described as quasi-ideological, we would expect to find high correlations among a set of items organized around a common empirical referent of considerable political salience. Unlike ideologically based politics, which draws empirically diverse items together, quasi-ideological politics binds a relatively narrow range of beliefs and attitudes into a consistent, rhetorical whole. High correlations indicating the presence of quasi-ideological or ideological politics would be found in population samples. On the other hand, in the case of mass or single-issue politics, high interitem correlations would be found only in subgroups or segments of the population.

As Converse (1964) points out, the matrix of high interitem correlations that would be observed in the case of ideological politics (and, by extension, quasi-ideological politics) is the type of matrix that "would be appropriate for factor analysis, the statistical technique designed to reduce a number of correlated variables to a more limited set of organizing dimensions. . . . Of course, it is the type of broad organizing dimension to be suggested by factor analysis of specific items that is usually presumed when observers discuss 'ideological postures' [liberal or conservative, for example] of one sort or another" (1964:230). Converse thus suggests that factor analysis provides the basis for a formal test of the hypothesis that ideological (or quasi-ideological) politics is present in a population. A slight reformulation of that notion defines the properties of an elementary baseline analysis pursued in this chapter in order to test the hypothesis that responses to a set of items represent data drawn from a population characterized by ideological or quasi-ideological politics.

The simplest model of a political arena assumes that individuals are divided into two camps—usually labeled "liberal" and "conservative"—and that all individuals in the arena hold consistently liberal or conservative positions on a set of issues (Simpson 1983, 1988b). That model implies the nominal or categorical level of measurement, that is, respondents are either for or against an issue, liberal or conservative in terms of their views, and so forth. An elementary baseline analysis, then, examines relations among a set of dichotomous positions.

The analog of correlation for dichotomous (or polytomous) categorical variables is cross-classification, and the analog of factor analysis for cross-classified variables is latent structure analysis (McCutcheon, 1987; Eliason, 1988). In keeping with Converse's suggestion regarding factor analysis, latent structure analysis would, then, be an appropriate statistical technique for performing an elementary analysis to test for the presence of ideological or quasi-ideological politics in a population. Like factor analysis, latent structure analysis posits unmeasured, unobserved categories in order to explain the observed relations among a set of items. In the simplest or baseline case, where the latent structure analysis of a set of dichotomous items detects two latent classes, evidence would exist in favor of the hypothesis that a population supports ideological or quasi-ideological politics (depending on the diversity of the items analyzed). Thus, if a latent structure analysis of a set of dichotomous body-oriented items detects two latent classes (conservative and liberal) in samples of the American and Canadian populations, there would be evidence in favor of the hypothesis that a quasi-ideological politics of the body exists in those populations.

It should be noted that were a baseline elementary analysis to fail, that is, if a two-class latent structure model did not fit observed data in a particular case, it would not necessarily follow that quasi-ideological politics was absent from the population where the data were obtained. A baseline elementary analysis tests the simplest model. Complex models of more than two latent classes and data sets with variables of more than two categories could be consistent with the notion that a quasi-ideological (or ideological) political arena exists in a population. In this chapter, however, the analysis is limited to the simplest case of dichotomous variables and two latent classes.

The body-oriented items analyzed here are taken from the 1984 Canadian National Election Study (Lambert et al., 1986; hereafter CNES1984) and the 1984 General Social Survey (Davis and Smith, 1984; hereafter GSS1984) of the American population.[1] As is the case with most secondary analysis, not all items in the original surveys conform precisely to the measurement assumptions of models that are fitted to test hypotheses. In the case of an elementary baseline analysis, the models that are fitted test the notion that a population is divided into two opposing camps on each of the issues that are under consideration. In measurement terms, an elementary baseline analysis assumes that nominal or categorical dichotomies best describe divisions in a population on a set of issues. In order to meet that assumption, some variables from CNES1984 and GSS1984 are collapsed to form dichotomies.

Another measurement consideration arises in terms of the questions pertaining to the issues under examination in the two surveys. Issue-specific questions are not the same in the two surveys. Since comparisons between the countries regarding a capacity for body politics is a goal of this chapter, the matter of question comparability deserves comment.

The problem of comparability can be put in terms of risk patterns. Where the same question pertaining to an issue—typically, a question developed by researchers in one location—is asked in two different countries or political jurisdictions, the risk of missing the differences between the expression and articulation of the issue in the two jurisdictions is high. The same issue, in other words, can be constructed somewhat differently in different political jurisdictions. Exact replication of question wording would miss those differences and possibly render a question somewhat "offbeat" in a jurisdiction. On the other hand, questions that are tailored to local specificities and understandings may be truly incomparable even though the manifest issues that they address appear to be the same. In that case, the risk of posing an invalid question is minimized, but the risk of incomparability is increased.

There is, of course, no general rule that tells the researcher how to proceed in order to achieve the best possible outcome, namely, the simultaneous minimization of both the risk of incomparability and the risk of posing an invalid, population-specific question that misses respondents' understandings of an issue. In terms of the items examined in the surveys considered here (CNES1984 and GSS1984), there was, of course, no attempt to resolve the incomparability/validity dilemma since the questions were designed locally and independently. That, presumably, means that the risk of invalidity in each case has been minimized, but it leaves open the question of comparability. Question wordings from the two surveys and the uncollapsed univariate distributions for each question are presented in Tables 8.2 and 8.3.[2]

Four body-oriented items are examined. Three items focus on abortion, homosexual rights, and pornography. The fourth item taps respondents' attitudes toward capital punishment. That item is included for several reasons. First, the issue of capital punishment can be viewed as an anchor item for body politics since it poses the question of the existence of the body and the state's right to deprive a person of her or his body. Considered in that way, the issue of capital punishment can be construed as the fundamental body-oriented issue, since it defines the limits of the exercise of legitimate power vis-à-vis body. In the second place, there is evidence that capital punishment is salient for those who are conservative or liberal on the other issues. In the United States, the conservative Moral Majority,

Table 8.2
Attitudes toward Social Issues in Canada: 1984 Canadian National Election Study

GAYTEACH   -   "People who are homosexuals should be permitted to teach school."

	N	%
Agree strongly	561	16.6
Agree some	772	22.9
Disagree some	373	11.1
Disagree strongly	1077	31.9
Neutral	246	7.3
No opinion	320	9.5
Refused	28	0.8

EXECUTE   -   "There should be capital punishment for anyone convicted of murder."

	N	%
Agree strongly	1453	43.0
Agree some	746	22.1
Disagree some	367	10.9
Disagree strongly	417	12.4
Neutral	179	5.3
No opinion	187	5.5
Refused	28	0.8

ABORTION   -   "The decision to have an abortion should be the responsibility of the pregnant woman."

	N	%
Agree strongly	1643	48.7
Agree some	678	20.1
Disagree some	264	7.8
Disagree strongly	518	15.3
Neutral	101	3.0
No opinion	145	4.3
Refused	28	0.8

CENSORSHIP -   "Pornographic magazines and movies should be censored."

	N	%
Agree strongly	1750	51.8
Agree some	746	22.1
Disagree some	322	9.5
Disagree strongly	275	8.1
Neutral	119	3.5
No opinion	137	4.1
Refused	28	0.8

Table 8.3
Attitudes toward Social Issues in the United States: 1984 General Social Survey

HOMO.TCH - "There are always some people whose ideas are considered bad or dangerous, for instance, a man who admits that he is a homosexual. Should such a person be allowed to teach in a college or university or not?"

	N	%
Allowed	864	58.7
Not allowed	545	37.0
Don't know	59	4.0
No answer	5	0.3

EXECUTE?2 - "Do you favour or oppose the death penalty for persons convicted of murder?"

	N	%
Favour	1029	69.9
Oppose	347	23.6
Don't know	86	5.8
No answer	11	0.8

ABORTANY - "Please tell me whether you think it should be possible for a pregnant woman to obtain a legal abortion if the woman wants it for any reason."

	N	%
Yes	548	37.2
No	872	59.2
Don't know	42	2.9
No answer	11	0.8

PORN.LAW? - "Which of these statements comes closest to your feelings about pornography laws?" 1) There should be laws against the distribution of pornography whatever the age; 2) There should be laws against the distribution of pornography to persons under 18; 3) There should be no laws forbidding the distribution of pornography."

	N	%
Yes: all	595	40.4
Yes: <18	790	53.6
No laws	61	4.1
Don't know	18	1.2
No answer	9	0.6

for example, supported capital punishment as a plank in its sociomoral platform (Falwell, 1980) while some liberals today actively oppose capital punishment and simultaneously agitate in favor of gay rights ("Lawrence Mikkelsen," 1993:69). Finally, some analysts have noted that, taken together, capital punishment and abortion raise the question of ethical consistency (Johnson and Tamney, 1988). Is it consistent to oppose (or favor) capital punishment and at the same time favor (or oppose) abortion, one

position supporting the continuation (or termination) of life, the other call-
ing for its termination (or continuation)? Clearly, a quasi-ideological politics of the body would have to provide for the rhetorical resolution of that
inconsistency. A rhetorical quasi-ideology, however, that underwrites a
general politics of the body would presumably only be useful in a political
arena where an elementary analysis uncovers an affinity between abortion
and capital punishment *and* other body-oriented issues. The analysis that
follows explores those relationships in the American and Canadian populations.

Tables 8.2 and 8.3 contain the questions, response categories, and univariate distributions for the items from the CNES1984 and GSS1984, respectively, pertaining to gay rights, capital punishment, abortion, and pornography. In all cases an attempt was made to choose items from the two
surveys that were as closely matched as possible. Responses to the gay
rights item (teaching in school, CNES1984; teaching in college or university, GSS1984) indicate that Americans appear to be more liberal than
Canadians on this particular issue. Fifty-nine percent (59 percent) of the
American respondents say that a homosexual should be allowed to teach
in a college or university, while only 39 percent of the Canadians agree
somewhat or strongly agree with the notion that homosexuals should be
allowed to teach in the schools. Caution, however, should be exercised
regarding the comparability of the figures. The GSS1984 question can be
interpreted as an indicator of attitudes toward civil rights and, specifically,
the desirably of freedom of expression in a venue where ideas are supposed
to receive free reign (the college or university classroom). While the
GSS1984 question may evoke some thoughts about the risk of corrupting
the morals of youth, it is prima facie more likely, given the marked emphasis on the norm of free speech in American society, to raise the question
of the extent to which limits should be imposed on the expression of "dangerous" ideas. The CNES1984 question, on the other hand, evokes the
risks involved in exposing school-age children to homosexuals. The emphasis is not on free speech but rather on the potential for child abuse and
the recruitment of "innocent youngsters" to a deviant life-style.

Canadians and Americans appear to be remarkably similar in their attitudes toward capital punishment. Seventy per cent (70 percent) of Americans queried in the GSS1984 favor the death penalty, while 65 percent of
the Canadian respondents said that they agree strongly or agree somewhat
that there should be capital punishment for anyone convicted of murder.
Despite the similarity of attitudes toward capital punishment in the mass
publics of the two countries, there is a major difference between Canada
and the United States regarding the legal status and legislative control of
criminal law and the sanction of capital punishment. In Canada criminal
law is a federal enactment. In the United States criminal law pertaining to
murder is under the jurisdiction of state legislatures subject to review by

the federal court system. Furthermore, capital punishment was abandoned in Canada as a legal sanction in 1967. Hence, to favor capital punishment in Canada means that one is taking a position against existing law, whereas in the United States a person who favors capital punishment generally has the (state) law on his or her side. While capital punishment was declared to be "cruel and unusual punishment" by the United States Supreme Court in 1972 and execution was suspended, it resumed when that decision was effectively reversed by the Court in 1976.

Regarding abortion, 37 percent of the American respondents think that legal abortion should be available on demand. Among Canadians, 69 percent think that a pregnant woman should have the power to make the decision to abort. Abortion on demand and the woman's right to decide regarding abortion are somewhat different indicators, with one focused on the range of circumstances where abortion, in the respondent's opinion, should be legally possible and the other on the locus of decision making regarding abortion. Of course, the absolute right of a woman to make the abortion decision would amount to abortion on demand. Based on the items examined here, Canadians appear to be considerably more liberal than Americans on the abortion issue. That difference, however, should be viewed with caution, given the equivocal comparability of the items.

Regarding pornography, Canadians appear to be much more conservative than Americans. Seventy-four per cent (74 percent) of the respondents in the CNES1984 survey indicate that they agree strongly or agree somewhat that pornographic magazines and movies should be censored. Forty per cent (40 percent) of the American respondents say that there should be laws restricting the distribution of pornography to persons of all ages, in other words, an absolute ban on the distribution of pornography. While it is unlikely that Americans are more prurient than Canadians, it is very likely that the lack of a long-established and constitutionally entrenched tradition in Canada of freedom of the press plus a record of seizure and ban and concerns regarding the relationship between pornography and violence toward women account for some of the large difference between Canadians and American on the pornography issue.

Are there conservative-liberal divisions in the Canadian and American populations that result in a high degree of consistency among the items in Tables 8.2 and 8.3? In order to answer the question, two-class latent structure models are fitted to the four-way tables that arise when the variables in Tables 8.2 and 8.3 are cross-classified. In each case, only respondents with clear opinions on either side of an issue are included in the cross-classifications. Each variable is dichotomized. For the items from CNES1984, "neutral," "no opinion," and "refused" are excluded. "Agree strongly" and "agree some" are collapsed to form one category. "Disagree some" and "disagree strongly" are collapsed to form the other category. In the case of GSS1984, "don't know" and "no answer" are excluded, leaving dichotomized variables in the cases of gay rights, capital punishment, and abortion. In the case of pornography, "yes: <18" and "no laws" were collapsed to form a single category. Given the large difference in sample sizes (CNES1984, n = 3377; GSS1984, n = 1473), CNES1984 was randomly sampled in order to make the number of cases run in each latent structure analysis comparable for the purpose of determining the relative goodness-of-fit of the models, a procedure that is sensitive to sample size. The four-way tables that are analyzed contain 1,339 (CNES1984) and 1,285 (GSS1984) cases.

Two sets of results from the analysis will be examined in order to determine whether there is any basis for a quasi-ideological politics of the body in Canada or the United States. If a two-class latent structure model fits the observed data, that would be evidence in favor of the presence of body politics. The fit of the model, then, is the first result that will be examined. It is possible, however, for the two-class model to fit the data but the composition of the latent classes themselves to be inconsistent with the hypothesis that the population is divided into substantively meaningful camps. That would be the case where one latent class or the other cannot be described as composed only of those who are conservative or liberal on the issues. The ideological composition of the latent classes can be determined by inspecting the conditional probabilities. A conditional probability is the probability that a respondent is at one of the levels of a manifest variable, given that she or he is in one of the latent classes. Conditional probabilities are analogous to factor loadings. For there to be unequivocal evidence that a basis for quasi-ideological politics is present in a population, the two-class latent structure model would have to fit the observed data *and* the pattern of conditional probabilities or loadings would have to be such that one latent class was highly loaded on the conservative responses to an item while the other class was highly loaded on the liberal responses.

Table 8.4 contains goodness-of-fit statistics for two models for the two four-way cross-classifications. The first model for each table is the independence model (H–1). The independence model tests the hypothesis that there are no interactions or associations between any of the variables in a table. If the independence model fits a table, there is nothing going on in the table, so to speak. The fit of a model can be assessed in terms of the ratio of the chi-square statistic to the degrees of freedom for a model: the smaller the ratio, the better the fit. Excellent fit occurs where the ratio is near one. As can be seen, the independence model does not fit either the CNES1984 table or the GSS1984 table. Were the independence model to fit, the presence of quasi-ideological politics could be ruled out. Since it does not fit either the CNES1984 table or the GSS1984 table, the presence of quasi-ideological politics cannot be ruled out.

The second model in Table 8.4 (H–2) tests the hypothesis that a quasi-

Table 8.4

Some Models Pertaining to the Cross-Classification of the Variables in Table 8.2 (CNES1984) and Table 8.3 (GSS1984)

Survey	Model	LR Chi-square	Degrees of Freedom
CNES 1984*	H-1 Independence	164.24	11
	H-2 2 Latent Classes	24.03	6
GSS 1984	H-1 Independence	284.47	11
	H-2 2 Latent Classes	11.74	6

*Random subsample of 1,339 cases.

ideological politics of the body is present in the Canadian and American populations. In each case the model is a two-class latent structure model with no restrictions on the parameters in the model. Clearly, in each case the model provides a substantially better fit to the data than the model of independence. While the two-class latent structure model fits the American data better than the Canadian data, in neither case do we observe an unequivocal excellent fit with the chi-square/degrees-of-freedom ratio approaching 1. Nevertheless, given the fairly good fit of the model to American data, one can with caution assert that a quasi-ideological politics of the body may be more or less characteristic of the general American population. In the case of Canada, there is considerably less evidence that the assertion holds.

Additional insight into the nature of the political arenas in the two countries can be gained by inspecting the table of conditional probabilities for the two models (Table 8.5). Those parameters represent the probability of a respondent in a given latent class being at a particular level or category of an observed variable. As noted above, they are analogous to factor loadings in factor analysis. There is, for example, a 0.86 probability that a respondent in latent class 1 of the analysis for CNES1984 is liberal on the gay rights issue. Being liberal on the gay rights issue is associated with a high loading on latent class 1. Inspection of the other conditional probabilities for CNES1984 shows that latent class 1 also includes those who tend to be conservative on capital punishment and pornography but liberal on abortion. Respondents in CNES1984 latent class 2 are conservative on gay rights, capital punishment, and pornography while liberal on abortion. Taken together, then, the results in Table 8.5 suggest that the Canadian population is seriously divided only on the gay rights issue. As far as abortion goes, there is a liberal tendency in both camps of a putative two-camp political arena where persons in both camps also tend to be conservative on capital punishment and pornography. Neither the fit of the two-class

Table 8.5
Conditional Probabilities Pertaining to Models H–2 in Table 8.4

VARIABLE	CATEGORY	CNES1984 LATENT CLASS		GSS1984 LATENT CLASS	
		1	2	1	2
GAYTEACH/	LIBERAL	0.86	0.01	0.88	0.27
HOMO. TECH	CONSERVATIVE	0.14	0.99	0.12	0.73
EXECUTIVE/	LIBERAL	0.38	0.13	0.24	0.26
EXECUTIVE?2	CONSERVATIVE	0.62	0.87	0.76	0.74
ABORTION/	LIBERAL	0.82	0.67	0.59	0.14
ABORTANY	CONSERVATIVE	0.18	0.33	0.41	0.86
CENSORSHIP/	LIBERAL	0.27	0.11	0.82	0.31
PORN.LAW?	CONSERVATIVE	0.73	0.89	0.18	0.69

model nor the pattern of conditional probabilities provides evidence favoring the hypothesis that a quasi-ideological politics of the body exists in Canada.

Turning now to the conditional probabilities in Table 8.5 for GSS1984, it can be seen that Americans in a hypothetical two-camp political arena are divided on gay rights, abortion, and pornography, with respondents in latent class 1 being liberal on those issues and respondents in latent class 2 taking conservative positions. Respondents in both latent classes 1 and 2, however, are conservative on the issue of capital punishment. Thus, with the exception of capital punishment, there is more division in the American population on a liberal-conservative body politics dimension than is the case in Canada. Regarding abortion, in particular, Americans divide into two camps, whereas Canadians as measured by the item in CNES1984 tend, on the whole, to be liberal on the issue.

CONCLUSION

The most general conclusion to be drawn from the preceding analysis is that Americans were divided more sharply and distinctly into two camps vis-à-vis body politics than were Canadians in 1984. While conservative overall on capital punishment—an issue that does not scale well with the other issues in the analysis—Americans in 1984 were divided in a consistent fashion on the issues of gay rights, abortion, and pornography. Canadians, on the other hand, were less polarized on those issues and overall tended to be conservative on capital punishment and censorship, liberal on abortion, and only divided on gay rights.

The analysis suggests, then, that in 1984 America had a greater capacity for a quasi-ideological politics of the body than Canada. That conclusion is consistent with both the visibility of so-called family values in the American political arena in recent years and arguments that have been made on historical and theoretical grounds that a politics of the body is much less likely to appear in Canada than in the United States (Simpson and Mac-Leod, 1985; Simpson, 1987).

NOTES

1. The 1984 Canadian National Election Study was funded by the Social Sciences and Humanities Research Council of Canada (SSHRCC) (microdiskette and codebook prepared and distributed by MicroCase Corporation, Bellevue, Wash.). The study investigators, SSHRCC, and MicroCase Corporation bear no responsibility for the analyses and interpretations presented here.

The 1984 General Social Survey was produced by the National Opinion Research Center, Chicago (tape distributed by the Roper Public Opinion Center, Storrs, Conn.; microdiskette and codebook prepared and distributed by MicroCase Corporation, Bellevue, Wash.).

2. The distributions reported in Tables 8.2 and 8.3 and the cross-tabulations that were analyzed to fit the models in Table 8.4 and estimate the parameters reported in Table 8.5 were computed by the MicroCase Analysis System (created and sold by MicroCase Corporation, Bellevue, Wash.; formerly Cognitive Development, Inc., Seattle).

The statistics and parameters reported in Tables 8.4 and 8.5 are output from the Categorical Data Analysis System (CDAS) (Eliason, 1988).

9 Attitudes toward Abortion and Capital Punishment: Prolife, Prochoice, Seamless Garment, and Inconsistency

Bradley R. Hertel

LINKING ABORTION AND CAPITAL PUNISHMENT

In an address at Fordham University in December 1983, Cardinal Joseph Bernadin outlined his "seamless garment" for a "consistent ethic of life" to include opposition to abortion, capital punishment, euthanasia, and the buildup of nuclear weapons. In later addresses on consistency in attitudes toward human life, Bernadin called attention to the need to alleviate suffering, particularly in the Third World but also at home, due to hunger, inadequate health care, and human rights violations (Bernadin, n.d.:3–8, 9–23). His call for concern for human life "from womb to tomb" has also been extended from present to future by applying the principle of seamless garment to environmental issues so as to preserve the potential for well-being of future generations. In emphasizing the importance of supporting all persons whose lives are threatened, Bernadin has said, "The church's social policy role is at least as important in *defining* key questions in the public debate as in *deciding* such questions" (ibid.:4). Clearly, he believes that to be genuinely prolife, one must show such concern in whatever context human lives are threatened. One who has that concern in some contexts but not in others, if "prolife," is inconsistent and has fallen short of the values with which he or she identifies.

Opponents of the seamless garment have countered with numerous arguments, including the impossibility of preserving *all* life, for example, in the case of a pregnant woman whose life is threatened by the pregnancy; and with a call for concern for quality of life, for example, in the case of a fetus expected to be deformed, in withholding life support systems for brain-dead patients, and by maintaining a nuclear arsenal to preserve peace. Former Nixon aide Charles Colson (1988:72) has argued that, if adopted as governmental policy, the seamless garment's rejection of nuclear weapons could undermine American military preparedness, which in turn could result in attack by our enemies, defeat for the United States, and slavery for American survivors. Advocates of the death penalty have contended that its net effect is to save lives by discouraging would-be wrongdoers from committing heinous acts.

These arguments underscore the complexity of the issues at hand and helped to determine the two courses followed in this chapter, both of which have to do with the meaning of concepts of fundamental importance to the abortion and related life issues debates: The first course is to consider the meaning of "inconsistent." Is there a logic applicable to assessing combinations of beliefs and values that enables theologians, governmental policymakers, social scientists, and the lay public to distinguish between a consistent set of stands and an inconsistent set? More specifically, are prolife supporters of the death penalty inconsistent for valuing the preservation of life in one context but not the other? Conversely, are prochoice opponents of the death penalty inconsistent? Second, this chapter seeks to determine through empirical analysis the demographic profiles and political identity of individuals holding various combinations of views on abortion and capital punishment. In this way, it will be possible to learn the relative size of each segment and to gain some idea of what makes each combination of positions make sense for the holders of those views.

Inconsistency—From Whose Perspective?

Is favoring capital punishment inconsistent with being prolife on abortion? This question is often asked, and has been the subject of recent research (Johnson and Tamney, 1988). In expressing dismay over the one-sidedness of the charge of inconsistency, Kelly (1987) asks, If being prochoice is a mark of political liberalism, are prochoice supporters of the death penalty—a conservative position—inconsistent? His point is well taken. Inconsistency is much more likely to be recognized by those who reject a given set of beliefs or values. Far from perceiving inconsistency, holders of a given set of so-called inconsistent values imply that for them those values are compatible.

In their analysis of national data on attitudes toward abortion and capital punishment, Johnson and Tamney (1988:45) concluded that what might appear to be inconsistent values probably reflect differences in salience of the several issues in which there is an apparent conflict.[1] Their conclusion has been reached by scholars researching inconsistency in other contexts, including the Thai Buddhist practice of wearing protective amulets despite their confidence in *kamma,* or the doctrine of works (Piker, 1972), and Mormons' willingness to shop on Sundays despite their high valuation of keeping the Sabbath (Donahue and Wood, 1985).

By using his "hierarchy of needs" as an analytical framework, Maslow (1969, 1971) is able to partially account for important differences in human behavior. Those who do not feel secure in terms of the fundamental need of safety are likely to spend much of their energy in pursuit of safety while those who are well beyond that need are likely to pursue higher needs and, ultimately, the more intellectual, creative goals of self-actualization. I believe that there also are innumerable—rather than one universal— "hierarchies of values" whereby, acting in accord with her or his values, each individual chooses what to think, say, and do in such a way as to avoid violating those values closest to the core of his or her being. What other observers may identify as inconsistency is probably explainable in terms of individuals' attempts to optimize support for the sum of their values, which often clash, especially in a modern pluralist society such as our own but, as past research has found, also in culturally more homogeneous societies.

Typically, one or more unstated assumptions needs to be made explicit for the conclusion that a set of values, beliefs, or practices is inconsistent to be more than an expression of the observer's dissonance. Take, for example, the perception that someone who identifies as prolife but favors capital punishment is inconsistent. This conclusion rests on at least two assumptions—that the observer and observed share more or less the same understanding of "prolife" and that the observed individual places greater value on being prolife than on being a supporter of capital punishment. If either or both of these assumptions do not hold, then the observed can hold the stated views without feeling dissonance.

To understand how a set of values are compatible for their holders, observers who view those values as incompatible must suspend their own worldview and logic and seek to understand the problem at hand from the perspective of those who hold what may seem inconsistent values. If researchers begin by assuming presence of a hierarchy of values and go on to identify and rank those values, the "inconsistency" that may have launched an inquiry is likely to be replaced by awareness of the consistency of the given views for those being observed. I believe that a hierarchy of values approach to studying attitudes and behavior is probably of very broad utility in making sense of apparent inconsistency in many contexts, including the life issues of the present study.

ABORTION AND CAPITAL PUNISHMENT IN THEORETICAL PERSPECTIVE

Let us consider support and opposition for abortion and capital punishment in order to arrive at expectations of the characteristics of holders of

Figure 9.1
Attitudes toward Abortion and Capital Punishment in Theoretical Perspective

Abortion

		Opposes	Favors
Capital Punishment	Opposes	Seamless garment	Political liberals
	Favors	Political conservatives	?

each combination of views. Support and opposition for abortion and capital punishment can be thought of in terms of the life issues typology of Figure 9.1. Those who oppose abortion *and* capital punishment are likely to hold other positions of advocates of the seamless garment. Accordingly, at this point as a hunch to help in hypothesis formulation, I think of such persons as likely to be "seamless garment" and, where possible, in Figure 9.1 offer summary labels based on my expectations for other of the combinations as well. The bases for these expectations are spelled out in greater detail in the hypothesis section that follows.

In terms of life-or-death concerns, the questions addressed in this chapter might at first appear to be limited to the right to live of fetuses and condemned convicts. However, pregnancy can threaten the life of women and, even in the absence of such threats, the availability or nonavailability of abortion for a woman wanting one has the potential to impact significantly on her life for many years. Thus, each of the four combinations of attitudes in Figure 9.1 pertains to three lives—the condemned convict, the fetus, and the pregnant woman.

Each of the four combinations of views represented in this figure is an expression of priority in concerns for at least one of these three lives and a lower priority for at least one. Those who are seamless garment advocates show concern for the condemned convict and the fetus over the right of the woman to control her body. Those who oppose abortion but favor capital punishment express concern for the fetus but not for the condemned individual and less concern for the pregnant woman than for the fetus; as explained below, these individuals are likely to be political conservatives. Prochoice opponents of capital punishment are concerned with the life of the convict and the pregnant woman but show lower concern for preserving the life of the fetus; these individuals are likely to be found to be political liberals. Finally, those who support both capital punishment and abortion rights could be viewed as consistently prodeath, but one would hardly expect to find them identifying with that label. Making sense of this combination of life values is one of the goals prompting the empirical analysis for this report.

Although issues of abortion and capital punishment are commonly debated in terms of abstract principles having to do with human life in general, when examined in terms of the individuals directly affected by the availability or nonavailability of these practices, these issues are found to have far greater direct impact on individuals from disadvantaged segments of society than on middle- and upper-class whites. When abortion is made more difficult in one state, it is typically women of color and/or women who are who poor and less educated who are unable to go out of state to obtain a safe and legal abortion. Application of the death penalty is concentrated in groups not defined solely by behavior. It is imposed almost exclusively on men, and—well beyond their proportion of the U.S. population—black men in particular. Of the 2,347 death row inmates in the United States in 1990, all but 30 were male and some 49 percent were nonwhite. Moreover, 60 percent of convicts executed between 1976 and 1990 were nonwhite and—as a further indication of the relevance of race to capital punishment in the United States—during this same period 84 percent of the victims of those executed were white (Worsnop, 1990:405; for still more recent figures confirming these patterns, see *Roanoke Times & World-News*, 1992, A6). Such findings have led some researchers to conclude that since the reinstatement of the death penalty in 1976, the death sentence has come to be more closely linked to race of victim than to race of defendant (Pasternoster, 1983; Gross and Mauro, 1984).

Through exposure to media coverage of these issues, discussions with friends, and reflection, many Americans have probably become aware of the relevance of race and social class to laws on abortion and capital punishment. Indeed, in a study of attitudes toward capital punishment, nearly half the supporters were found to believe that the death penalty is reserved for the poor and unfortunate (Ellsworth and Ross, 1983:153). My initial characterization and expectations concerning the holders of the various combinations of attitudes toward abortion and capital punishment rest on the assumption that many Americans are at least somewhat aware of the relevance of social class to the likelihood of being personally affected by the application of the death penalty or by laws restricting access to abortion.

Hypotheses

Seamless Garment. Owing to mothers continuing to be the chief care givers in American families,[2] I expect that married women will more often be sympathetic to preserving the life of those unable to fend for themselves and will more often than men or single women oppose both abortion and capital punishment.

Legal abortion has been seen by elites within the black community as a possible threat of genocide against blacks (Petchesky, 1990; cf. Cook, Jelen, and Wilcox, 1992:115). I believe that a similar argument can be made for capital punishment and therefore expect to find blacks more often than whites opposed to both abortion and capital punishment. I expect blacks to be pronatal in order to bolster their number and, in turn, their political power, and I expect them to oppose the ultimate sanction in order to preserve their numbers, minimize state violence toward minorities, and discourage any ripple effect whereby some members of society, responding to cues from state violence, might conclude that some offenses warrant a violent or even lethal response.

Supporters of capital punishment may contend that the latter fear is unjustified because, unlike a court-ordered execution, private acts of violence are not legal; thus, if most Americans are law-abiding, they will make the distinction between legal versus illegal taking of life and not regard the former as encouragement for the latter. However, grounds for such fears are evident in research that has shown increases in the murder rate in the state of New York during the month after an execution (Bowers and Pierce, 1980). It may well be that capital punishment does more to increase than discourage violence. Further, the distinction between legal versus illegal violence is likely to be lost for many blacks who, more so than whites, are aware that in earlier times, lynchings and other acts of violence were supported by the legal system through officials' participation and by their reluctance to enforce the law, and in more recent times, by numerous acts of police brutality, including beatings and deaths of blacks in the custody of white police officers, whose punishment is often no greater than dismissal from their jobs. The reality of black-on-black violence within the urban gang subculture can also be expected to lead blacks to oppose capital punishment, so as not to reinforce norms supporting killing as an acceptable act of retribution.

On the basis of research identifying two factions of opponents of abortion—those who oppose on the basis of the right to life and those who do so to voice their concern for sexual morality (Jelen, 1984)—I expect to find that opponents of abortion on the principle of right to life are better educated, disproportionately Catholic, and more regular in church attendance than those who oppose abortion for other reasons. Compared with prolife supporters of the death penalty, seamless garment proponents are also likely to be less rural, less southern, and less Republican.

Prolife Supporters of the Death Penalty Versus Prochoice Opponents of the Death Penalty. The two groups in this study who might be expected to be most dissimilar in ideology are the seamless garment advocates and those who do not support the preservation of either the fetus or the convict. However, I expect that the sharpest contrasts in social class and other demographics and political and religious identity will be found between prolife supporters of the death penalty and their opposites—the prochoice opponents of capital punishment.

By favoring preservation of the life of only the fetus or the condemned convict but not both—to borrow the term that Cook and her colleagues (1992) used for individuals who support abortion in some but not all circumstances—persons holding either combination of values could be considered "situationalists" of sorts, and they might have a good deal in common in their overall worldviews. However, I expect to find that those who favor abortion rights and oppose capital punishment are political liberals, whereas those who oppose abortion but favor the death penalty are likely to be political conservatives. Through their stands on both issues, prochoice opponents of capital punishment have expressed sympathy for individuals who are poor and minorities, whereas prolife supporters of the death penalty, in rejecting the seamless garment, have suggested that so far as life issues are concerned, their hierarchy of values is dominated by other than keen desire to preserve all life.[3] I hypothesize that these individuals are political conservatives who will show strong leanings toward the Republican party in contrast to prochoice opponents of the death penalty, who I expect will show the lowest support of the Republican party.

In addition to having the highest proportion of Republicans among all groups, prolife supporters of the death penalty, as political conservatives, are likely to be disproportionately white, male, rural, southern, and—as Jelen (1984) found of opponents of abortion on other than the right-to-life principle—less educated, disproportionately Protestant fundamentalists, and infrequent church attenders. I expect political liberals who favor abortion rights and oppose capital punishment to be the group most unlike the prolife supporters of capital punishment in all of these characteristics.

Prochoice Supporters of Capital Punishment. As a result of their holding the most common position on each life issue (see Table 9.1), prochoice supporters of the death penalty are by far the largest of the four groups. Their sheer size implies considerable diversity, which hinders attempts to anticipate defining characteristics of this broad segment of American society. If, however, their size is a basis to regard them as within "mainstream America," this group is likely to be found to be generally proestablishment and, as such, to be disproportionately male, nonsouthern, urban, rather well educated, and not to have large numbers who are Catholic or Protestant fundamentalist. This group's support of women but lack of sympathy for convicts is likely to result in some canceling out of liberal and conservative tendencies so that, while often Republican, they are likely to show less affinity to that party than prolife supporters of capital punishment.

Table 9.1
Attitude toward Capital Punishment, Suicide, and Abortion 1987–1991

| | Attitude toward Abortion | | | | | | | |
| | Whites (%) | | | | Blacks (%) | | | |
	Prolife	Middle	Prochoice	Total	Prolife	Middle	Prochoice	Total
Attitude toward Capital Punishment								
Oppose	5.8	5.0	9.1	19.9	16.1	15.2	17.7	49.0
Favor	17.0	25.7	37.4	80.1	15.1	14.6	21.3	51.0
Total	22.8	30.7	46.5	100.0	31.2	29.8	39.0	100.0
				(N=3,737)				(N=769)
Attitude toward Suicide if Incurable Disease								
Not Allow	18.1	14.6	9.5	42.2	23.5	19.8	15.0	58.3
Would Allow	5.7	16.0	36.1	57.8	1.6	11.2	28.9	41.7
Total	23.8	30.6	45.6	100.0	25.1	31.0	43.9	100.0
				(N=1,394)				(N=187)

Measurement

Prolife Versus Prochoice. In that my interest is in studying inconsistency of definite positions on capital punishment and abortion, I excluded those in the middle from most of the analyses. This was possible for attitudes on abortion but not for those on capital punishment, which the GSS has assessed in terms of support versus opposition rather than in terms of situations in which individuals either support or oppose that action.

Initially, I had planned on employing Cook and her colleagues' approach to defining prolife and prochoice by excluding all situationalists. In the end, however, I employed looser definitions of both prolife and prochoice. Factor analysis of GSS data for the six situations in which abortion is dealt with in that annual survey reveals two distinct sets of situations—extreme (mother's life, rape, defect) and nonextreme (single, economics, child not wanted);[4] see Hertel and Hughes (1987). That these are two quite different sets of issues is evident in the much higher levels of support for abortion under extreme circumstances (Davis and Smith, 1991:247–48). In that the vast majority of Americans approve of abortion in at least one of the extreme conditions, I reasoned that by prevailing norms, anyone who opposes abortion in even one of these conditions is prolife.[5] Similarly, I reasoned that strong tendency toward a given pole rather than purity of that expression should be the test as to whether an individual is to be regarded as prochoice. Accordingly, I have regarded as prochoice anyone who approves of abortion in at least two of three nonextreme circumstances.[6]

Analysis

The General Social Surveys have asked Americans their opinions on abortion since 1972 and capital punishment since 1974. The present report makes use of these data to look at trends in attitudes toward life issues through 1991. However, in order to focus primarily on current times and to have findings that facilitate comparison with Cook, Jelen, and Wilcox's (1992) study of attitudes toward abortion, I have utilized only data for 1987 through 1991 for most of the analysis in this report.

The statistical analyses in this report are of three kinds. When examining trends in attitudes toward abortion and capital punishment, I sought (1) unstandardized regression coefficients (or, "b") which indicate the average annual increase or decrease in proportion of Americans favoring a given position, say, prochoice. I also did (2) cross-tabulations to learn the relative size of each of six groups—the four of primary interest in this study plus supporters and opponents of the death penalty, who are neither clearly prolife nor clearly prochoice. I also used cross-tabular analysis to identify differences in the four categories of the life issues typology with respect to sex, marital status, education, work status, and place of residence. For the remaining analyses, I employed an analysis of variance (ANOVA) procedure known as (3) multiple classification analysis, or MCA, which produces means on ordinal or higher variables within categories of a nominal scale variable with and without controls for other variables (which are treated as nominal scale even if interval); for another application of MCA in the study of abortion values and other family issues, see Hertel and Hughes (1987).

MCA provides two summary measures, eta and beta,[7] which measure strength of association between one or more predictor variables—here, the typology for values on abortion and capital punishment—and a given dependent variable with controls (beta) and without (eta) for other possible influences. In light of the relevance of gender, marital status, and education to values on life issues, I have controlled for each of these factors. Combining gender and marital status into a single four-category variable (single men, married women, etc.) controls not only for the main effects but for any interaction effects of gender and marital status. The adjusted means indicate how the four groups would compare on a given dependent variable if those groups were to be alike in proportion of single men, married women, and so on for the other control variables and predictor variables.

Owing to the importance of the black church and to blacks' continued minority status in American society, rather than simply compare overall racial differences in support of each of the life issues, I have examined racial differences in the impact of all of the predictor variables' relationships with life issues. For some variables, blacks were too few to allow for meaningful analysis; findings are not reported if the available number of cases having complete data on dependent, independent, and control variables is less than 200.

Findings

Determining the relative size of groups of holders of each combination of attitudes on abortion, capital punishment, and suicide is a helpful step in considering the relationship between attitudes on these life issues (see Table 9.1). By the definitions employed in this study, prochoice is by far the largest group for whites, at nearly 50 percent, and the largest group for blacks as well but by a relatively small margin over prolife and those in the middle. In accord with hypothesized racial differences in life values, white support of capital punishment (80 percent) is far greater than black support (51 percent). Support for the race hypothesis is further evident in blacks' aligning with the seamless garment at a rate nearly three times as high as for whites (16 percent for blacks versus 5.8 percent for whites). Also supporting the race hypothesis, the political conservatives, that is, prolife supporters of the death penalty, are nearly twice as common among whites as among blacks (37.4 percent versus 21.3 percent).

It is interesting to note that despite significant differences in life values, whites and blacks show about 30 percent who are neither prolife nor prochoice. These holders of middling positions will receive little attention in the rest of this report because of the greater relevance of those who have definite leanings on both abortion and capital punishment to identifying and explaining consistency and inconsistency.

Compared with the broad support of capital punishment, support in the GSS samples for suicide—even in the case of someone with an incurable disease—is relatively low, at 58 percent among whites and 42 percent among blacks. Supporters of both suicide and abortion are more numerous than holders of any other combination of views on these two life issues; this is true for both blacks and whites. At 24 percent of blacks versus only 18 percent of whites favoring preservation of life under both circumstances, the findings for suicide support the prediction that blacks are more inclined than whites to endorse the seamless garment.

Table 9.1 shows the relative size of the segments of the American public holding each combination of attitudes on basic life issues and also reveals racial differences in the prevalence of those attitudes. However, the relationship of abortion values to each of the other life issues can be seen more clearly by comparing the prolife, prochoice, and "middlings" in terms of the proportions of each group that approve capital punishment and suicide. These findings are presented in Table 9.2.

Before considering these findings, I would like to call attention to an earlier report on abortion and capital punishment in which James Kelly (1987:154) noted that analysis of GSS data for 1982 by Ralph Lane revealed that only 45 percent of prolife individuals approved capital punishment compared with the much higher 73 percent approval within the total sample. In short, while far from universal in their rejection of capital punishment, compared with American society as a whole, those who were prolife were found to be much less supportive of the death penalty.

The present analysis for more recent times reveals similar patterns but with important qualifications. In the 1987 through 1991 GSS samples, for whites and blacks alike, abortion values are positively related to values on capital punishment as well as suicide. That is, those who oppose the taking of life in one situation tend to oppose the taking of life in each of the other situations. Like Kelly's report, these findings support the conclusion that, despite contrary popular images, Americans tend toward consistency on life issues. But this pattern is weak, at best. It is very clear-cut in the association between abortion and suicide (Pearson r's above .4 for both races), but the relationship between positions on abortion and capital punishment is very small at .045 for whites (statistically significant at the .001 level), and .054 for blacks (due to small sample, not significant even though

Table 9.2
Attitudes toward Capital Punishment and Suicide by Attitudes toward Abortion, 1987–1991

| | Attitude toward Abortion | | | | | |
| | Whites (%) | | | Blacks (%) | | |
	Prolife	Middle	Prochoice	Prolife	Middle	Prochoice
Attitude toward capital punishment						
Oppose	25.4	16.2	19.5	51.7	51.1	45.3
Favor	74.6	83.8	80.5	48.3	48.9	54.7
Total	100.0	100.0	100.0	100.0	100.0	100.0
	r = .045 sig. = .01			r = .054 sig.: N/S		
Attitude toward suicide if incurable disease						
Not Allow	93.6	63.8	34.1	76.1	47.8	20.9
Would Allow	6.4	36.2	65.9	23.9	52.2	29.1
Total	100.0	100.0	100.0	100.0	100.0	100.0
	r = .448 sig. = .001			r = .488 sig. .001		

larger than the r for whites). The low strength of association between attitudes toward abortion and those on capital punishment is underscored by
the fact that prochoice whites who are middling on abortion are slightly
more inclined to favor capital punishment than those who are prochoice,
while among blacks, the prolife are no more inclined to oppose the death
penalty than the middling on abortion. The much closer ties between attitudes toward abortion and suicide than those between abortion and capital punishment recalls the fact that the National Right to Life Committee
has taken official stands against both abortion and euthanasia but not
against capital punishment (Kelly, 1987:152).

The positive relationship between abortion values and attitudes toward
the death penalty and suicide is basis to conclude that Americans are *not*
generally inconsistent on life values. Even so, the popular image of widespread inconsistency is not without basis. Attitudes on abortion fail to
explain even 1 percent of the variance in attitudes on capital punishment
for either race. This is to say that knowledge of individuals' positions on
one of these two life issues is of nearly no utility in predicting positions on
the other. Clearly, both as individuals and as a formal institution, many
who identify with the cause of protecting human life do not extend their
concern to condemned convicts.

Before turning to further relationships among life issues attitudes, I
looked at trends in attitudes toward abortion, capital punishment, and
suicide of someone with an incurable disease; see Figures 9.2a and 9.2b.
Examining these trends is useful because of their relevance to making sense
of present relationships and to anticipating future relationships. For example, if there were to be continuous growth in support of the death penalty,
then that variable would eventually come to be more nearly a constant
and, in turn, the association between attitudes toward abortion and those
toward capital punishment would necessarily decline. For each year for
which data are available, Figure 9.2a shows the percentage of whites who
are prolife, middle, prochoice, in favor of capital punishment, and who
would allow suicide in the case of someone with an incurable disease.
Figure 9.2b does the same for blacks.

Among whites, the prolife grew an average of 0.20 percent per year
between 1972 and 1991, an increase that is significant at the .001 level.
The proportion who are in the middle on abortion grew by a somewhat
smaller amount, 0.15 percent per year, which was significant but only at
the .05 level. Growth in popularity of both of these positions implies comparable erosion in strength of the prochoice of 0.35 percent per year,
which was significant at the .001 level.

For blacks, there was a sizeable and significant decline of 0.66 percent
per year in the proportion who are prolife. Together, the increase in white
support of prolife and decrease in black support provide evidence of convergence and decline in the relevance of race to attitudes toward abortion.

Figure 9.2a
Trends in Attitudes toward Life Issues, 1972–1991 (Whites only)

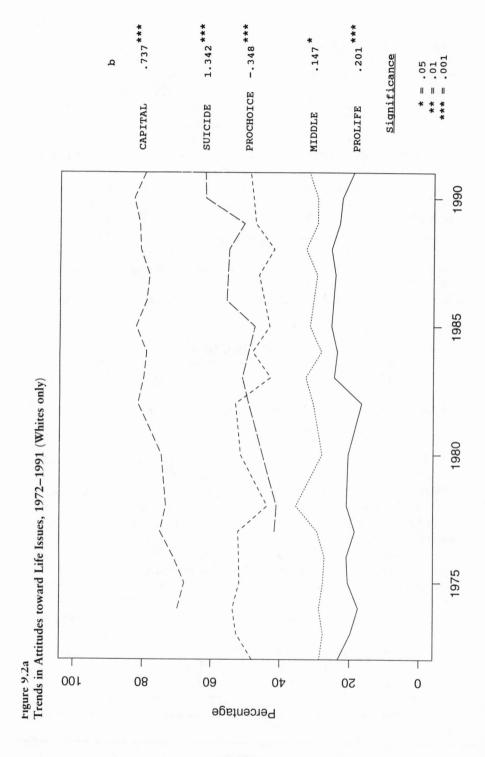

174

Figure 9.2b
Trends in Attitudes toward Life Issues, 1972–1991 (Blacks only)

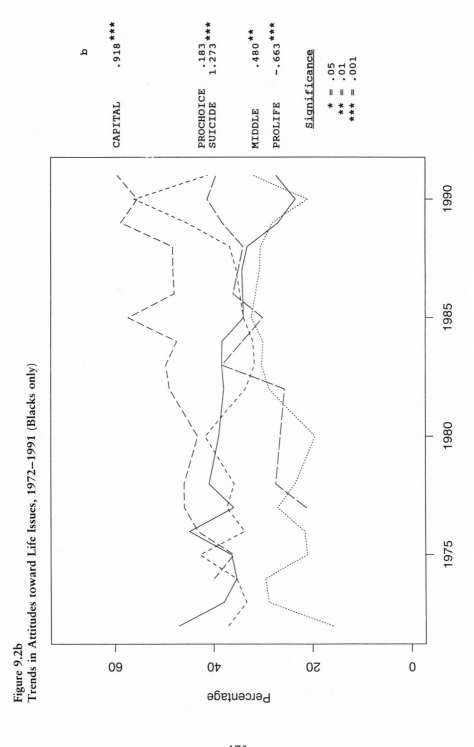

That race is coming to matter less in shaping life values is also evident in the 0.48 percent per year growth in support for middle views among blacks, which by 1991 resulted in black and white support for these positions being nearly the same. Finally, while white support of prochoice has declined, black support has gained slightly, further resulting in trends toward convergence of blacks and whites on attitudes toward abortion.

Considerable growth in support of capital punishment is evident for both whites (0.74 percent increase per year) and blacks (0.92 percent per year). Just as blacks and whites are converging in abortion attitudes through shifts in opposite directions, racial differences are also disappearing for attitudes toward the death penalty, due to the sharper rise in blacks' acceptance of capital punishment.

Support of suicide by those with an incurable disease is growing even more rapidly than support of the death penalty, by about 1.3 percent per year for both blacks and whites. Thus, even while prolife has grown among whites, within both races support for capital punishment and suicide has also increased. These opposing trends suggest that Americans regard these life issues as distinct from each other; only a small minority of Americans regard these issues as threads of a seamless garment.

Determining the gender, marital status, education, and other characteristics of each of the four categories of the life issues typology can help reveal how each of these combinations of values is cohesive for its holders. The sheer scope of the GSS data—which by 1991 included more than 600 items!—provides opportunity for a much more detailed profile of the ideological group of seamless garment advocates and the other groups in this study than can be dealt with in this chapter. Here, it is possible only to consider the demographic backgrounds of each group along with their political and religious identities.

Gender, Race, and Life Values. As shown in Table 9.3, compared with single whites, married whites of both sexes are decidedly more inclined to favor only the death penalty; as already noted, blacks are much more often seamless garment (23 percent of those individuals not holding middle positions on abortion) than are whites (8 percent). Both races show pluralities in favor of both abortion and the death penalty, but this preference is much more common for whites (54 percent) than for blacks (30 percent).

Single men show the greatest racial differences on life issues. Single black men are decidedly more in favor of protecting both the fetus and the convict than are white single men. Among persons holding other than middle positions on abortion, only 5 percent of single white men hold seamless garment views, versus more than 26 percent of single black men. Moreover, among holders of clear positions on abortion and capital punishment, 61 percent of single white men versus only 14 percent of single black men approve of both abortion and the death penalty.

For women of both races and white men, compared with their married counterparts, the single are more commonly in favor of abortion. Single black women show higher support of abortion than any other group of blacks (64 percent), but not as high as that of single white women (73 percent). The strongest support of abortion, however, is shown by single white men (78 percent). The exceptionally high support for only abortion among single black men—which at 35 percent is higher than that among single black women and twice as high as that among single white women—might at first seem surprising. However, along with the high support of seamless garment views by single black men, this finding underscores black single men's disapproval of the death penalty. The more general pattern of single people showing higher support of abortion can be explained by the greater relevance of abortion to single people.

Regional and Rural-Urban Effects. Whites raised in the South are much more often in favor of only the death penalty (33 percent) than those born outside the South (22 percent). Blacks show a similar effect of region on likelihood of approving of only capital punishment: 25 percent of southern-raised versus 17 percent of nonsouthern favor only the death penalty. By contrast, for both races, those favoring only abortion are disproportionately of nonsouthern roots. The hypothesized tie of southern origin to the seamless garment position is clearly present for blacks (29 percent of southern versus 16 percent of nonsouthern are seamless garment advocates) but only weakly, if at all, present for whites (10 percent versus 8 percent). In general, the findings for rural-urban differences in values on life issues are parallel to those for southern-nonsouthern differences and somewhat more pronounced. For example, compared with blacks raised in urban areas, rural blacks are much less likely to support both capital punishment and abortion (22 percent of rural versus 37 percent of urban, a difference of 15 percent), whereas the southern-nonsouthern difference in support of both is not as large (28 percent versus 33 percent).

Education. Compared with better-educated persons, less educated persons are much more likely to favor the seamless garment position (31 percent of blacks and 16 percent of whites with less than high school education versus much lower figures for more educated persons). For both races, education is also strongly inversely related to the likelihood of favoring capital punishment and opposing abortion. For both races, support of abortion is strongly linked with high education levels. Support for the combination of capital punishment and abortion is appreciably more common among persons who have completed or gone beyond high school. Support for only abortion is especially likely among those who have completed college. Ties between education and life issues suggest two camps of supporters of abortion—well-educated civil libertarians who oppose capital punishment, and less highly educated proestablishment individuals who, in reflecting society's dominant norms, support capital punishment.

Employment. The impact of employment on life issues differs categori-

Table 9.3

Attitudes toward Abortion and Capital Punishment—Demographics, 1978–1991

A. Whites

	Seamless Garment	For CAPPUN only	For ABORT only	For both	N
All Whites	8.4	24.5	13.1	54.0	2591
Single men	4.9	17.0	17.2	60.9	430
Married men	5.3	27.9	9.7	57.1	753
Single women	10.4	16.5	18.0	55.2	473
Married women	11.4	29.4	11.4	47.7	935
Raised in south	9.9	32.6	8.5	49.1	639
Raised elsewhere	7.9	21.9	14.6	55.6	1952
Raised rural	10.0	29.2	11.1	49.6	1527
Raised elsewhere	6.0	17.8	15.9	60.2	1060
B.A. or higher	6.3	16.2	23.1	54.4	671
High School completed	7.2	24.6	10.8	57.4	1478
Less than High School	15.5	37.2	5.5	41.8	433
Men					
Full-time	4.6	23.8	10.9	60.7	782
Part-time	3.1	28.1	20.8	47.9	96
Not working	7.0	18.8	21.1	53.1	128
Women					
Full-time	8.7	18.5	15.8	57.0	584
Part-time	11.4	27.7	14.9	46.0	202
Not working	12.1	32.4	11.2	44.4	448
Republican	36.3	55.5	22.6	48.3	2582
					.2
					.0
Catholic	13.5	26.3	10.3	49.9	696
Protestant Fundamentalist	18.4	48.7	6.3	26.6	158
Attends at least weekly	55.2	53.6	12.4	14.4	2562
				Beta[1]	.4
				Significance	.C

178

B. Blacks (1987-91)

	Seamless Garment	For CAPPUN only	For ABORT only	For both	N
All Blacks	23.0	21.5	25.2	30.4	540
Single men	26.5	23.9	35.4	14.2	113
Married men	27.2	19.6	14.1	39.1	92
Single women	15.5	20.1	27.8	36.6	194
Married women	27.7	22.7	20.6	29.1	141
Raised in South	28.7	25.4	17.8	28.1	303
Raised elsewhere	15.6	16.5	34.6	33.3	237
Raised in rural places	29.4	27.0	21.8	21.8	252
Raised elsewhere	17.5	16.8	28.3	37.4	286
B.A. or higher	22.4	8.2	34.7	34.7	49
H.S. completed	18.4	17.5	27.3	36.8	315
Less than H.S.	31.2	32.9	19.1	16.8	173
Men					
Full-time	23.5	24.3	22.6	29.6	115
Part-time	20.0	25.0	40.0	15.0	20
Not working	28.9	13.2	31.6	26.3	38
Women					
Full-time	12.8	42.9	24.2	45.0	149
Part-time	26.5	1.6	44.1	26.5	34
Not working	25.2	55.6	22.0	25.2	127
Republican	10.0	9.6	13.2	10.8	537
				Beta	.04
				Significance	n.s.
Attends at least weekly	40.9	37.1	24.4	16.2	534
					.22
					.001

[1]This beta is a measure of nonlinear association with a range of 0 to 1.00. Whereas the related eta (not reported) measures zero-order relationships, beta measures association between an ordinal or interval scale variable and a nominal scale variable when one or more control variables are included in the analysis. Here, the controls are for sex, marital status, and education. For further discussion of this measure, see SPSS Inc. (1986: 461–62).

cally for men and women. For white men and women the unemployed are most in favor of the seamless garment position, and full-time workers are least in support of that position. This finding indicates that work encourages support for abortion or capital punishment or both. (Unfortunately, the number of cases of blacks is too low for several work categories of men and for part-time employed women, so it is not possible from these findings to draw clear conclusions for blacks.) Further inspection of the findings for whites reveals marked gender differences in relevance of work to life values: Employment bears on women's attitudes toward abortion and on men's attitudes toward capital punishment: Adding the percentages in columns 3 and 4, one finds that women's support of abortion increases with level of participation in the work force, but for men there is no clear pattern. Similarly, by adding the figures in columns 2 and 4 showing support for capital punishment, one finds that for men support of the death penalty increases with level of involvement in the work force, while for women there is no clear pattern.

It is interesting that for both men and women employment bears only on one but not the other life issue. Employment heightens women's consciousness and concern for women's rights in general. Working women's support of abortion can be explained in terms of the adverse impact of an unwanted pregnancy on opportunities to secure and retain jobs. Employed men's greater support for the death penalty may be due in part to poor and unemployed people having somewhat greater fear of themselves being the victims of this practice. A more plausible explanation is that the unemployed are more able to empathize with individuals even more disadvantaged than themselves, while full-time employed men may be more inclined to view harsh punishment as needed for maintaining order in society.

In the analysis reported thus far from Table 9.3, values on life issues have been treated as dependent on sex, marital status, education, and so on. This assumption was also made for the relationship between religious identity and life issues. Consequently, for these variables, the figures in each row sum to 100 percent. However, political identity and church attendance, both declining in the United States, are treated as more influenced by life issues than vice versa. This inversion led to the use of multiple classification analysis for these two variables. When addressing the question, "Controlling for sex, marital status, and education, what percent of seamless garments, conservatives, liberals, and establishments are Republican?" (rather than vice versa), row totals do not sum to 100 percent.

Political Identity. Supporters of capital punishment but not abortion were hypothesized to be political conservatives, with a high proportion of Republicans. Supporters of abortion who do not approve of the death penalty were expected to be liberals. These expectations are supported for whites. Whites who support only abortion showed by far the lowest identity with the Republican party (23 percent), while those who support only capital punishment had the highest identity with that party (56 percent).

At the outset, there was reason to expect that the seamless garment advocates would lean toward the Republican party, being more influenced in choice of political party by their conservative attitude toward abortion— an issue that has generated much more public debate and media coverage than capital punishment—than by their liberal attitude toward capital punishment. Also, I expected a relatively high proportion of supporters of both to identify as Republican because, as supporters of the dominant values on both issues, these individuals can be thought of as within the mainstream of American society and, as such, inclined to align with the party that stands for preserving the status quo. At 48 percent Republican, the "establishment" individuals conformed to my expectation. However, with a much lower proportion Republican (36 percent), the seamless garment advocates did not. Instead, despite the greater salience of the abortion issue, the seamless garment proponents were relatively liberal, being much closer in political affiliation to supporters of abortion only than to supporters of capital punishment only.

The unexpectedly low support of the Republican party among seamless garment advocates can be explained in a number of ways. It is likely that, despite fundamental differences in expression of such concern, both seamless garment advocates and liberals share a strong concern for others' well-being and share other basic values as well as political identity. Alternatively, having based their opposition to abortion on the principle of right to life, seamless garment advocates may have felt little inclination to identify with a party that in recent decades has been mired in the scandals of Watergate and Irangate, the savings and loan debacle, tax policies designed to favor the wealthy and punish the poor, and unwillingness to enforce civil rights legislation.

Among blacks, the Republican party has little appeal, and political identity does not appear to be related to values on life issues. All four groups in the life issues typology are within several points of being 10 percent Republican.

Religion. It has long been established that, compared with individuals of other religious identities, Catholics and Protestant fundamentalists are prolife,[8] with Catholics more than Protestants opposing abortion on the principle of right to life (Jelen, 1984). Among whites, both of these religious bodies were considerably more likely than whites in general to be seamless garment advocates (14 percent of Catholics and 18 percent of Protestant fundamentalists). This finding might be viewed as inconsistent with Jelen's findings, but such is not the case. As a proportion of all their members who oppose abortion, a higher proportion of Protestant fundamentalists than Catholics support capital punishment (72 percent versus

66 percent). While providing continuity with earlier research on religion and abortion, these findings provide fresh fuel for critics of the label prolife. The overwhelming support of the death penalty even among the "prolife" members of two denominations that have been at the forefront of the movement underscores the limited context to which that term applies. This is not to suggest that the prolife are hypocrites, but only that the values of many differ significantly from those implied by the label with which they identify.

For both whites and blacks, church attendance is related to abortion attitudes—opponents are far more likely to attend, especially among whites—but not to attitudes toward capital punishment. The pattern for abortion is a familiar one. That church attendance does not appear to be associated with low levels of support of the death penalty raises questions on what is being delivered from the pulpit on the Old Testament's "Thou shalt not kill" and the New Testament's "Love thy neighbor." The hypothesized low attendance among conservatives was not observed. More research is needed on a larger number of denominations and on attendance within those denominations to more fully understand the bearing of religion on combinations of life values.

CONCLUSIONS

Two concerns guided this study: (1) to consider the meaning of "inconsistency," an undertaking that led me to suggest that the inconsistents are probably consistent in terms of their own hierarchy of values, and (2) to learn through empirical analysis some of the important demographic and ideological characteristics of supporters and opponents of abortion and the death penalty, in order to arrive at tentative conclusions on how each combination of positions on those life issues is consistent for its holders.

In terms of the earlier research on inconsistency discussed and still other past and present research findings that could not be presented in this brief report, I am persuaded that the assumption of a hierarchy of values is a much more fruitful starting point than inconsistency per se for understanding combinations of values and/or behavior that may not appear coherent in terms of principles with which those studied identify, or in terms of the researcher's worldview or society's norms. By learning more about those who hold what may seem to be conflicting values, scholars can ordinarily expect to find consistency emerge to account for what was initially seen as inconsistency. In the present case, given their characteristics spelled out in detail, those who support only capital punishment can be characterized as political conservatives, those who support only abortion are political liberals, and opponents of abortion and capital punishment can be characterized as seamless garment advocates.

Those who support both capital punishment and abortion were most difficult to characterize at the outset but were found to be identifiable, as any of the other groups. They are disproportionately male, married, nonsouthern, urban, rather well educated, employed full-time, and Republican. In short, they are mainstream American society, or "establishment," and more than any other group, they embrace and define dominant norms. The rather high proportion of white Catholics and low frequency of church attendance among supporters of both abortion and capital punishment do not appear to fit well with an image of this group as "establishment"; additional research is needed to learn more about the religious and ideological leanings of each of the four groups in the life issues typology.

NOTES

The author wishes to thank Barbara Townley for typing the manuscript and tables and Donggeon Kim and Ruan Hoe for preparing the figures.

1. Johnson and Tamney (1988) confined their attention to attitudes toward capital punishment of prolife Americans; they did not study prochoice Americans. They did not identify the characteristics of either the advocates or the opponents of capital punishment among prochoice individuals. By comparing the characteristics of prolife and prochoice supporters and opponents of the death penalty, the present study provides more opportunity to understand the nature of relationship between these two life issues.

2. See Nock and Kingston (1988) for a detailed report that shows that American married women's increased involvement in the work force has resulted in increased parenting by fathers but that, in terms of time spent and levels of responsibility assumed, mothers continue to be far more active in parenting than fathers.

3. Prolife supporters of capital punishment commonly contend that they are for preservation of life in general but that (1) through heinous wrongdoing, the condemned criminal has forfeited his right to life, in marked contrast to the fetus, who is innocent of any wrongdoing, and (2) by serving to deter other would-be murderers, capital punishment saves lives in the long run.

4. Cook, Jelen, and Wilcox (1992:33), noting this same division in the GSS data on abortion, refer to extreme and nonextreme circumstances as "traumatic" and "elective."

5. Regarding as prolife only those who oppose abortion under all circumstances could exclude many people who identify as and are seen by others as prolife. Further, to confine that concept to those who oppose abortion under all circumstances would designate as prolife those who oppose abortion even when the mother's life is threatened; this is a criterion of debatable relevance to a literal prolife position.

6. Also excluded from the analysis are 268 individuals who, by the criteria mentioned, are both prolife (oppose abortion under at least one extreme circumstance) and prochoice (approve abortion under at least two nonextreme circumstances). As such, these individuals, who comprised only about 1 percent of the combined GSS samples, are more relevant to a methodological study of measurement of ambiguous response patterns than to a substantive study of inconsistency.

7. This beta is not the much more common beta used to assess change in an

ordinal and higher dependent variable associated with increase in an ordinal or higher predictor variable. Instead, the beta in Table 9.3 is a measure of association between a dichotomous or nominal scale independent variable in analysis that includes one or more control variables that may be nominal, ordinal, or interval scale but are treated as though nominal scale. For more discussion of this beta and its associated measure eta for assessing zero-order relationship, see SPSS Inc. (1986:461–62).

8. See Hertel and Hughes (1987) for discussion of Protestant fundamentalists and a list of denominations defined as Protestant fundamentalist.

10 Conclusion: The Future of the Abortion Debate

Ted G. Jelen

This volume has dealt with a number of different aspects of public debate about abortion in the North American democracies of Canada and the United States. Because of the highly volatile, emotional nature of the issue, abortion is often considered by some as typical of the type of controversy that democracies do not handle particularly well. Given the fact that abortion seems to embody a number of basic values, such as religion, sexuality, gender roles, and the value of life itself (see Staggenborg, 1987), it seems difficult to imagine how the abortion issue can be debated or resolved with respect for the values of democratic civility. The abortion debate has witnessed a great deal of unconventional and even illegal political activity. While most militant direct action has been performed by prolife activists (who are, so far, the losing side in the United States and Canada), it remains the case that activists on both sides of the abortion debate consistently disparage the values and the motives of their opponents (Luker, 1984).

While a precise definition of "civility" is difficult, the concept would seem to include, at a minimum, the following: a respect for the procedures of liberal democracy, a respect for the worthiness and motives of those with whom one disagrees, a tolerance for opposing viewpoints, a willingness to seek common ground, and (perhaps especially) a willingness to accept an unfavorable outcome if such results from a process to which one has attached legitimacy (see Shils, 1992). In other words, civility would seem to require that a citizen value membership in the political community that she inhabits more than the outcome of a particular controversy. To take a simple example, we expect the losing side in an election to accept the outcome with good grace (while continuing to organize for the next electoral opportunity) and to refrain from using fraud or violence to obtain a more desirable result. Obviously, being such a "good sport" is much easier if ultimate values are not at stake. The fact that some participants in the abortion debate do not seem able to conduct themselves with such civility suggests that the values involved are so basic and so important that adverse outcomes are not considered tolerable.

Is it the case, then, that the abortion issue will continue to be so divisive as to threaten the fabric of democratic citizenship? Is abortion an issue so emotional and so basic that compromise and acceptance of outcomes that are less than optimal will result in illegal and even violent political activity? It is to the relationship between the abortion debate and democratic civility that this concluding essay is devoted.

PROSPECTS FOR UNCIVIL POLITICS

For many observers, the murder of Dr. David Gunn in March of 1993 offered the strong probability of continuing violence against providers of abortion (See Gray, 1993; Lacayo, 1993; Salholz et al., 1993). Indeed, when considered along with earlier antiabortion violence in Pensacola (Blanchard and Prewitt, 1993), it seems entirely possible that "prolife" politics will likely contain elements of unconventional, illegal, and perhaps violent activity in the immediate future. Abortion may be an issue in which democratic civility is difficult to attain, since it constitutes an area in which a number of highly central values are at stake (Staggenborg, 1987).

Among the more important values at stake in the abortion controversy are religious beliefs. As Blanchard and Prewitt (1993) point out in their summary of activists who have been convicted of violent prolife activity, most such persons have claimed to be animated by religious zeal. While I remain skeptical of their claim that a propensity to violence is an intrinsic characteristic of fundamentalism (Jelen, 1994), it cannot be gainsaid that many people who engage in unconventional prolife activity believe themselves to be acting upon "God's will." Religious beliefs are often thought to be nonnegotiable and not subject to compromise (see Wald, 1989). Religion is based on divine revelation, which is often taken to be infallible. In a conflict between absolute truth and error, it is difficult to see why error should be accorded any deference. In the case of the abortion issue, either the fetus is human (in which case a murder is being committed by the act of abortion), or it is not. It is difficult for some to discern a middle ground within which a compromise on abortion can be reached.

Moreover, the incivility which might be occasioned by religious fervor might be exacerbated in the United States and Canada by the pervasiveness of the concept of rights. According to Mary Ann Glendon (1991), in Anglo-American political cultures, rights are often regarded as nonnegotiable prerogatives, which serve to inhibit rather than enhance political discussion. The assertion of a right involves a claim of individual sovereignty within which the autonomous individual need not answer to anyone (Goldwin, 1992). "Rights talk" essentially denies the legitimacy of opposing viewpoints. For example, the assertion of a right to free speech is thought to exempt the person claiming such a right from the need to defend herself from arguments that the speech in question is foolish, harmful, or pernicious. To the extent that the abortion controversy is couched in the language of rights, compromise is difficult, since the assertion of a right is (literally) an excuse for engaging one's opponents in arguments.

In the United States, both sides of the abortion controversy employ the language of rights (Cook, Jelen, and Wilcox, 1992). A presumed right to life on the part of the fetus is contrasted with a right to choose on the part of the pregnant woman. Each side of the controversy regards the right it asserts as paramount. Thus, since a right to life on the part of some (presumed) living being would trump any countervailing right the woman might have (save the right to self-defense), opponents of legal abortion may believe that they need not consider the possible reasons a woman might have for wishing to terminate her pregnancy. (For contrary arguments, see Thompson, 1971, and McDonagh, 1993). Conversely, the assertion of a right to choose implies that any reason a woman may have for choosing abortion is sufficient and is a private matter for which she need not account. From the standpoint of someone asserting that access to legal abortion is a right, it is not a legitimate part of public discourse to distinguish between sufficient and insufficient reasons for terminating a pregnancy. Even to make such arguments is to impose a public, political character on what is regarded as an essentially private action.

To the extent that the abortion controversy is described as a clash of competing rights (see Tribe, 1990), abortion proponents and opponents have little incentive to engage in constructive dialogue. Indeed, as conducted at the activist level in the United States, the abortion debate consists of spokespersons offering caricatures of their opponents' positions. To compare legal abortion to the Nazi Holocaust, or to compare restricting abortion to slavery, is to employ rhetorical strategies that are designed to anger and mobilize rather than persuade (Cook, Jelen, and Wilcox, 1992). Activists within the abortion debate are likely to denigrate the motives of their opponents rather than to address their arguments (Luker, 1984). Moreover, the successful assertion of a right is often to deny the legitimacy of the values of those on the losing side (Glendon, 1987; Calebresi, 1985). For example, the majority opinion in *Roe v. Wade* permitted some regulation of abortion based on when in the pregnancy an abortion was contemplated but allowed no regulation based on why a woman might wish to terminate her pregnancy. Since most Americans would like to make precisely the latter sort of distinction (see Cook, Jelen, and Wilcox, 1992), a Court decision such as *Roe* would seem to exclude widely held values from even being considered in public debate. To the extent that people with moral reservations about abortion come to feel that their values are accorded no weight in public policy, they may feel justified in resorting to extralegal activity to promote their values. It is, perhaps, one thing to lose a public debate, and quite another to be told that one's participation is unwelcome or irrelevant.

According to Glendon (1987), the notion that the ability to obtain an abortion is a right is more or less unique to the United States. In most other Western countries, abortion is available under varying circumstances, but is always subject to regulation by government. In other words, legal abortion may be a matter of public policy, but is not generally considered to be a (nonnegotiable, inalienable?) *right*. In most of the Western world—with the possible exception of Germany (*Chicago Tribune*, 1993)—abortion policy is made by legislatures rather than by courts. Legislatures are thought to be more responsive to public opinion and are permitted to fashion compromises not available to courts. However, some observers have suggested that the "rights culture" that characterizes the United States has crept over the border into Canada. The decision of the Canadian Supreme Court in *Morgentaler v. Regina* suggested to some that the 1982 Canadian Charter of Rights and Freedoms had ushered in a substitution of American-style judicial review for Canada's tradition of parliamentary supremacy. (For a superb account of the *Morgentaler* decision as well as an analysis of the possible effects of the Charter on the Canadian legal culture, see Morton, 1992.) To the extent that the abortion issue in Canada is contested in courts rather than popularly elected branches of government, the possibility exists that the incivility that characterizes the behavior of some U.S. prolife activists might extend to Canada as well.

Further, it is possible that some election outcomes might exacerbate the tendency of prolife activists to engage in extralegal activity. As this is being written, newly elected President Bill Clinton (a prochoice Democrat) has appointed Ruth Bader-Ginsberg successor to Supreme Court Justice Byron White (a dissenter in *Roe*). For the first time in over a decade, abortion opponents lack the symbolic support of the president of the United States. Moreover, the fact that the core abortion right in *Roe* has recently been upheld in *Planned Parenthood of Southeastern Pennsylvania v. Casey* (with the support of Reagan appointee Sandra Day O'Connor and Bush appointee David Souter) suggests the possibility that prolife activists may find little support among any of the three branches of the federal government. To the more militant proponents of direct action, illegal activity may seem the only alternative to acquiescence (see Gray, 1993).

Thus, the combination of religious zeal and the pervasiveness of "rights" in North America suggest that abortion politics may continue to be characterized by obstinance, civil disobedience, and perhaps physical violence. In one form, religion may provide the moral certitude necessary to defy the law, while the culture of rights may render compromise on the abortion issue extremely problematic. While it must be admitted that most prolife activists do not engage in illegal activity, it may not take many participants in such lawbreaking to change the climate in which abortion is discussed. Many prolife activists, while not willing to engage in violent activities on their own, nonetheless seem willing to offer tacit support to their colleagues who engage in direct action (Gray, 1993; Salholz et al., 1993). To the extent that the destruction of property and physical intimidation replace compromise, bargaining, and negotiation, the abortion issue threatens to alter the character of North American politics.

PROSPECTS FOR CIVIL POLITICS

However, the possibility that abortion politics will increasingly become uncivil politics is not inevitable. Other characteristics of the issue suggest that the abortion issue may not be all that unusual in democratic political systems. The controversy may ultimately lend itself to compromise, and the abortion issue may eventually no longer occupy center stage in Canadian or United States politics.

Most people in both North American nations are neither consistently prolife nor consistently prochoice. In the United States, for example, a large majority of the population favors legal abortion in at least some circumstances. Conversely, many people who hold very permissive attitudes toward legal abortion favor restrictions on access to abortion, such as waiting periods, parental notification, and so forth (Cook, Jelen, and Wilcox, 1992). Similarly, in Chapter 7 of this volume, it was shown that an intermediate stance on abortion was the modal position in Canada as well. It seems clear that most citizens of the United States and Canada value *both* the potential life of the fetus and the personal autonomy of women. There would thus seem to exist substantial public support for compromises on the abortion issue.

Further, it does seem clear that the possibility for legislative action may exist in both countries, placing the abortion issue on the agenda of the branch of government with the strongest incentive to find an intermediate policy. In Canada, of course, Parliament does have the power to override acts of the Canadian Supreme Court. While the *Morgentaler* decision posed the possibility of American-style judicial review, the decision remains binding primarily because of the failure of the Canadian Senate to pass compromise legislation (Wallace, 1991). Similarly, the U.S. Supreme Court, while quite explicit on the fact that abortion remains a constitutionally derived right, has nevertheless begun to permit state governments greater latitude in regulating the practice of abortion. In the cases of *Web-*

ster v. Missouri Reproductive Services and *Planned Parenthood of South-eastern Pennsylvania v. Casey,* the Court has upheld provisions such as requiring testing for fetal viability, parental notification, and waiting periods for women seeking to terminate pregnancies. Some of these restrictions seem likely to limit access to abortion, while others seem to promise benefits that are primarily symbolic. However, it might well be argued that symbols are important in making unconventional political activity less attractive.

An example might make this last point more clearly. In *Casey,* the Court upheld a Pennsylvania provision that would prohibit abortion for purposes of sex selection. It seems unlikely that such a law will be particularly effective in reducing the number of abortions actually performed. One might question the frequency of abortion for sex selection, since such a practice is likely to be quite unusual in the United States. Moreover, a woman who sought to abort to select the sex of her next child could simply lie once she learned that such grounds for abortion were impermissible. Does this mean that the Pennsylvania law is meaningless? Not at all, since such legislation allows for the expression of the moral sentiments of at least some members of the political community. The Pennsylvania state legislature is allowed to express publicly the idea that, in its view, abortion is a serious matter, with profound moral implications. The sex selection statute conveys the message that abortion should not be considered for selfish or frivolous reasons (Cook, Jelen, and Wilcox, 1992).

Thus the possibility exists that prolife activists may be able to make some limited progress through the channels of normal politics in both the United States and Canada. To the extent that the abortion issue is debated in legislatures rather than in courts, the possibility exists that a compromise might be reached on the issue. Unlike courts, legislatures are not normally charged with choosing winners and losers in disputes over rights, but are more likely to attempt to make policies acceptable to a broad spectrum of public opinion. Studies of public opinion in both countries suggest that the modal position on the issue may be "legal, but . . ." There is general support for access to legal abortion but considerable uneasiness about its frequency and (apparently) easy availability. As an empirical matter, there is support for debating the appropriateness of various restrictions, as is generally the case in Western Europe (see Glendon, 1987; Jelen, O'Donnell, and Wilcox, 1993). The possibility of such a debate may make extralegal direct action less attractive to prolife activists.

It should be noted that the possible compromise to which I have been alluding would likely not satisfy activists on either side of the issue, and would require the modification of "rights talk" on both sides. Those who regard abortion as murder would be forced to concede that some "murders" are less heinous than others. Conversely, those who believe abortion to be an application of a more general right to privacy would be required to admit that there does exist a public, communal aspect to the private nature of sexuality and pregnancy. To people who believe either in an absolute right to life or an absolute right to choose, any compromise on the abortion issue is likely to be unacceptable. This is simply to suggest that if the culture of rights contributes to the incivility of the abortion debate, there may exist a trade-off between the rights in question and appropriate styles of political discourse.

This, in turn, brings us to the final variable in any discussion of abortion politics: the role of religion. It has been shown that participants in direct prolife action are animated by religious fervor. However, it is not the case that religion inevitably leads to political incivility. In his insightful work *The Political Meaning of Christianity: An Interpretation* (1989), Glenn Tinder has argued that tolerance, humility, and respect for opposing viewpoints is authentically Christian as well as authentically democratic. For Tinder, the core propositions of Christianity are twofold: First, humans are inherently corrupt, due to the fall in the Garden of Eden. Second, Christ's substitutive atonement holds out the possibility for the redemption of beings with such fallen natures. The fallen, corrupt nature of humankind suggests that the judgment of humans is fallible and that the world may be constructed so as to preclude solutions that are unambiguously morally correct.

The fact of our fallible capacity for judgment, according to Tinder (1989), proscribes the very moral certainty required to engage in illegal activity. Discerning the message of the Scriptures is a complex, difficult task, for which corrupt, fallen humans are poorly equipped. The fact that the core text of the Bible—the Gospels—is cast in narrative form suggests that understanding the Gospel message is an ongoing process. Attempts to translate a divinely inspired text into propositional form inevitably introduce human error. Thus, even if we take the Scriptures themselves to be inerrant (a controversial proposition in itself), the task of finding particular prescriptions or proscriptions in the Bible alloys the divine with the fallibility of the carnal mind. Thus, if we try to show that the Bible prohibits abortion (for discussions of problems with the biblical case against abortion, see Cook, Jelen, and Wilcox, 1992, and Jelen, 1993), we risk substituting our human judgments for those that are taken to be divinely inspired.

Moreover, the one sin that would seem to be consistently condemned in the Bible is the sin of pride. The fall of Adam and Eve in Eden is ultimately based on the human desire to supplant and perhaps to replace God ("ye shall be as gods"). In the New Testament, Jesus consistently reserves his strongest condemnation for the Pharisees, who have attempted to codify past divine revelations. For one human to condemn the acts of another according to an imputed "will of God" is to commit an error of fundamental importance.

This is not to say that Christians are not to resist evil and injustice. However, Tinder argues that our fallen nature renders our capacity to do so extremely limited. We are called upon to resist particular injustices, and are required to do so by our standing as redeemable beings created in God's image. However, for Christians to resist injustice in a systematic way is to commit the sin of pride. Indeed, Tinder suggests that the most monstrous evils perpetrated by humans (Nazism, Stalinism, etc.) are precisely the results of systematic, global attempts to impose human solutions on the problems of a corrupt humankind. A humble, limited approach to combating evil is more consistent with our limitations as fallen creatures.

As fundamentally flawed beings, we have also (according to Tinder) constructed a world in which dilemmas (understood as necessary choices between bad alternatives) are quite common. Frequently, corrupt beings such as ourselves impose structures and alternatives in which people are forced to choose "the lesser of two evils." Tinder argues that such situations are necessary consequences of the fall. Part of the condition of sin is that a world comprised of sinful beings may not offer clear choices between right and wrong in particular instances. As much as certain fundamentalists may deplore "situational morality," such ambiguous moral choices seem to be an unavoidable feature of the world most of us inhabit. Thus, empirical studies that show that many people agree that "abortion is murder" *and* that "abortion is sometimes the best course" (Cook, Jelen, and Wilcox, 1992:154) may not indicate cognitive inconsistency but may simply show that people are familiar with situations in which no satisfactory alternative is available.

Thus there is a sense in which an authentic, and authentically conservative, Christianity may be able to accommodate relatively permissive policies on life-style issues such as abortion, or at least to permit devout believers to engage in political discourse on the issue. Tinder's elegant account of a humble, prophetic religious politics may ultimately boil down to a warning against passing judgment on the behavior of others. According to Tinder, Christianity poses the believer with both aspirations toward morality and limitations against imposing such morality on others. Christianity thus provides the basis for making judgments and reasons for tempering these judgments. To the extent that religious leaders emphasize the tentative, limited, and necessarily flawed character of human endeavor (see Jelen, 1992, 1993), religion could, in some sense, serve as a basis for civility rather than the source of prolife militancy. Even if some individual believers are tempted to engage in illegal or violent activities, a nonjudgmental political Christianity could, in principle, deny such people the implicit support they seem to attract.

IN LIEU OF CONCLUSION

The abortion issue derives its somewhat unique character in U.S. and Canadian politics from two broad sorts of considerations: the religious overtones that the issue has come to carry, and the nonnegotiable nature of "rights" asserted by both sides. Both of these forces carry the implicit threat of democratic incivility. Religion is thought by some to provide an infallible set of doctrines that are based in some form on divine revelation. Truth, so understood, may owe "error" no deference. Similarly, the culture of rights suggests a style of discourse in which the very legitimacy of opposing viewpoints is at issue. If one asserts a fundamental right, not only are one's opponents mistaken, but the opposition is considered to be prohibited from engaging in political conflict at all. To the bearer of a right, the flaw of the opposition is procedural rather than substantive. Therefore, opponents of a particular right not only are mistaken about a policy judgment but are cast as bad citizens, since they do not seem to understand the rules governing and limiting political engagement. If two sides are asserting competing rights (life versus choice), each side has the means to disparage the motives—rather than the arguments—of the other. Both religion and rights, therefore, have contributed to the apparently zero-sum nature of the abortion controversy, in which direct, illegal action may seem an attractive alternative. However, there is nothing inevitably uncivil about the politics of abortion. As described, religion can, in principle, serve as the basis for democratic civility as well as the basis for political militancy. Christianity, after all, does contain a diagnosis of our current condition (sin) and imposes limitations on our ability to defeat evil in this world. Even if one regards abortion as an evil, it is but one evil among many, and may not merit such concentrated attention on the part of religious activists.

Moreover, the prospects for a civil politics of abortion may be enhanced to the extent that the arena in which the abortion issue is debated shifts from courts to legislatures. As noted, legislatures are typically less concerned with the protection of fundamental rights and more concerned with determining policies acceptable to as many citizens as possible. Again, legislative policies about abortion seem likely to be based on compromise and bargaining, and may seem unacceptable and even incoherent to those who see the abortion issue as the site on which fundamental values are contested. Nevertheless, debates on abortion conducted in legislatures (and, by extension, in election campaigns) may have the effect of legitimating opposing viewpoints and of increasing acceptance of policies reached in the more manifestly political branches of government.

References

Annas, George. 1982. "Forced Caesareans: The Most Unkindest Cut of All." *Hastings Center Report* 12, no. 3 (June): 16, 45.

Apple, R. W., Jr. 1989. "Supreme Court: Ruling on Abortion May Transform Campaigns into Referendums on Sexual Politics," *New York Times*, July 5, A18.

———. 1992. "Republicans Form Group to Regain Centrist Votes." *New York Times*, December 16, A24.

Arditti, Rita, Renate Klein, and Shelley Minden. 1984. *Test Tube Women: What Future for Motherhood?* London, Boston: Pandora Press.

Avery, Byllye. 1990. "A Question of Survival/A Conspiracy of Silence: Abortion and Black Women's Health." In *From Abortion to Reproductive Freedom: Transforming a Movement*, ed. Marlene Gerber Fried, 75–81. Boston: South End Press.

Back, Kurt W. 1988. "Metaphors for Public Opinion in Literature." *Public Opinion Quarterly* 52: 278–88.

———. 1989. *Family Planning and Population Control: The Challenges of a Successful Movement*. Boston: Twayne.

Balzar, John. 1989. "Justices Open Door to Change in California," *Los Angeles Times*, July 4, A1.

Barnartt, Sharon N., and Richard J. Harris. 1982. "Recent Changes in Predictors of Abortion Attitudes." *Sociology and Social Research* 66 (April): 320–34.

Barringer, Felicity. 1989. "Minnesota, Scene of Abortion Battles, Watches High Court for Key Moves," *New York Times*, June 25, L20.

Baudrillard, Jean. 1983. *Simulations*. New York: Semiotext(e).

Behrens, David. 1989. "Planned Parenthood Boosted by Aggressive Leadership," *Los Angeles Times* (special to the *Times* from *Newsday*), Oct. 5, E1.

Bell, Tina. 1987. "What Hath Woman Wrought." *The Human Life Review* 13, no. 1 (Winter): 14–21.

Bennett, Tony. 1982. "Media, 'Reality,' Signification." In *Culture, Society and the Media*, ed. Michael Curevitch, Tony Bennett, James Curran, and Janet Woollacott. London: Methuen.

Berton, Pierre. 1982. *Why We Act Like Canadians*. Toronto: McClelland and Stewart.

Benson, Peter, and Dorothy Williams. 1982. *Religion on Capitol Hill*. San Francisco: Harper & Row.

Bernadin, Cardinal Joseph. N.d. *The Seamless Garment*. Kansas City, Mo.: National Catholic Reporter Publishing.

———. 1988. *Consistent Ethic of Life*. Kansas City, Mo.: Sheed and Ward.

Best, Joel. 1987. "Rhetoric in Claims-Making: Constructing the Missing Children Problem." *Social Problems* 34, no. 2 (April): 101–21.

Blanchard, Dallas A., and Terry J. Prewitt. 1993. *Religious Violence and Abortion: The Gideon Project*. Gainesville: University of Florida Press.

Bowers, William J., and Glenn L. Pierce. 1980. "Deterrence or Ritualization? What is the Effect of Executions?" *Crime and Delinquency* 26: 453–84.

Boyarski, Bill. 1989. "The Times Poll: Public Is Deeply Divided over Ruling on Abortion," *Los Angeles Times*, July 4, A1.

Broder, David. 1989. "Desecration," *Washington Post*, July 9, B7.

Bromley, David, and Anson Shupe, eds. 1984. *New Christian Politics*. Macon, Ga.: Mercer University Press.

Brown, Wendy. 1983. "Reproductive Freedom and the Right to Privacy: A Paradox for Feminists." In *Families, Politics, and Public Policy*, ed. Irene Diamond. New York: Longman.

Burtachaell, James Tunstead. 1982. *Rachael Weeping*. Fairway, Kan.: Andrews and McMeel, Inc.

Cable, Sherry. 1984. "Professionalization in Social Movement Organizations: A Case Study of Pennsylvanians for Biblical Morality." *Sociological Focus* 17 (October): 287–304.

Calebresi, Guido. 1985. *Ideals, Beliefs, Attitudes, and the Law*. New York: Syracuse University Press.

Callahan, Daniel. 1986. "How Technology Is Reframing the Abortion Debate." *Hastings Center Report* 16, no. 1 (February): 33–42.

———. 1990. "An Ethical Challenge to Prochoice Advocates," *Commonweal*, November 23, 681–87.

Chancer, Lynn. 1990. "Abortion without Apology." In *From Abortion to Reproductive Freedom: Transforming a Movement*, ed. Marlene Gerber Fried. Boston: South End Press.

Chicago Tribune. 1993. "Germany Abortions Ruled Unconstitutional," May 29, sec. 1, p. 3.

Chilton, Paul. 1987. "Metaphor, Euphemism, and the Militarization of Language." *Current Research on Peace and Violence* 10: 7–19.

Cima, Anthony. 1973. "Letters to the Times: The Supreme Court's Ruling on Abortion," *Los Angeles Times*, Jan. 30, B6.

Cisler, Lucinda. 1970. "Unfinished Business: Birth Control and Women's Liberation." In *Sisterhood Is Powerful,* ed. Robin Morgan. New York: Vintage Books/Random House.

Cleghorn, J. Stephen. 1986. "Research Note on Cardinal Bernardin's 'Seamless Garment.' " *Review of Religious Research* 28, no. 2: 129–42.

Cohen, Richard. 1989. "When Abortion Is Illegal Again," *Washington Post,* July 6, A17.

Cohen, Stanley, and Jock Young, eds. 1973. *The Manufacture of News.* Beverly Hills, Calif.: Sage.

Colson, Charles. 1988. "Seamless Garment or Straitjacket?" *Christianity Today* 32, 72.

Condit, Celeste. 1990. *Decoding Abortion Rhetoric: Communicating Social Change.* Urbana: University of Illinois Press.

Conover, Pamela, and Stanley Feldman. 1981. "The Origins and Meaning of Liberal/Conservative Self-Identifications." *American Journal of Political Science* 25, no. 4: 617–45.

———. 1986. "Religion, Morality, and Politics." Paper presented at the annual meeting of the American Political Science Association, Washington, D.C.

Conover, Pamela Johnston, and Virginia Gray. 1983. *Feminism and the New Right: Conflict over the American Family.* New York: Praeger.

Converse, Philip E. 1964. "The Nature of Belief Systems in Mass Publics." In *Ideology and Discontent,* ed. David Apter, pp. 206–61. New York: Free Press.

Cook, Elizabeth Adell, Ted G. Jelen, and Clyde Wilcox. 1992. *Between the Absolutes: Public Opinion and the Politics of Abortion.* Boulder, Colo.: Westview Press.

———. 1993a. "Catholicism and Abortion Attitudes in the American States: A Contextual Analysis." *Journal for the Scientific Study of Religion* 32: 223–30.

———. 1993b. "Generational Differences in Attitudes Toward Abortion." *American Politics Quarterly* 21, no. 1: 31–53.

Cuneo, Michael W. 1989. *Catholics Against the Church: Anti-Abortion Protest in Toronto, 1969–1985.* Toronto: University of Toronto Press.

Cutler, Lloyd. 1989. "Pro-Life? Then Pay Up," *New York Times,* July 7, A29.

Daniels, Everett. 1992. "Letters to the Times: Supreme Court on Abortion," *Los Angeles Times,* July 8, B6.

Dart, John. 1973a. "Abortion Decision Expected to Have Little Effect in California," *Los Angeles Times,* July 23, A12.

———. 1973b. "High Court 'Out-Herods' Herod on Abortions, Archbishop Says," *Los Angeles Times,* July 26, B1.

Davis, Angela. 1983. *Women, Race and Class.* New York: Vintage Books/Random House.

Davis, James A., and Tom W. Smith. 1991. *General Social Survey.* (Machine-readable data file). Chicago: National Opinion Research Center.

Davis, Nanette J. 1985. *From Crime to Choice: The Transformation of Abortion in America.* Westport, Conn.: Greenwood.

Dellinger, Walter. 1989. "The Abortion Decision: Monument to Confusion," *Washington Post,* July 9, B1.

Dionne, E. J., Jr. 1989. "On Both Sides, Advocates Predict a 50-State Battle: Many Legislatures Will Try to Follow Example Set by Missouri Law," *New York Times*, July 4, A1.

Donahue, Michael J., and Philip K. Wood. 1985. "Inconsistent Religious Beliefs in a Sample of Young Adolescents." Paper presented at the annual meetings of the American Psychological Association, Los Angeles, August.

Donaldson, Peter J. 1990. *Nature Against Us: The United States and the World Population Crisis, 1965–1980*. Chapel Hill, N.C.: University of North Carolina Press.

Drucker, Peter F. 1993. *Post-Capitalist Society*. New York: HarperCollins.

Durkheim, Emile. 1964. *The Elementary Forms of the Religious Life*. London: George Allen and Unwin.

Edsall, Thomas, and Helen Dewar. 1989. "A Bloody Battle: Divisive Issue Likely to Move to Center Stage in State Elections," *Washington Post*, July 4, A1.

Egan, Timothy. 1989. "Judge Gives Abortion Protesters a Painful Choice," *New York Times*, June 23, A6.

Eliason, Scott R. 1988. *The Categorical Data Analysis System Version 3.00A Users' Manual*. State College, Pa.: Department of Sociology and Population Issues Research Center, Pennsylvania State University.

Ellsworth, Phoebe C., and Lee Ross. 1983. "Public Opinion and Capital Punishment: A Close Examination of the Views of Abolitionists and Retentionists." *Crime and Delinquency* 29: 116–69.

Faludi, Susan. 1989. "Where Did Randy Go Wrong?" *Mother Jones* 14, no. 9, November, 22–28, 61–64.

———. 1991. *Backlash: The Undeclared War against American Women*. New York: Crown Publishers.

Falwell, Jerry, 1980. *Listen America!* New York: Doubleday.

Farrell, William. 1973. "Ruling Seems to Forestall Abortion Debate in Albany," *New York Times*, Jan. 23, 1.

Faux, Marian. 1988. *Roe v. Wade*. New York: New American Library.

Ferraro, Geraldine. 1989. "Abortion: The Issue Can't Be Ducked," *New York Times*, July 15, Sec. 1, p. 25.

Fisher, Walter. 1984. "Narration as a Human Communication Paradigm: The Case of Public Moral Argument." *Communication Monographs* 51: 1–23.

Flanigan, William, and Nancy Zingale. 1987. *Political Behavior of the American Electorate*. Boston: Allyn and Bacon.

Foucault, Michel. 1981. *The History of Sexuality, Volume 1: An Introduction*. New York: Vintage Books.

Fox-Genovese, Elizabeth. 1991. *Feminism without Illusion*. Chapel Hill, N.C.: University of North Carolina Press.

Francome, Colin. 1984. *Abortion Freedom: A Worldwide Movement*. London: George Allen and Unwin.

Fried, Marlene Gerber, ed. 1990. *From Abortion to Reproductive Freedom: Transforming a Movement*. Boston: South End Press.

Fulwood, Sam. 1989. "Black Women Reluctant to Join Pro-Choice Forces," *Los Angeles Times*, Nov. 27, A1.

Gallagher, Janet. 1987. "Prenatal Invasions and Interventions: What's Wrong With Fetal Rights." *Harvard Women's Law Journal* 10: 9–58.

Gamson, William, and Andre Modigliani. 1989. "Media Discourse and Public Opinion on Nuclear Power: A Constructionist Approach." *American Journal of Sociology* 95, no. 1 (July): 1–37.

Gans, Herbert. 1979. *Deciding What's News*. New York: Pantheon.

———. 1988. *Middle-American Individualism*. New York: Free Press.

Gilder, George. 1981. *Wealth and Poverty*. New York: Basic Books.

Gilligan, Carol. 1982. *In a Different Voice: Psychological Theory and Women's Development*. Cambridge, Mass.: Harvard University Press.

Ginsburg, Faye. 1989. *Contested Lives: The Abortion Debate in an American Community*. Berkeley: University of California Press.

Ginsburg, Faye, and Anna Lowenhaupt Tsing, eds. 1990. *Uncertain Terms: Negotiating Gender in American Culture*. Boston: Beacon Press.

Gitlin, Todd. 1980. *The Whole World Is Watching*. Berkeley: University of California Press.

Glendon, Mary Ann. 1987. *Abortion and Divorce in Western Law*. Cambridge, Mass.: Harvard University Press.

———. 1991. *Rights Talk: The Impoverishment of Political Discourse*. New York: Free Press.

Glick, Mario, and Edward Zigler. 1985. "Self-Image: A Cognitive-Developmental Approach." In *The Development of the Self*, ed. Robert L. Leahy. New York: Academic Press.

Goldwin, Robert A. 1992. "Rights, Citizenship, and Civility." In *Civility and Citizenship in Liberal Democratic Societies*, ed. Edward C. Banfield. New York: Paragon House: 39–56.

Goodman, Ellen. 1989a. "Counting the Votes," *Washington Post,* July 4, A23.

———. 1989b. "Trust Not in the Constitution, but in Votes," *Los Angeles Times,* July 4, B7.

Goodman, Leo A. 1974. "The Analysis of Systems of Qualitative Variables when Some of the Variables Are Unobservable. Part I: A Modified Latent Structure Approach." *American Journal of Sociology* 79: 1179–1259.

Granberg, Donald. 1981. "The Abortion Activists." *Family Planning Perspectives* 13, no. 4 (July/August): 157–63.

———. 1982. "What Does It Mean to Be 'Pro-Life'?" *Christian Century* 99, May 12, 562–66.

Grant, Janet. 1974. *National Right to Life News*, September.

Grant, John Webster. 1973. "At Least You Knew Where You Stood with Them: Reflections on Religious Pluralism in Canada and in the United States." *Studies in Religion* 2: 340–51.

Gray, Paul. 1993. "Thou Shalt Not Kill," *Time* 141, March 22, 44–46.

Green, John, James Guth, and Kevin Hill. 1993. "Faith and Election: The Christian Right in House Races, 1978–1988." *Journal of Politics* 55, no. 1: 80–91.

Greenhouse, Linda. 1989. "Justice: Crowds Gather, Suspense Mounts. Due at 10 A.M. Today: A Legal Drama's Long-Awaited Finale," *New York Times,* July 3, A10.

Gross, Samuel R., and Robert Mauro. 1984. "Patterns of Death: An Analysis of Racial Disparities in Capital Sentencing and Homicide Victimization." *Stanford Law Review* 37: 27–153.

Gusfield, Joseph. 1963. *Symbolic Crusade: Status Politics and the American Temperance Movement.* Urbana: University of Illinois Press.

Guth, James, Corwin Smidt, Lyman Kellstedt, and John Green. 1993. "The Sources of Antiabortion Attitudes: The Case of Religious Political Activists." *American Politics Quarterly* 21, no. 1: 65–80.

Hadden, Jeffrey K., and Anson Shupe. 1988. *Televangelism: Power and Politics on God's Frontier.* New York: Henry Holt.

Hagner, Thomas, Jr. 1973. "Letters to the Editor: 'Positive Programming,'" *Washington Post,* Feb. 3, A15.

Hall, Stuart. 1984. "The Narrative Construction of Reality: An Interview with Stuart Hall." *Southern Review* 17 (March): 3–17.

Hall, Stuart, Chas Critcher, Tony Jefferson, John Clarke, and Brian Roberts. 1978. *Policing the Crisis.* New York: Holmes and Meier Publishers.

Harrison, Beverly Wildung. 1983. *Our Right to Choose.* Boston: Beacon Press.

Hart, Daniel, and William Damon. 1985. "Contrasts between Understanding Self and Understanding Others." In *The Development of the Self,* ed. Robert L. Leahy. New York: Academic Press.

Harter, Susan. 1985. "Competence as a Dimension of Self-Evaluation: Toward a Comprehensive Model of Self-Worth." In *The Development of Self,* ed. Robert L. Leahy. New York: Academic Press.

Hartley, John. 1982. *Understanding News.* London: Methuen.

Hartman, Betsy. 1987. *Reproductive Rights and Wrongs.* New York: Harper and Row.

Hatfield, Mark. 1989. "Ending *Roe v. Wade* Wouldn't End Abortion," *Washington Post,* July 2, C7.

Helgesen, Martin. 1973. "Letters to the Editor: Abortion and the Court," *New York Times,* 28.

Henshaw, Stanley K., and Jane Silverman. 1988. "The Characteristics and Prior Contraceptive Use of U.S. Abortion Patients." *Family Planning Perspectives* (July/August): 158–60.

Hentoff, Nat. 1989. "Dred Scott, Abortion, and Jesse Jackson." *The Human Life Review* 15, no. 2 (Spring): 108–12.

Hershey, Marjorie. 1984. *Running for Office.* Chatham, N.J.: Chatham House.

Hertel, Bradley R., and Michael Hughes. 1987. "Religious Affiliation, Attendance, and Support for Pro-Family Issues in the United States." *Social Forces* 65: 858–80.

Hibbard, Julie. 1992. "Letters to the Times: Supreme Court on Abortion," *Los Angeles Times,* July 8, B6.

Himmelstein, Jerome L. 1983. "The New Right." In *The New Christian Right,* ed. Robert C. Liebman and Robert Wuthnow, 13–30. New York: Aldine.

———. 1986. "The Social Basis of Antifeminism." *Journal for the Scientific Study of Religion* 25, no. 1: 1–15.

Hodgson, Dennis. 1991. "The Ideological Origins of the Population Association of America." *Population and Development Review* 17, no. 1 (March): 1–34.

Hubbard, Ruth. 1984. "Legal and Policy Implications of Recent Advances in Prenatal Diagnosis and Fetal Therapy." *Women's Rights Law Reporter* 3 (Spring): 201–18.

Hyer, Marjorie. 1973a. "Cardinal O'Boyle Asks Pastors to Preach Against Abortion Rule," *Washington Post,* Jan. 25, B1.

———. 1973b. "Ruling on Abortions Criticized in Sermons," *Washington Post,* Jan. 29, C1.

Inglehart, Ron. 1990. *Cultural Shift.* Princeton, N.J.: Princeton University Press.

Japenga, Ann, and Elizabeth Venant. 1989. "Underground Army: Abortion" (special to the *Los Angeles Times*), Nov. 30, E1.

Jelen, Ted G. 1982. "Sources of Political Intolerance: The Case of the American South." In *Contemporary Southern Political Attitudes and Behavior,* ed. Robert Steed, Laurence Moreland, and Tod Baker, 73–91. New York: Praeger.

———. 1984. "Respect for Life, Sexual Morality, and Opposition to Abortion." *Review of Religious Research* 30: 40–46.

———. 1987. "The Effects of Religious Separatism on White Protestants in the 1984 Presidential Election." *Sociological Analysis* 48: 30–45.

———, ed. 1989. *Religion and Political Behavior in the United States.* New York: Praeger.

———. 1990. "Religious Belief and Attitude Constraint." *Journal for the Scientific Study of Religion* 29, no. 1: 118–125.

———. 1991. *The Political Mobilization of Religious Belief.* Westport, CT: Praeger.

———. 1992. "The Clergy and Abortion." *Review of Religious Research* 34, no. 2: 132–51.

———. 1993. *The Political World of the Clergy.* Westport, CT: Praeger.

———. 1994. Review of Dallas A. Blanchard and Terry J. Prewitt, *Religious Values and Abortion,* in *Review of Religious Research.*

Jelen, Ted G., John O'Donnell, and Clyde Wilcox. 1993. "A Contextual Analysis of Catholicism and Abortion Attitudes in Western Europe." *Sociology of Religion.*

Johnsen, Dawn. 1986. "The Creation of Fetal Rights: Conflicts with Women's Constitutional Rights to Liberty, Privacy, and Equal Protection." *The Yale Law Journal* 95: 599–625.

Johnson, Sonia. 1989. *Wildfire: Igniting the She/Volution.* Albuquerque, N.M.: Wildfire Books.

Johnson, Stephen D. 1986. "The Christian Right in Middletown." In *The Political Role of Religion in the United States,* ed. Stephen D. Johnson and Joseph B. Tamney, 181–89. Boulder, Colo.: Westview Press.

Johnson, Stephen D., and Joseph B. Tamney. 1988. "Factors Related to Inconsistent Life-Views." *Review of Religious Research* 30: 40–46.

Johnson, Stephen D., Joseph B. Tamney, and Ronald Burton. 1992. "Economic Satisfaction vs. Moral Conservatism in the 1988 Presidential Election." *Sociological Focus* 24: 303–14.

Johnston, David. 1989. "Confusion Followed by Confrontation as Ruling Stirs the Waiting Crowd," *New York Times,* July 4, A10.

Joseph, Gloria. 1981. "Styling, Profiling, and Pretending: The Games before the Fall." In *Common Differences: Conflicts in Black and White Feminist Per-*

spectives, ed. Gloria Joseph and Jill Lewis, 179–230. Garden City, N.Y.: Anchor/Doubleday.

Joyner, Brenda. 1990. "Fighting Back to Save Women's Lives." In *From Abortion to Reproductive Freedom: Transforming a Movement,* ed. by Marlene Gerber Fried, 205–11. Boston: South End Press.

Kaiser, Donn L. 1991. "Religious Problem-Solving Styles and Guilt." *Journal for the Scientific Study of Religion* 30, no. 1: 94–98.

Kamen, Al. 1989. "Supreme Court Restricts Right to Abortion, Giving States Wide Latitude for Regulation: 5–4 Ruling Short of Overturning 'Roe'," *Washington Post,* July 4, A1.

Kegan, Robert. 1985. "The Loss of Pete's Dragon: Developments of the Self in the Years Five to Seven." In *The Development of the Self,* ed. Robert L. Leahy. New York: Academic Press.

Kellstedt, Lyman, and Mark Noll. 1990. "Religion, Voting for President, and Party Identification, 1948–1984." In *Religion and American Politics,* ed. Mark Noll, 355–79. New York: Oxford University Press.

Kelly, James R. 1981. "Beyond the Stereotypes: Interviews with Right-to-Life Pioneers," *Commonweal,* November 1981: 655.

———. 1987. "AIDS and the Death Penalty as Consistency Tests for the Prolife Movement," *America* 157, September 26, 151–55.

———. 1988. "The Vanishing Middle in Abortion Politics," *The Christian Century,* August 3–10, 708–11.

———. 1989a. "Ecumenism and Abortion: A Case Study of Pluralism, Privatization, and the Public Conscience." *Review of Religious Research* 30, no. 3: 225–35.

———. 1989b. "Toward Complexity: The Right to Life Movement." *Research in the Social Scientific Study of Religion* 1: 79–83.

———. 1989c. "Winning *Webster v. Reproductive Health Services:* The Crisis of the Prolife Movement," *America,* August 19, 79–83.

———. 1990. "A Political Challenge to the Prolife Movement," *Commonweal,* November 23, 692–96.

———. 1991a. "Learning and Teaching Consistency: Catholics and the Right to Life Movement." In *The Catholic Church and the Politics of Abortion,* ed. Mary C. Segers and Timothy Byrne, 152–68. Boulder, Co: Westview Press.

———. 1991b. "Abortion: What Americans Really Think," *America,* November 3, 310–16.

———. 1993a. "Prolife and Prochoice after Reagan-Bush," *America,* February 6: 11–15.

———. 1993b. "Consistency and Common Ground in the Post-Casey Abortion Era." In *The Politics of Abortion in the American States,* ed. Mary C. Segers and Timothy Byrne. Armonk, N.Y.: ME Sharpe.

Kirkpatrick, Jeane J. 1982. *Dictatorships and Double Standards.* New York: Simon & Schuster.

Klecka, William. 1980. *Discriminant Analysis.* Beverly Hills, Calif.: Sage.

Kocka, Jurgen. 1974. "Organiserter Kapitalismus oder Staatsmonopolistischer Kapitalismus? Begriffliche Vorbemerkungen." In *Organiserter Kapitalismus,* ed. H. Winckler, 20–24. Gottingen: Vandenhoeck & Ruprecht.

Kollar, Nathan R. 1989. "Controversial Issues in North American Fundamental-
ism." Unpublished paper, St. John Fisher College, Rochester, New York.
Koop, C. Everett. 1984. "The Slide to Auschwitz." In *Abortion and the Conscience
of the Nation*, ed. Ronald Reagan, 41–72. Nashville: Thomas Nelson Pub-
lishers.
Kraft, Joseph. 1973. " 'Conservative' on Abortion," *Washington Post*, Jan. 25,
A15.
Krauthammer, Charles. 1989. "A Middle Ground on Abortion," *Washington Post*,
July 7, A17.
Kroker, Arthur, and David Cook. 1986. *The Postmodern Scene: Excremental Cul-
ture and Hyper-Aesthetics*. Montreal: New World Perspectives.
Krol, John Cardinal. 1973. "Statements by 2 Cardinals" (issued by Cardinal
Cooke and John Cardinal Krol, Archbishop of Philadelphia and President
of the National Conference of Catholic Bishops), *New York Times*, Jan.
23, 20.
Lacayo, Richard. 1993. "One Doctor Down, How Many More?" *Time* 141,
March 22, 46–47.
Lader, Lawrence. 1971. *Breeding Ourselves to Death*. New York: Ballantine
Books.
————. 1973. *Abortion II: Making the Revolution*. Boston: Beacon Press.
Lake, Randal A. 1986. "The Metaethical Framework of Anti-Abortion Rhetoric."
Signs 11, no. 3: 478–99.
Lambert, Ronald D., Steven D. Brown, James E. Curtis, Barry J. Kay, and John M.
Wilson. 1986. *The Canadian National Election Study*. Waterloo, Ontario:
Department of Sociology, University of Waterloo.
LaPiere, Richard T. 1934. "Attitudes vs. Actions." *Social Forces* 13: 230–37.
Lash, Scott, and John Urry. 1987. *The End of Organized Capitalism*. Madison:
University of Wisconsin Press.
Lauter, David, and Karen Tumulty. 1989. "GOP Seen as Having Most to Lose in
Abortion 'War,' " *Los Angeles Times*, July 6, A20.
Law, Sylvia. 1984. "Rethinking Sex and the Constitution." *University of Pennsyl-
vania Law Review* 132, no. 5: 955–1040.
"Lawrence Mikkelsen, '64, Parish Priest." 1993. *Stanford* 21, no. 2, 69. Stanford,
Calif.: Stanford Alumni Association.
Leahy, Peter. 1975. "The Anti-Abortion Movement." Ph.D. diss. on microfilm.
Ann Arbor, Mich.: University Microfilms International.
Leahy, Robert L., ed. 1985. *The Development of the Self*. New York: Academic
Press.
Lee, Nancy Howell. 1969. *The Search for an Abortionist*. Chicago: The University
of Chicago Press.
Legge, Jerome. 1983. "The Determinants of Attitudes toward Abortion in the
American Electorate." *Western Political Quarterly* 36, no. 3: 479–90.
Lenski, Gerhard. 1971. "Conservatives and Radicals." In *Contemporary Sociologi-
cal Theory*, ed. Fred E. Katz, 220–22. New York: Random House.
Levin, Michael. 1988. "Abortion, Homosexuality, and Feminism." *The Human
Life Review* 14, no. 3 (Fall): 35–43.
Levinson, Daniel J., and Phyllis E. Huffman. 1955. "Traditional Family Ideology
and Its Relation to Personality." *Journal of Personality* 23, no. 3: 251–73.

Liebman, Robert C., and Robert Wuthnow, eds. 1983. *The New Christian Right: Mobilization and Legitimation.* Hawthorne, N.Y.: Aldine.

Lipset, Seymour Martin. 1990. *Continental Divide: The Values and Institutions of the United States and Canada.* New York: Routledge.

Lipset, Seymour, and Carl Everett Ladd. 1975. *The Divided Academy: Professor and Politics.* New York: Norton.

Los Angeles Times. 1973. "Abortions and the Right of Privacy" (editorial), Jan. 23, A4.

———. 1989. "Excerpts: 'The Signs Are . . . Ominous, a Chill Wind Blows.' " (excerpts from the majority and dissenting opinions in *Webster v. Missouri Reproductive Services*), July 4, A24.

———. 1992. "Text: Duty 'To Define Liberty of All.' " (excerpts from the majority and dissenting opinions in *Planned Parenthood of Southeastern Pennsylvania v. Casey.*), Times Wire Services, June 30, A11.

Luker, Kristin. 1984. *Abortion and the Politics of Motherhood.* Berkeley: University of California Press.

Lynd, Robert S., and Helen M. Lynd. 1929. *Middletown.* New York: Harcourt, Brace, and World.

Lynn, Suzanne. 1982. "Technology and Reproductive Rights: How Advances in Technology Can Be Used to Limit Women's Reproductive Rights." *Women's Rights Law Reporter* 7, no. 3 (Spring): 223–27.

MacKenzie, John. 1973. "Supreme Court Allows Early-Stage Abortions," *Washington Post*, A1.

Mandel, Ernest. 1975. *Late Capitalism.* London: NLB.

Mann, Judy. 1989a. "Abortion-Rights Clout," *Washington Post*, July 12, D3.

———. 1989b. "Sickening Display," *Washington Post*, July 7, C3.

Marcus, Ruth. 1989. "A New Majority: Blackmun Assails 'Reversal,' " *Washington Post*, July 4, A1.

Marsden, George. 1980. *Fundamentalism and American Culture.* New York: Oxford University Press.

Martin, Douglass. 1989. "Women Given Cruelest Choice Now Fight Back," *New York Times*, October 21, p. 1, sec. 1.

Marx, Karl. 1954. *Capital.* Moscow: Foreign Language Publishing House.

———. 1990. *Selected Writings in Sociology and Social Philosophy*, ed. T. B. Bottomore and Maxilien Rubel. London: Penguin Books.

Maslow, Abraham H. 1969. "Toward a Humanistic Biology." *American Psychologist* 24: 734–35.

———. 1971. *Motivation and Personality.* New York: Viking Press.

Mathews, Linda. 1973. "Supreme Court Rule Gives Women Right to Have Abortions," *Los Angeles Times,* Jan. 23, A1.

Matkin, James. 1986. "The Negotiation of the Charter of Rights: The Provincial Perspective." In *Litigating the Values of a Nation: The Canadian Charter of Rights and Freedoms*, ed. Joseph Weiler and Robin Elliot, 27–48. Toronto: Carswell.

Mayer, Maria. 1992. "Letters to the Times: Supreme Court on Abortion," *Los Angeles Times,* July 8, B6.

McAdam, Doug, John D. McCarthy, and Mayer N. Zald. 1988. "Social Movements." In *Handbook of Sociology*, ed. Neil J. Smelser. Beverly Hills, Calif.: Sage.

McCarthy, John D. 1987. "Pro-Life and Pro-Choice Mobilization." In *Social Movements in an Organizational Society*, ed. Mayer N. Zald and John D. McCarthy. New Brunswick, N.J.: Transaction Books.

McCutcheon, Allan L. 1987. *Latent Class Analysis*. Newbury Park, Calif.: Sage.

McDonagh, Eileen. 1993. "Recasting the Politics of Personhood: Does the Humanity of the Fetus Matter?" Paper presented at the Conference on the Politics of Abortion, Illinois Benedictine College, Lisle, Illinois, April 14.

McGrory, Mary. 1989. "Coathangers and Roses," *Washington Post*, July 4, A2.

McKeegan, Michele. 1992. *Abortion Politics: Mutiny in the Ranks of the Right*. New York: Free Press.

Mead, George H. 1934. *Mind, Self and Society*. Chicago: The University of Chicago Press.

Meehan, Mary. 1980. "Abortion: The Left Has Betrayed the Sanctity of Life." *The Progressive*, September, 13–34.

Merelman, Richard M. 1991. *Partial Visions: Culture and Politics in Britain, Canada, and the United States*. Madison: University of Wisconsin Press.

Merton, Robert K. 1949. "Discrimination and the American Creed." In *Discrimination and National Welfare*, ed. R. H. MacIver, 99–126. New York: Harper & Row.

Mill, John Stuart. 1975. "On Liberty." In *John Stuart Mill: Three Essays*, introduction by Richard Wollheim, 5–41. New York: Oxford University Press.

Mills, C. Wright. 1963. "Situated Actions and Vocabularies of Motive." In *Power, Politics and People*, ed. Irving Horowitz, 439–52. New York: Oxford University Press.

Moen, Matthew. 1989. *The Christian Right and Congress*. Tuscaloosa: University of Alabama Press.

Mohr, James. 1978. *Abortion in America: The Origins and Evolution of National Policy, 1800–1900*. New York: Oxford University Press.

Molotch, Harvey. 1979. "Media and Movements." In *The Dynamics of Social Movements*, ed. Mayer Zald and John McCarthy, 71–93. Cambridge, Mass: Winthrop.

Morrison, Robert G. 1982. "Choice in Washington: The Politics of Liberalized Abortion." Master's thesis, University of Virginia.

Morton, F. L. 1992. *Pro-Choice vs. Pro-Life: Abortion and the Courts in Canada*. Norman: University of Oklahoma Press.

Mumby, D., and L. Spitzack. 1985. "Ideology and Television News: A Metaphoric Analysis of Political Stories." *Central States Speech Journal* 34, no. 3: 162–71.

Nathanson, Bernard. 1979. *Aborting America*. New York: Pinnacle Books.

———. 1983. *The Abortion Papers: Inside the Abortion Mentality*. New York: Frederick Fell.

National Conference of Catholic Bishops. 1975. *Pastoral Plan for Prolife Activities*. Washington, D.C.: U.S. Catholic Conference.

Neitz, Mary Joe. 1981. "Family, State, and God: Ideologies of the Right-to-Life Movement." *Sociological Analysis* 42, no. 3: 265–76.

Neuhaus, Richard. 1988. "The Return of Eugenics." *The Human Life Review* 14, no. 3 (Summer): 81–107.

New York Times. 1973. "Governor Scores Buckley's Move: Says Abortion Amendment Would Be 'Divisive,' " 39.

———. 1989a. Internal Memorandum, July 3.

———. 1989b. "Excerpts from Court Decision on the Regulation of Abortion," July 4, L12.

———. 1989c. "No Abortion Decision Yet," June 30, A8.

———. 1989d. "Respect for Privacy" (editorial), Jan. 24, 40.

———. 1989e. "What Is Right and Wrong with *Roe vs. Wade?* The View from Friends of the Court," April 23, E6.

———. 1989f. "A Woman's Right, Barely Visible" (editorial), July 4, A28.

———. 1990. "Recognition of Language May Begin in the Womb," August 14, C8.

———. 1991. "Canadian Priests Are Asked to Boycott Speech By Cuomo," September 19, B2.

———. 1992. "Excerpts from the Justices' Decision in the Pennsylvania Case," (special to the *New York Times,* no byline), June 30, A8.

Newsweek. 1991. "How Kids Grow," Special Edition, Summer.

Nock, Steven L., and Paul Williams Kingston. 1988. "Time with Children: The Impact of Couples' Work-time Commitments." *Social Forces* 67: 59–85.

Noonan, John, Jr. 1970. "An Almost Absolute Value in History." In *The Morality of Abortion,* ed. John Noonan, Jr., 1–59. Cambridge: Harvard University Press.

Nsiah-Jefferson, Laurie. 1989. "Reproductive Laws, Women of Color, and Low-Income Women." *Women's Rights Law Reporter* 11, no. 1 (Spring): 15–38.

Oehme, Chris. 1973. "Letters to the Editor: 'Perceptive Ruling,' " *Washington Post,* Feb. 3, A15.

Oliner, Samuel P., and Pearl M. Oliner. 1988. *The Altruistic Personality: Rescuers of Jews in Nazi Europe.* New York: Free Press.

Paige, Connie. 1983. *The Right to Lifers.* New York: Summit Books.

Pasternoster, Raymond. 1983. "Race of Victim and Location of Crime: The Decision to Seek the Death Penalty in South Carolina." *Journal of Criminal Law and Criminology* 74: 754–85.

Pedhazur, Elazar. 1982. *Multiple Regression in Behavioral Research.* New York: Holt, Rinehart, and Winston.

Petchesky, Rosalind. 1987. "Foetal Images: The Power of Visual Culture in the Politics of Reproduction." In *Reproductive Technologies: Gender, Motherhood, and Medicine,* ed. Michelle Stanworth, 57–80. Oxford, UK: Polity Press.

———. 1990. *Abortion and Women's Choice: The State, Sexuality and Reproductive Freedom.* Rev. ed. Boston: Northeastern University Press.

Peters, Cynthia. 1990. "Every Sperm Is Sacred." In *From Abortion to Reproductive Freedom: Transforming a Movement,* ed. Marlene Gerber Fried, 187–93. Boston: South End Press.

Phillips, Kevin. 1991. *The Politics of Rich and Poor.* New York: HarperCollins.

Piker, Steven. 1972. "The Problem of Consistency in Thai Religion." *Journal for the Scientific Study of Religion* 11: 211–29.

Pollitt, Katha. 1990. "Fetal Rights: A New Assault on Feminism." *The Nation,* March 26, 409–18.

———. 1992. "In the Middle of the Muddle." *The Nation,* May 25, 718–26.

Poloma, Margaret, and George Gallup, Jr. 1991. *Varieties of Prayer: A Survey Report.* Philadelphia: Trinity Press International.

Rapp, Rayna. 1990. "Constructing Amniocentesis: Maternal and Medical Discourses." In *Uncertain Terms: Negotiating Gender in American Culture,* ed. Faye Ginsburg and Anna Lowenhaupt Tsing. Boston: Beacon Press.

Raspberry, William. 1989. "A 'Breath of Life' Test for Abortion," *Washington Post,* July 12, A23.

Reagan, Ronald. 1984. *Abortion and the Conscience of the Nation.* Nashville: Thomas Nelson Publishers.

Ridgeway, James. 1985. "The Prolife Juggernaught," *The Village Voice,* July 16, 28–29.

Roanoke Times & World-News. 1992. "Profile of Capital Punishment in the U.S. since 1976," April 22, A6.

Rogers, Ann Gaile. 1987. "Gender Differences in Moral Reasoning: A Validity Study of Two Moral Orientations." Ph.D. diss., Washington University, St. Louis.

Rolata, Gina. 1989. "Doctors' Tools Limited in Testing Fetal Viability," *New York Times,* July 4, A10.

Roof, Wade Clark, and William McKinney. 1987. *American Mainline Religion.* New Brunswick, N.J.: Rutgers University Press.

Rosen, Judith. 1989. "A Legal Perspective on the Status of the Fetus: Who Will Guard the Guardians?" In *Abortion Rights and Fetal Personhood,* ed. Ed Doerr and James Prescott, 35–36. Long Beach, Calif.: Centerline Press.

Rosenstiel, Thomas. 1989. "Abortion Issue Quickly Segues into the TV Spotlight," *Los Angeles Times,* July 4, A27.

Rossi, Alice. 1966. "Abortion Laws and Their Victims." *Trans-Action* (Sept./ Oct.): 8.

Rubin, Alissa. 1991. "Interest Groups and Abortion Politics." In *Interest Group Politics,* 3rd ed., ed. Allan J. Cigler and Burdett A. Loomis, 239–55. Washington, D.C.: CQ Press.

Rubin, Eva R. 1987. *Abortion, Politics, and the Courts: "Roe v. Wade" and Its Aftermath.* Westport, Conn.: Greenwood Press.

Saffire, William. 1989. "Option 3: 'Pro-Comp,' " *New York Times,* July 6, A21.

Salholz, Eloise, Peter Kater, Spencer Reiss, Daniel Glick, and John McCormick. 1993. "The Death of Dr. Gunn," *Newsweek,* March 22, 34–35.

Savage, David. 1989a. "No Ruling Yet on Key Abortion Case: Monday Is Last Day of This Term that Court Can Issue Decision," *Los Angeles Times,* June 30, A4.

———. 1989b. "5-4 Vote OKs Missouri Ban on Use of Public Facilities," *Los Angeles Times,* July 4, A1.

Schmeiser, Douglas. 1973. "The Case against Entrenchment of the Canadian Bill of Rights." *Dalhousie Law Journal* 1: 23.

Schneider, William. 1989. "Rehnquist and Company: Courting Controversy," Los Angeles Times, July 9, E1.

Schwartz, Amy E. 1985. "Bitter Pill," *The New Republic,* February 18, 10–12.

Scott, Jacqueline. 1989. "Conflicting Beliefs about Abortion: Legal Approval and Moral Doubts." *Social Psychology Quarterly* 52, no. 4: 319–26.

Scott, Jacqueline, and Howard Schuman. 1988. "Attitude Strength and Social Action in the Abortion Dispute." *American Sociological Review* 53, no. 4: 785–95.

Scott, Janny. 1989. "Viability Called 'Non-Issue' Affecting 1% of Abortions," *Los Angeles Times,* July 4, A22.

Shapiro, Michael. 1989. "The Abortion Decision: Monument to Confusion," *Washington Post,* July 9, B1.

Shaw, David. 1990a. "Bias Sweeps into News on Abortion: Media Coverage Shifted after *Webster* Decision in '89" (first of four articles on "Abortion and the Media"), *Los Angeles Times,* July 1, A1.

———. 1990b. Three-Part Series on Abortion Reportage, *Los Angeles Times,* July 1–4.

Sheeran, Patrick. 1987. *Women, Society, the State and Abortion.* New York: Praeger.

Shils, Edward. 1992. "Civility and Civil Society." In *Civility and Citizenship in Liberal Democratic Societies,* ed. Edward C. Banfield, 1–16. New York: Paragon House.

Sigal, Leon V. 1973. *Reporters and Officials.* Lexington, Mass: D. C. Heath.

Simpson, John H. 1983. "Moral Issues and Status Politics." In *The New Christian Right: Mobilization and Legitimation,* ed. Robert C. Liebman and Robert Wuthnow, 187–205. Hawthorne, N.Y.: Aldine.

———. 1987. "Globalization, the New Religious Right, and the Politics of the Body." *The Psychohistory Review* 15: 59–75.

———. 1988a. "Religion and the Churches." In *Understanding Canadian Society,* ed. James Curtis and Lorne Tepperman, 345–69. Toronto: McGraw-Hill Ryerson.

———. 1988b. "A Reply to 'Measuring Public Support for the New Christian Right: The Perils of Point Estimation.'" *Public Opinion Quarterly* 52: 338–42.

———. 1992a. "Fundamentalism in America Revisited: The Fading of Modernity as a Source of Symbolic Capital." In *Religion and Politics in Comparative Perspective: Revival of Religious Fundamentalism in East and West,* ed. Bronislaw Misztal and Anson Shupe, 10–27. Westport, Conn.: Greenwood/Praeger.

———. 1992b. Review of *Communities of Discourse,* by Robert Wuthnow (Cambridge, Mass.: Harvard University Press). *International Journal of Comparative Sociology* 23, nos. 1–2: 147–49.

———. 1993. "Religion and the Body: Sociological Themes and Prospects." In *A Future for Religion? New Paradigms for Social Analysis,* ed. William H. Swatos, Jr., 149–64. Newbury Park, Calif.: Sage.

Simpson, John H., and Henry G. MacLeod. 1985. "The Politics of Morality in Canada." In *Religious Movements: Genesis, Exodus, and Numbers,* ed. Rodney Stark, 221–40. New York: Paragon.

Sipe, Kerry. 1989. "Labeling: Are Newspaper Terms Neutral in Abortion Debate?" *Virginia-Pilot and Ledger-Star,* November 19, 6.

Sister Christine. 1973. "Letters to the Editor: The Supreme Court's Ruling on Abortion," *Los Angeles Times*, January 30, B6.

Smith, Beverly. 1990. "Choosing Ourselves: Black Women and Abortion." In *From Abortion to Reproductive Freedom: Transforming a Movement*, ed. Marlene Gerber Fried, 83–86. Boston: South End Press.

Smith, Janet Farrell. 1983. "Rights-Conflict, Pregnancy, and Abortion." In *Beyond Domination*, ed. Carol C. Gould, 265–73. Totowa, N.J.: Rowman & Allenheld.

Smithey, Shannon K. 1991. "Public Opinion, Courts, and Civil Liberties in Canada: An Initial Examination." Paper presented at the annual meeting of the Midwest Political Science Association, Chicago, April.

Smothers, Ronald. 1989. "Organizer of Abortion Protests Is Jailed in Atlanta," *New York Times*, July 12, A10.

Snow, David, and Robert Benford. 1988. "Ideology, Frame Resonance, and Participant Mobilization." *International Social Movement Research, Volume 1*. Greenwich, Conn.: Jai Press.

Snow, David, E. Burke Rochford, Jr., Steven Worden, and Robert Benford. 1986. "Frame Alignment Processes, Micromobilization, and Movement Participation." *American Sociological Review* 51, no. 4 (August): 464–81.

Spitzer, Robert J. 1987. *The Right to Life Movement and Third Party Politics*. Westport, Conn.: Greenwood Press.

Sprague, Joey. 1991. "The Reproductive Debate: Gender, Class and Ethnic Standpoints." Paper presented at the 86th annual meeting of the American Sociological Association, Cincinnati, Ohio.

SPSS Inc. 1986. *SPSS User's Guide*. 2nd ed. Chicago: SPSS.

Staggenborg, Suzanne. 1987. "Life-Style Preferences and Social Movements Recruitment: Illustrations from the Abortion Conflict." *Social Science Quarterly* 68 (1987): 779–98.

———. 1991. *The Pro-Choice Movement: Organization and Activism in the Abortion Conflict*. New York: Oxford University Press.

Stark, Rodney, and Charles Y. Glock. 1968. *American Piety: The Nature of Religious Commitment*. Berkeley: University of California Press.

Stark, Rodney, and William Sims Bainbridge. 1985. *The Future of Religion*. Berkeley: University of California Press.

Stenson, James. 1973. "Letters to the Editor: 'Protecting the Unborn,' " *Washington Post*, Jan. 31, A19.

Stewart, Charles, Craig Allen Smith, and Robert Denton, Jr. 1984. "A Rhetoric of Transcendence: Pro-Life Responds to Pro-Choice." In *Persuasion and Social Movements*, ed. Charles Stewart and Craig Allen Smith, 121–35. Prospect Heights, Ill.: Waveland Press.

Swatos, William H. 1991. "Cultural-Historical Factors in Religious Economies: Further Analysis of the Canadian Case." *Review of Religious Research* 33: 60–75.

Swidler, Ann. 1986. "Culture in Action: Symbols and Strategies." *American Sociological Review* 51 (April): 273–86.

Tamney, Joseph B. 1986. "Religion and the Abortion Issue." In *The Political Role of Religion in the United States*, ed. Stephen D. Johnson and Joseph B. Tamney, 159–80. Boulder, Colo.: Westview Press.

————. 1992. *The Resilence of Christianity in the Modern World*. Albany, N.Y.: State University of New York Press.

Tamney, Joseph B., and Stephen D. Johnson. 1985. "Consequential Religiosity in a Modern Society." *Review of Religious Research* 26: 360–78.

————. 1988. "Explaining Support for the Moral Majority." *Sociological Forum* 3, no. 2: 234–56.

Tamney, Joseph B., Stephen D. Johnson, and Ronald Burton. 1992. "The Abortion Controversy: Conflicting Beliefs and Values in American Society." *Journal for the Scientific Study of Religion* 31, no. 1: 32–46.

Tamney, Joseph, Jennifer Mertens, Stephen Johnson, Robert Burton, and Rita Caccamo. 1992. "Personal Experience, Ideology, and Support for Feminism." *Sociological Focus* 25: 203–16.

Teck, Katherine. 1973. "Letters to the Editor: 'Ruling of the Supreme Court on Abortion,' " *New York Times*, Feb. 3, 28.

Terdiman, Richard. 1985. *Discourse/Counter-Discourse*. Ithaca, N.Y.: Cornell University Press.

Terry, Jennifer. 1989. "The Body Invaded: Medical Surveillance of Women as Reproducers." *Socialist Review* 19, no. 3: 13–43.

Tesh, Sylvia. 1984. "In Support of Single-Issue Politics." *Political Science Quarterly* 99, no. 1: 27–44.

Thomas, Cal. 1989. "Trust Not in the Constitution, but in Votes," *Los Angeles Times*, July 4, B7.

Thompson, Judith Jarvis. 1971. "A Defense of Abortion." *Philosophy and Public Affairs* 1: 45–61.

Time. 1981. "The Battle over Abortion," April 6, 20–24.

————. 1992. "Letters: Abortion," May 25, 11.

Tinder, Glenn. 1989. *The Political Meaning of Christianity: An Interpretation*. Baton Rouge: Louisiana State University Press.

Toner, Robin. 1989. "Personalities Eclipse Legalism in Abortion Debate," *New York Times*, July 11, A17.

Tooley, M. 1974. "Abortion and Infanticide." In *The Rights and Wrongs of Abortion*, ed. M. Cohen, T. Nagel, and T. Scanlon. Princeton, N.J.: Princeton University Press.

————. 1983. *Abortion and Infanticide*. New York: Oxford University Press.

Tordella, Beth. 1973. "Letters to the Editor: 'The Abortion Ruling,' " *Washington Post*, Jan. 31, A19.

Torres, Ada, and Jacqueline Darroch Forrest. 1988. "Why Do Women Have Abortions?" *Family Planning Perspectives*, July/August.

Toubia, Nahid. 1991. "Redefining Survival." *Conscience* 12, no. 5, Sept.–Oct.

Treadwell, David. 1989. "Abortion Plaintiffs Now on Opposite Sides: Similar Pasts, Different Viewpoints for *Roe, Doe*," *Los Angeles Times*, June 25, A1.

Trew, Tony. 1979. "What the Papers Say: Linguistic Variation and Ideological Difference." In *Language and Control*, ed. Robert Booth Fowler, Bob Hodge, and Gunther Kress, 117–56. London: Routledge & Kegan Paul.

Tribe, Laurence. 1990. *Abortion: The Clash of Absolutes*. New York: Norton.

Trinkhaus, Walter. 1975. "Dred Scott Revisited," *Commonweal*, Feb. 14, 388.

Tuchman, Gaye. 1978. *Making News: A Study in the Construction of Reality*. New York: Free Press.

Tumulty, Karen. 1989a. "Illinois Takes Center Stage in Abortion Battle," *Los Angeles Times,* July 17, A1.

———. 1989b. "States Will Be Less Able to Finesse Issue," *Los Angeles Times,* July 4, A23.

Turner, Bryan S. 1984. *The Body and Society: Explorations in Social Theory.* Oxford: Basil Blackwell.

USA Today. 1986. "Inquiry Topic: Abortion." June 12, A9.

Van Gelder, Lawrence. 1973. "Cardinals Shocked—Reaction Mixed," *New York Times,* Jan. 23, 1.

Verba, Sidney, and Norma Nie. 1972. *Participation in America: Political Democracy and Social Equality.* Chicago: The University of Chicago Press.

Wald, Kenneth D. 1987. *Religion and Politics in the United States.* New York: St. Martin's.

———. 1989. *Religion and Politics in the United States.* Washington, D.C.: CQ Press.

Wallace, Bruce. 1991. "Back to Square One: The Senate Rejects New Abortion Legislation," *Maclean's* 104, no. 6, February 11, 15.

Washington Post. 1973. "Catholic Groups Hits Justice Brennan," Jan. 26, A12.

———. 1989. "*Webster v. Reproductive Health Services:* Excerpts from the Supreme Court Decision," July 4, A8.

Weaver, Warren, Jr. 1973. "High Court Rules Abortions Legal: State Bans Ruled Out until Last 10 Weeks—National Guidelines set by 7 to 2 Vote," *New York Times,* Jan. 23, 1.

Westfall, David. 1982. "Beyond Abortion: The Potential Reach of a Human Life Amendment." *American Journal of Law and Medicine* 8, no. 2 (Summer): 97–135.

Wicker, Tom. 1989. "Abortion and the GOP," *New York Times,* July 7, 1.

Wilcox, Clyde. 1989. "Political Action Committees and Abortion: A Longitudinal Analysis." *Women and Politics* 9, no. 1: 1–19.

———. 1992. *God's Warriors: The Christian Right in Twentieth-Century America.* Baltimore, Md.: The Johns Hopkins University Press.

Wilcox, Clyde, and Ted G. Jelen. 1993. "Catholicism and Gender Equality in Western Europe: A Contextual Analysis." *International Journal of Public Opinion Research* 5: 40–57.

Wilcox, Clyde, Sharon Linzey, and Ted Jelen. 1991. "Reluctant Warriors: Premillennialism and Politics in the Moral Majority." *Journal for the Scientific Study of Religion* 30, no. 3: 245–58.

Wilkerson, Isabel. 1989. "Abortion Foes Discuss Plans for 'Post-*Roe* Era.'" *New York Times,* July 3, A8.

Will, George F. 1989. "Trust Not in the Constitution, but in Votes," *Los Angeles Times,* July 4, A8.

Willis, Ellen. 1983. "Abortion: Is a Woman a Person?" In *Powers of Desire,* ed. Ann Snitow, Christine Stansell, and Sharon Thompson, 471–76. New York: Monthly Review Press.

———. 1985. "Putting Women Back into the Abortion Debate," *The Village Voice* 30, July 16, 15–16, 24.

———. 1990. "Putting Women Back into the Abortion Debate." In *From Abor-*

tion to Reproductive Freedom: Transforming a Movement, ed. Marlene Gerber Fried, 131–38. Boston: South End Press.

Wills, Garry. 1989. "Evangels of Abortion." *New York Review of Books* 36, June 15, 15–21.

Wirthlin Group. 1990. *A National Benchmark Survey of Public Attitudes on the Issue of Abortion.* McClean, Va.: Wirthlin Group.

Worsnop, Richard L. 1990. "Death Penalty Debate Centers on Retribution," *Congressional Quarterly,* July 13, 398–410.

Wuthnow, Robert. 1989. *Communities of Discourse: Ideology and Social Structure in the Reformation, the Enlightenment, and European Socialism.* Cambridge, Mass.: Harvard University Press.

Yost, Paula. 1989. "As Abortion-Rights Groups Rally Support, Foes Set Legislative Drive in 4 States," *Washington Post,* July 5, A10.

Zald, Mayer, and John D. McCarthy. 1987. *Social Movements in an Organizational Society.* New Brunswick, N.J.: Transaction Books.

Zepezauer, Frank. 1988. "The Masks of Feminism." *The Human Life Review* 14, no. 3 (Fall): 28–34.

Index

About the Contributors

RONALD BURTON received his Ph.D. from Michigan State University. He has published extensively in the area of the relationships among religion, social class, and politics. He is currently preparing an article on "Individualism, Communalism, and the Political Right."

MARTHE A. CHANDLER is Professor of Philosophy and Religion at DePauw University in Greencastle, Indiana. She works in logic and the philosophy of science.

ELIZABETH ADELL COOK is Assistant Professor at the American University. Her research interests include public opinion, women and politics, and feminist consciousness in America. She co-authored, with Ted G. Jelen and Clyde Wilcox, *Between Two Absolutes: Public Opinion and the Politics of Abortion*.

JOHN C. GREEN is Director of the Ray C. Bliss Institute of Applied Politics and Assistant Professor of Political Science at the University of Akron. He has published extensively on religion and politics at the mass and elite level. Along with James L. Guth, he is co-editor of *The Bible and the Ballot Box: Religion and Politics in the 1988 Election* (1991).

LAURA GRINDSTAFF is a doctoral candidate in Sociology and Women's Studies at the University of California, Santa Barbara, where she teaches courses in the departments of Film, Sociology, and Women's Studies. She considers herself a cultural studies scholar, specializing in popular culture, film, and television.

JAMES L. GUTH is Professor of Political Science at Furman University. He has served in the past as chair of the department and chair of the university faculty. His work on religion and politics has appeared in many journals and edited collections.

BRADLEY R. HERTEL is Associate Professor of Sociology at the Virginia Polytechnic Institute and State University. His research interests are on problems of measurement and theory testing in the sociology of religion. He recently completed a pair of studies on the impact of employment on church attendance, including a chapter that will appear in Nancy Ammerman and Wade Clark Roof's edited volume, *Work, Family, and Faith.*

TED G. JELEN is Professor of Political Science at Illinois Benedictine College in Lisle. He is the author of *The Political Mobilization of Religious Belief* (1991) and *The Political World of the Clergy* (Praeger 1993), among other scholarly books and articles. With Elizabeth Adell Cook and Clyde Wilcox, he co-authored *Between Two Absolutes: Public Opinion and the Politics of Abortion.*

STEPHEN D. JOHNSON is Professor of Sociology at Ball State University. He has published over twenty articles and one book on religion and politics.

LYMAN A. KELLSTEDT is Professor of Political Science at Wheaton College. He is the co-author (with David C. Leege) of *Rediscovering the Religious Factor in American Politics* (1993). He has published numerous articles in the field of religion and politics, with a more specific focus on religious activists, electoral politics, and policy areas such as abortion and the environment.

JAMES R. KELLY is Professor of Sociology at Fordham University. He has written on social policy, social movements, and the sociology of religion for a variety of journals, including *The Journal for the Scientific Study of Religion, Sociological Analysis,* and *Review of Religious Research,* as well as for *Commonweal, America,* and *The Christian Century.* He contributed an essay on "Right-to-Life Groups" for the forthcoming *The New Dictionary of Catholic Social Thought.*

CAROL J. C. MAXWELL is a doctoral candidate in Anthropology at Washington University in St. Louis. She is Project Coordinator for the National Cooperative Inner City Asthma Study at St. Louis University (NIH-

NIAID). Her research interests include ethnicity and class, self-identity, religious experience, activism, and oral history. She is the author of *White Like Them: Asian Refugees in a White Christian Congregation* (1989).

JOHN H. SIMPSON is Professor of Sociology and Chair of the Department of Sociology in the University of Toronto. His recent publications include articles on globalization and religion, postmodernity and Fundamentalism, America's attitudes toward socio-moral issues in the 1980s, and religion and the body.

CORWIN E. SMIDT is Professor of Political Science at Calvin College, Grand Rapids, Michigan. He has authored or co-authored a variety of research articles, which have focused on the empirical relationship between religion and politics generally and on the political attitudes and behavior of American evangelical Christians specifically. He is presently working, along with his co-authors, on completing two books. The first book focuses on religious political activists, and the second book focuses on the political attitudes and behavior of clergy across different Protestant denominations.

JOSEPH B. TAMNEY is Professor of Sociology at Ball State University. Recent publications include *The Resilience of Christianity in the Modern World* and *American Society in the Buddhist Mirror*. He is editor-elect of *Sociology of Religion: A Quarterly Review*.

CLYDE WILCOX is Associate Professor at Georgetown University, and is the author of numerous scholarly publications, including *God's Warriors: The Christian Right in Twentieth Century America*. He is the co-author, with Ted G. Jelen and Elizabeth Adell Cook, of *Between Two Absolutes: Public Opinion and the Politics of Abortion*.